SOCIAL WORK
and the Unemployed

SOCIAL WORK

And the Unemployed

KATHARINE HOOPER BRIAR

National Association of Social Workers, Inc.
Silver Spring, MD 20910

This book is dedicated to the unemployed and their families and to the many social workers who, constrained in addressing the needs of the jobless, have been rendered underemployed in our society.

Library of Congress Cataloging-in-Publication Data

Briar, Katharine Hooper.
    Social work and the unemployed.

    1. Family social work—United States. 2. Unemployed—
Services for—United States. 3. Unemployment—Social
aspects—United States. I. Title.
HV699.B73 1988   362.8'5'0973   87-34846
ISBN 0-87101-153-0

Printed in the United States of America

 3

Contents

Foreword

Social workers witness the human tragedies created by unemployment and underemployment on a daily basis. Their clients may seek treatment for depression, substance abuse, stress-related health disorders, or other manifestations of the consequences of joblessness. Too often, social workers are placed in the reactive position of treating the symptoms and stresses of job displacement and exclusion.

The National Association of Social Workers (NASW) is taking steps to address the policy and programmatic issues surrounding employment. In 1985, the Board of Directors established the Commission on Employment and Economic Support to guide policy formulation and program development in this field of practice. In November 1987, NASW's governing body, the Delegate Assembly, approved a policy statement on "Full and Equitable Employment" that calls for a national policy to ensure constitutionally and legally guaranteed rights to freely chosen, socially useful employment suited to individual capacity. NASW advocates a national policy to promote caregiving resources, such as comprehensive health care, child care, and respite services, that enable full employment and to support initiatives that can reverse the destruction caused by instability in the national and global economies.

The publication of *Social Work and the Unemployed* is another step in NASW's programmatic efforts on behalf of clients who have suffered from the economic chaos and stresses caused by long-term or multiple spells of unemployment. In this new book, Katharine Briar addresses the clinical, programmatic, and policy issues related to employment, and she provides pragmatic, explicit strategies for effecting change.

SUZANNE DWORAK-PECK, *President*
MARK G. BATTLE, *Executive Director*

February 1988

Acknowledgments

This book is a culmination of the numerous stories, experiences, and ideas of the jobless and the many creative visions of colleagues—all of which, in one way or another, have helped to seed and furnish the ideas in this book. I have been fortunate to be surrounded by students, especially doctoral students, who have contributed to the development of my ideas. Nancy Dickinson, Marie Hoff, Kristin Knighton, Paule McNicholl, Joanne Ray, Rosemary Ryan, Angie Van Ry, Michele Vinet, and Spencer Zeiger have been pioneers in their own right and most helpful to me. Kristin Knighton's research assistance has been invaluable.

Fellow academics who have been of enormous assistance are Pamela Day, Ronald M. Dear, Moya Duplica, Naomi Gottlieb, Jim Herrick, Nancy Hooyman, Judy Kopp, Robert Plotnick, and Florence Stier. I am especially appreciative of Judy Kopp's help with the clinical chapters. Community colleagues who have advised me and collaborated on visions for aiding the jobless include Roland Barach, Jane Bidstrup, Ann Blalock, Tom Croft, Marilyn Farrell, Barbie Faubion, Decky Feidler, Mary Gentry, Larry Gossett, Bill Hagens, Noel Hagens, Larry Kinney, Bill Knowles, Mark McDermott, Thelma Payne, Dorothy Pitkin, Mimi Rappley, Kay Thode, Rodger Vandegrift, and Marvin Williams.

At the national level of the National Association of Social Workers, Inc. (NASW), staff members Thom Gauthier and Norma Taylor and such colleagues on national committees as Ruth Antoniades, Sue Bellinger, Jim Francek, Grace Harris, Otto Jones, Dan Lanier, Jim Parham, and Sandra Turner have served as reality checks for some of my ideas. In addition, I have been fortunate to be part of a creative and energetic team of NASW members in Washington State, who are promoting innovations in labor and industry and designing services for the jobless. Members of NASW's Coordinating Committee for Social Work in Labor and Industry, the Counselor Referral Network for the unemployed, and the Work Institute have greatly supported my work and sparked visions and demonstration projects that attest to the changes that social workers can help bring about. Especially critical to my work have been Amandalei Bennett, Sally Carlson, Larry Crump, Elaine Darling, Laura Taylor Degnan, Bill Dethlefs, Penny Herrick, Connie Jones, Billie Lawson, and Greg Long.

Another great source of inspiration has been the members of the International Network for Social Work and the Unemployed. As scholars and practitioners, they have helped me to germinate or confirm many ideas that have been incorporated in this book. Outside the United States, such leaders as Hans Berglind, Yvonne Dhooge, Christine Labonté-Roset, Sharon McKay, George Maslany, Jennie Popay, Ann and Don Pilcher, Graham Riches, and Keith Windschuttle have been a growing collaborative network of support to me, while within the United States, I have depended on the help of Mimi Abramowitz, Joyce Beckett, Michael Borrero, Mary Bricker-Jenkins, Trudy Goldberg, Ken Root, Lee Schore, Essie Trammel Seck, Michael Sherraden, Kusim Singh, and Greg Weeks.

I owe a great intellectual debt to Bertram Gross, for his wide-ranging knowledge and historic work to promote full employment in this country. Similarly, Lou Ferman and David Gil have helped me anchor my work in multiple perspectives and visions for change. Will Richan first encouraged me to write this book, and Chuck Wilder has been a mentor and colleague from the start. Sheila Akabas and Paul Kurzman especially have been helpful regarding proposals for improved workplaces. Although ideas get filtered through many lenses and experiences, they may not come out necessarily just the way many of my collaborators and mentors might have wished. Nevertheless, we all can be enriched by the many talents and diverse perspectives in the social welfare community that add to the debates about how to serve the unemployed.

This book has had several caretakers, including Diane Bernard, former executive director of the Council on Social Work Education, and at NASW, Beatrice Saunders and Jacqueline Atkins, former directors of publications; Wendy Almeleh, former senior editor; and Linda Beebe, the current director of publications, and staff. Its production would not have occurred so effectively had it not been for the patience and help provided by Jeannette Ashby, Suzanne Condict, Mary Grembowski, Chris Hoffman, Karen Miller, Laurie Pollack, and Gail Nyman York.

Without support from my family, I could not even have envisioned this book. My daughter Jenny and her friends, especially Jenny Patzold, not only have been helpful, but have endured summer vacations dominated by the book. Nancy Briar helped with the research; Keith Briar, my parents, grandparents, brothers, and sisters provided multiple perspectives on the economy. On the Patzel side of my family, I have gained invaluable insights into the farming crisis and the consequences of the decline in the U.S. fishing industry. Finally, my husband Scott has been a continual source of encouragement, patience, and scholarly advice.

Introduction

It has been eight months that I've been out of work. I look endlessly for work but get knocked down each time I apply for a job. My family is about to give up on me, and I want to give up altogether. It's so bad that I don't even want to look for a job anymore. My biggest problem is that I'm stuck and have nowhere to turn for help. Last year, when I broke my arm, I was given immediate medical attention and advice on how long it would tie me up, what to expect, and how to cope. Well, now I'm at the breaking point and hurt worse than I did with my broken arm. This time, I have no one to give me attention and advice on my work future, on training possibilities, how long I'll be stuck like this, and how I can survive until I get a job.

—Susan, a jobless 23-year-old

Last week, the boss called us out to the parking lot and said that he had sold the plant and that we had a half hour to pack up our tools and get our last check. He said that the new owner would run the plant nonunion. We could apply for our old jobs, but he couldn't be certain we would be hired back. With the news and the way our boss treated us, I felt like I'd been knifed in the back after 15 years of hard work for this guy. Is this all it adds up to? That's the end of things for me, I think. Isn't there any justice left in the world?

—Fred, a jobless 52-year-old

Susan and Fred's plaints may go unheeded by many social workers because, for the most part, traditional social services have not focused on the jobless. Even so, Susan and Fred may have appeared in social service agencies not as jobless workers but as depressed, possibly suicidal persons who were seeking help for substance abuse or some other problem. As their pain suggests, unemployment is one of the most debilitating human conditions, scarring those who are its victims and leaving few untouched in their lifetime. It causes irretrievable losses, blunted dreams, and shattered social functioning. Ironically, this condition, which is so destructive of effective individual, family, and community functioning, is one of the few truly preventable calamities that afflict us. Given the social work profession's concern for special populations and high-risk groups, it is time for social workers to intensify their clinical, programmatic, and policy missions to aid the jobless. Moreover, there may be no greater opportunity to renew the profession's earlier concerns for this disenfranchised population than this time of increased awareness of the effects of unemployment and the need for full and equitable employment for all who wish to work.

Rationale for the Book

This is a book about the strengths and stresses of the millions of people whose lives, families, and communities have been disrupted, impaired, or deformed by unemployment. It is written in the hope that social workers will be able to address more explicitly the economic and employment conditions that force many to seek their help. In the chapters that follow, various dynamics, dilemmas, and practice modalities are presented. This book is intended to serve clinicians, planners, agency directors, researchers, and the jobless clients served by the profession. However, it also lays out ways that direct service practitioners may intensify their influence on policy because they are so clearly cognizant of the consequences of the deficits of policy and services—especially those that affect the unemployed.

The suggested practice scenarios for extending the current breadth of social work practice are designed more to stimulate dialogue and debate in the field about relevant responses to joblessness and underemployment than to provide a ready-made textbook of practice. At this time, prescriptions for all realms of practice would be premature, given the pioneering that must be done to combat the loss of livelihood, the demise of communities, and the effects of a restructuring of the global economy. Rather than burden social workers with more initiatives and work, it is hoped that some shortcuts to meeting the needs of workers, families, and communities will be evident. At the heart of the book is the belief that many social workers have fallen prey to some of the same outcomes of industrialization that are engulfing other workers whose repertoires of skills and talents remain untapped.

This book addresses unemployment and underemployment as byproducts of labor market regulation, disadvantage, marginalization, and exclusion. These processes involve not only the exclusion of some persons from the labor market, but underutilization and insufficient compensation for the skills and contributions of many who labor both in the labor market and outside it. Such dynamics also involve definitions of who is employable and whose work warrants wages versus who is conscripted as free labor.

Chapter 1 examines some of the stresses and scars of unemployment, which often are the reasons that the jobless and their families seek help. Chapter 2 explores the dynamics of the decline of individuals, families, and communities, as well as the constructive reactions of these groups to unemployment. These dynamics suggest the delivery of multiple types of services and the development of policies. Clinical practice, once it is grounded in the documented effects of joblessness and underemployment and the dynamics and stages of deterioration, then may be expanded to promote occupational development.

Chapter 3 describes the facets of an occupational problem-solving role that could be performed by most clinicians. Chapter 4 presents tools that can be used to enhance family functioning and that address some of the multigenerational consequences of unemployment. Chapter 5 addresses the changes in agency services and programs that might contribute to more comprehensive responses to the jobless and complement the repertoire of clinicians. Such suggestions also include a community economic development role for social service agencies whose services could be linked to workplaces and to unions. Chapter 6 discusses the roles that social workers and social service agencies can play in documenting the effects of unemployment, not just on individuals but on their families, support networks, and communities. Such documentation, in turn, may lead to new standards of services that are based on critical thresholds and strategies to prevent the often-inevitable unraveling of the functioning of individuals, groups, and communities. Chapter 7 addresses workplace- and union-based innovations. It suggests a partial pathway of care for help seekers and attempts to ensure early and more relevant services to victims of labor market disadvantage. Chapter 8 analyzes the "welfare to wages" dilemma and offers prescriptions for social work advocacy and occupational development strategies for public assistance recipients. Chapter 9 suggests some policy avenues that address preventive strategies, entitlements, and the injustices that now dominate current labor market policies. Globally relevant practice, covered in chapter 10, is becoming increasingly important, given the effects of clinical programs and policies at the local level on the well-being of workers, families, and communities throughout the world.

Threaded throughout these chapters are proposed multimodal interventions on behalf of the jobless, their families and communities. Such multidimensional interventions suggest new clinical services and programs, collective empowerment strategies, and policy reform. Social work has the heritage, professional education, and mandate to promote both clinical and systemic interventions.

Rather than retooling, practitioners must recognize that they may have many of the skills needed to aid the jobless. Informed by knowledge of the causes, phenomenology, and consequences of joblessness, underemployment, and community economical decline and the cures for these conditions, social workers may be readily able to adapt their skills to this neglected population.

Many of the ideas for serving the unemployed are conditioned by the realities of the capitalist economic system in the United States and in most parts of the world. Nevertheless, the thrust and intent of the multimodal approaches suggested in the chapters that follow are that of humanizing and democratizing the economic system, rather than solely cushioning its casualties. Because the economies of the United States, Canada, and Western European nations are at a crossroads, some of the suggestions offered may, nonetheless, be shaped by what is possible within the confines of capitalism, especially in the United States. Whether such multimodal proposals can be transformational remains to be researched and tested in practice as we attempt to craft a better future for those we serve.

1

Stress of Unemployment

Susan doesn't know where to seek help for the underwriter's job she wants. She looks as systematically as she can, only to find that unadvertised jobs are filled by insiders or she is not as competitive as those with more experience. She is persuaded by her family to seek counseling for her depression and bouts of insomnia. At the multiservice agency in her town, the counselor assisting her is attuned to her depression and gives her an array of tools for combating it.

Jobless, depressed, and poor six months after his plant closed, Fred is arrested for theft from a liquor store. He now is identified as a "polydrug" abuser and a criminal—two labels that seemingly are removed from the jobless condition that may have set in motion or reinforced his substance-abusing proclivities.

As Susan receives treatment from a mental health counselor, it is not clear that her joblessness will be addressed. After all, just helping her cope with her depression may be a treatment goal in itself. Like Susan, Fred has acquired two "labels"—(1) criminal and (2) substance abuser—and a new set of problems that may preempt his getting help with reemployment. To those who help him deal with his substance-abusing and criminal activities, the trauma of his job loss and the plant's closure may seem far removed and even irrelevant.

In this chapter, the human costs of unemployment and underemployment that produce many of the symptoms reflected in the stresses and problems of persons like Susan and Fred are discussed. By laying out some of the well-documented correlates and by-products of unemployment, this chapter will set the stage for the array of social work innovations that must be mounted to ensure that practice addresses not just symptoms but their precipitants.

Assaults and Scars of Unemployment

Unemployment incurs multiple traumas in and challenges the ability of individuals, families, and communities to cope with the stress it engenders. Dealing with the personal stresses of unemployment may exhaust quickly one's psychological, social, and financial resources; may bring irreversible damage to one's self and to loved ones; and may result in the loss of possessions built up over a lifetime. The consequences of unemployment for communities may include increased bankruptcies and business failures, as well as lost tax revenues that lead to cutbacks in such services as public welfare, job-search aid, housing, and mental health.

Many jobless workers may be able to adapt easily to a short period of unemployment. For those who experience several weeks without work while changing jobs, unemployment may leave few scars and even may be a positive experience. For others, especially those who are out of work 15 weeks or more or who lack the resources to cushion their financial stress, unemployment may be debilitating. Mounting evidence from research, to update the findings of the 1930s, has specified some of the direct and indirect consequences of unemployment, including depression, suicide, mental illness, psychiatric hospitalization, spouse and child abuse, parent–child conflict, divorce, substance abuse, delinquency, crime, homicide, and eating and sleeping disorders.[1]

Research also has documented the physiological incapacitation of immune systems because of stressful life events. Although the debate continues over which illnesses and diseases are stress induced, studies have found that hypertension, cardiovascular and cerebrovascular disease, and kidney disease are stress-based outcomes of joblessness.[2] However, research by Liem, Liem, and Hauser, among others, has shown that when the unemployed can turn to support systems, some of these negative effects may be mitigated.[3] Nevertheless, in some cases, husbands or wives may exhibit symptoms that are similar to those of their jobless spouses. Children may develop somatic and gastrointestinal disorders, as well as behavior-management problems.[4] When there are two jobless members, the stresses on the family often are compounded.

The loss of structure to one's day owing to the loss of a job and the difficulty in creating meaningful and productive use of one's time afflicts many workers. Even the structuring of behavior and thoughts may become impaired in the ensuing sense of disorganization and drifting and the absence of social and economic cohesion. Although little research has been conducted on how the temporal changes caused by unemployment lead to changes in cognitive functioning, such researchers as Jahoda have made beginning inquiries.[5] For example, time rationality may become impaired among the jobless; jobless workers and their families may focus increasingly on the past and present and develop a blunted, if not obfuscated, sense of the future. It also has been shown that passive leisure-time behavior (involving behaviors that may constitute social withdrawal) increases with joblessness.[6]

The emotional, social, and financial toll of unemployment may be exacerbated by the rejections and related stresses experienced in the job search. Amundsen and Borgen likened the job search to stages of burnout.[7] Sometimes unemployment benefits will prolong the worker's search for work because the benefits make it possible to hold out for a desirable job. Many persons, however, are plunged immediately into underemployment—a condition that is as corrosive as unemployment, especially when one is unable to claim unemployment benefits.

Depleted life savings, bankruptcy, poverty, and homelessness are but a few of the by-products of one or multiple spells of unemployment. Economic deprivation, in turn, may set in motion a chain of losses that compound the psychological and social stresses associated with joblessness. Fewer than half and at many times only a third of the jobless receive unemployment benefits. And even if they receive such benefits, workers and their families with no other source of income are plunged below the poverty line.[8] Assertions that the jobless can weather their plight or that a second wage earner significantly cushions such economic losses need to be tempered by knowledge that inadequate benefits may alter drastically their life-styles, family functioning, and living standards. As economic assaults mount, cars may be sold or repossessed, insurance is foregone, and homes are sold or lost; these and many other setbacks often create insurmountable impediments to reemployment.

Much work has been undertaken to liken the stages of unemployment to stages of grief. Ferman, others, and this author find grief analysis helpful but limited to a focus on psychological adjustments when economic loss, adaptation, and devastation may be the more overarching destabilizer and crippler in long-term joblessness.[9]

Policymakers frequently claim that plenty of jobs are available for those who will look harder for them or are willing to work for lower wages. If they accept this claim of policymakers, unemployed workers may begin to blame themselves, not for their layoff but for their inability to find new jobs. Society gives workers few options other than self-blame. Although self-blame suggests that one has the power to control and change the situation, it also may blunt political advocacy because many jobless workers personalize, rather than politicize, their plight.

Like those who have been laid off, reentering workers who have been in school or in family work roles also may be prone to self-blame and depression, not just because of rejections during their job search but by their inability to acquire leads for job openings. This problem is exacerbated by the finding that only 12 percent of the available jobs are listed with employment services and want ads in newspapers may be inaccurate.[10] Some workers may land a job through what may seem like random or aimless job seeking. Others may withdraw from the labor market, discouraged by the increased rejections from random job seeking and their consequent toll.

During recessions, many workers expect to be recalled to their former line of work, as was the case in the past. Today, however, unlike former recessions and the depression of the 1930s, the labor market in the United States is undergoing a major restructuring. Obsolescence in plants and in equipment, poor management, and less expensive sources of labor in other regions or nations have intensified the flight of capital and the closure of plants. Workers may not return to their former jobs; thus, the loss of a livelihood—not just of a job—has become a major problem.

Some jobless workers may seek retraining or may attempt to start their own businesses. However, retraining and self-employment sometimes are risky routes to gaining economic and employment security. Retraining for livelihoods that are in decline is one of the more ineffective routes to reemployment. Small businesses, although critical to economic redevelopment, may not receive the marketing and technical assistance and loans they require. Thus, they are liable to fail. Therefore, many of the "solutions" forced on jobless workers actually may set them further astray.

Just as workers may become more impaired as they try to cope with joblessness and a prolonged job hunt, their families may become incapacitated. Declining resources may undercut the caregiving and provider roles of families. The jobless worker eventually may be seen as a liability and, in some cases, may be expelled from the family through divorce or separation. In some families, the withdrawal of support for a member may necessitate the placement of an elderly relative in a nursing home or a younger member in foster or group care.

Increasing joblessness, along with the rise of the service economy and its laggard wages, impede the emancipation of some adolescents while forcing some adult children and their offspring to return home. It has been estimated that since 1970 there has been a 10-percent increase nationally in the number of persons aged 18 to 34 who live with their parents.[11]

Like the jobless and their families, communities often cope with unemployment in ways that exacerbate their condition. For example, to attract new businesses during recessions and when plants close, local and state governments may reduce or eliminate corporate taxes to induce new businesses to come to the area. Yet tax cutting may further erode support for services to the jobless because of declining revenues and make tax reinstatements more difficult. In addition, as social services are cut back, community agencies may face escalating demands for services. Moreover, the jobless are not the only members of the community who are affected; shopkeepers, most wage earners, and other community residents are afflicted by the rise in crime and declining community services. Brenner's research on unemployment and morbidity suggests that mortality rates increase with each percentage-point rise in the jobless rate, the rate of business failures, and the decline in per capita income.[12]

Thus the lives of many, not just the jobless, are affected by the economic insecurity and financial loss that accompany recessions and the restructuring of economies. Unemployment and economic decline threaten the well-being of multiple generations—not just of those who depend on the jobless worker as a provider and caregiver, but those who consider him or her a role model.

Human Costs of Job Rationing: Oppressed Populations

The human costs of unemployment are compounded for the oppressed groups in our society. Although research has not tracked systematically these differential human costs, it is critical that they be recognized. What middle-class white men now are experiencing with intensity has long affected the lives of groups that have been excluded from or disadvantaged in the labor market. The absence of full employment policies to guarantee decent-paying jobs for all has resulted in defacto job rationing. Thus, those who are last in line for jobs historically have been the victims of other forms of societal discrimination. Gender, race, age, disability, sexual affiliation, and class are some of the attributes that society has used to divide and disproportionately ration jobs.

To understand where the "majority" members of society are heading as the economy restructures and the welfare state experiences cutbacks is to understand the plight of groups that often have been pushed to the margins of society, especially in hard economic times. Although some of their stories are threaded throughout the chapters that follow, it is important to frame discussions of unemployment in the context of how oppressed groups have been afflicted disproportionately. Once a group is pushed to the margins, society then may insidiously use the attributes of gender, race, or age against which jobs are rationed as the causal explanation for the group's poor integration in the labor market. Persons who are excluded or disadvantaged in the labor market because of discrimination owing to their sexual affiliation, disability, gender, race, class, or age then are blamed for their inability to be well integrated and to seize opportunities and for their disproportionate use of government benefits.

Oppressed groups thus must deal with discrimination, job rationing, and the consequences of exclusion and labor market disadvantage that undercut their ability to care for themselves and their dependents and forces some into a life of chronic unemployment, underemployment, poverty, and, in some cases, institutionalization.

The human and societal costs of wholesale exclusion from and disadvantage in the labor market have not been well documented. If such costs were well documented, we would look at prisoners, patients in hospitals, high school dropouts, welfare recipients, homeless people, abused women and children, children in foster care—and even mentally ill patients—from a new perspective. We would see many of these populations as major indexes of the aggregate human and societal costs of inequitable labor market policies and benefits.

Ethnic Minorities

Unemployment and underemployment have long been experienced disproportionately by ethnic minorities and often have hurt all facets of their lives. In fact, chronic unemployment may be endemic to ethnic minorities because of the absence of full employment and the consequent job rationing based on labor market discrimination. The National Urban League has claimed that unemployment is the top problem in the black community.[13] The historic Kerner Commission report on racial disturbances similarly concluded that adequate employment is of critical significance.[14] Limited achievement in school, illiteracy, crime, disability, and the inability to form or stabilize families are well known by-products of labor market discrimination and disadvantage.[15]

Like blacks, Hispanics not only face similar labor market barriers but are cordoned off disproportionately into migrant labor jobs involving deplorable wages, harmful working conditions, frequent joblessness, and inequitable access to unemployment compensation.[16] Migratory patterns of labor undercut family stabilization, children's school performance, and the capacity to be a permanent part of a community. Destitution brought about by subminimum wages and the intimidation and exploitation of non-English-speaking workers aggravates strife at work and in the family.

The restructuring of the economy suggests an even more precarious economic future. Moreover, if trends in poverty-level wages continue, Hispanics will replace blacks in 1990 as the group with the highest poverty rate among ethnic minorities because of the especially low-paying jobs that are most pronounced in the Southwest. Hispanics are also 21 percent more likely than are whites to experience dislocation from their jobs.[17]

Joblessness and underemployment among native Americans often is pegged at 80 percent or above. Like black and Hispanic workers, native Americans are hurt doubly by the current restructuring of the economy because many resource-based industries on which their livelihoods and tribal futures have depended—agriculture, fishing, timber, mining—are all in a sharp and, in some cases, irreversible decline.[18]

Native American populations are victims of fatal accidents and diseases at far higher rates than those of the U.S. population as a whole.[19] The rates of cirrhosis of the liver, accidental death often in motor vehicles, suicide, and homicide have increased over the years. Deaths from cirrhosis of the liver among native Americans are five times higher than those in the general population. Brenner found that suicide, homicide, and cirrhosis of the liver are correlates of unemployment; the fact that Indian populations are so greatly afflicted may stem, in part, from their high rates of joblessness and occupational distress.[20]

Immigrant groups, especially from Asia, have had an exceptionally difficult time becoming integrated into the U.S. labor market, not because of a lack of industriousness but because of the absence of job guarantees in this restructuring economy. Asian workers fall into some of the same patterns of unemployment and underemployment as do other oppressed groups. However, some of the economic progress among Asian workers and their families, including newly immigrated workers, is due to multiple family wage earners and 60-hour-or-more workweeks—not to equal wages with white workers. Asian families may have more members working, but all at the minimum wage.[21] Moreover, 21 to 32 percent or more of Chinese parents may not see their children during the week because of their long working hours.[22] Thus, the rise of gangs is attributed partially to the excessive workloads that Chinese families must bear to bring home a living wage. Moreover, immigrants may be grossly underemployed, because, over the decades, immigration officers reputedly have selected the most skilled to enter the country, who then must start at the bottom of the job ladder. Thus, the human costs of underemployment may be revealed dramatically in a Vietnamese or Korean father's depression over his inability to provide for his family as he did in his homeland, which necessitates that all working-age members of his family seek employment in the United States.[23]

Persons with Disabilities, Youths, and Older Persons

All the well-documented human costs of unemployment are multiplied for workers with disabilities. Disability caused by an illness or injury may compound the problems of reentering the labor market not only because of the retooling that may be required but because of the hopelessness and depression that impede access to jobs and even special aid for workers with disabilities. The intricate interplay of workers' compensation, when and if it is available, with the return to work further compounds the human costs of long-term unemployment and marginalization in the labor market.[24] The most prominent harm faced by workers with disabilities is the attitudes of others toward their condition.

Working-age persons with disabilities constituted 17 percent of the working-age population in 1978.[25] A disproportionate number of these workers were black or members of other ethnic minority groups. Proportionately more women than men exist among such workers as well.

High school dropouts (25 to 50 percent) are indicators of the effect of an unstable economy and jobless future on youths, especially those in regions of poverty and job discrimination because of their ethnic minority status. Teenage pregnancy is not the cause of some of the high dropout rates but may be the consequence of joblessness among those who drop out and do not find work because they believe that the only valued role left to them is parenting, even in rock-bottom poverty. This problem is not unique to the United States. As the British economy declines, school superintendents are facing increased barriers to keeping their youths in school as well.[26]

Older workers have been long-time victims of labor market discrimination through forced retirement, dislocation before retirement, and underemployment, especially when they reach retirement age. Despite attempts to rescind mandatory retirement requirements, older workers are disproportionately downgraded or expelled from their jobs. No less immune to the human costs of unemployment than are other groups, older jobless workers may have higher rates of stress-related health problems, suicidal preoccupation, and depression.[27] Moreover, the heavy attrition of workers below age 65 will not be reversed, despite the predicted decline in labor market entrants in the next decade.[28]

Women, Gays, and Lesbians

Labor market discrimination may involve the differential treatment and labor market exclusion of women and persons whose sexual affiliation is gay or lesbian. Nevertheless, the widespread human costs of and harms to women and sexual minorities from unemployment and underemployment are not well documented. Despite the increasing recognition of the economic setbacks faced by women because of underemployment and the absence of comparable worth, the harms of joblessness and temporary or dead-end jobs still are ill defined. Research has shown, however, that women endure many of the human costs of joblessness that men experience.[29] Because women are more likely to be affected by segregation in and exclusion from the labor market, they, like other oppressed groups, may endure profound effects and scars.

The fact that little research exists on the effects of joblessness and underemployment on gay and lesbian workers reveals the degree of disadvantage these groups may experience in the labor market. Their inequitable treatment when their sexual affiliation or affection preference is disclosed may cause them to experience compounding wounds of underemployment and unemployment. The deliberate expulsion tactics practiced by workplaces when they disclose their affiliation compounds the disadvantages they confront.

Public opinion studies have revealed severe patterns of discrimination among employers, co-workers, and the public at large in hiring gay or lesbian workers. Because of public stereotypes, misinformation about sexual affiliation, and the heightened fear of AIDS, hiring, promotion, and firing processes all may hinder workers who are either suspected of homosexuality or who disclose their sexual affiliations.[30]

Oppressed groups may share with the majority universal cultural responses to underemployment and unemployment involving similar psychological, social, and health outcomes. However, the effects of discrimination and the human costs that ensue from being treated differently and inequitably because of an attribute that has nothing to do with work performance may compound enormously the painful consequences of joblessness and underemployment.

Low-Income People

Like discrimination against sexual minorities, class-based discrimination has long been used as a divisive mechanism to block the equal participation of many members of society in the workplace. Differential dress, speech, manners, and beliefs conspire to blunt careers and aggravate segregation patterns in the labor market.[31] Aspirations for mobility may be blocked by external barriers while self-doubts about ability and rights may slow activism to eliminate class-based discrimination. In England, consciousness about class-based discrimination has been so evident that, until the past two decades, working-class children were routed into vocational-technical schools while upper-class children were tracked into college preparatory educational programs. In contrast, the U.S. myth is that anyone can make it from the log cabin to the White House . . . if he or she tries hard. Thus, the human costs of unemployment and underemployment that are caused or aggravated by class-based discrimination, sometimes subtle and hence often more harmful, loom ahead for further study, exposé, and legislative and legal action.

Stress and Coping

The psychological, social, and economic outcomes of unemployment may be attributable, in part, not just to the human costs of labor market disadvantage but to individual reactions to the multiple stressors encountered in a period of joblessness. It has been hypothesized that the link between external stressors and personal outcomes consists of a series of cause-and-effect relationships involving individualized reactions to the external event or stressor (job loss, for example); along with one's appraisal of the event (for instance, a sense of failure); along with inadequate resources to deal with the stressor (insufficient unemployment compensation to stave off the sale or foreclosure of a house); followed by an emotional or behavioral coping response (such as depression or drinking).[32] Figure 1 depicts the flow of these reactions.

This paradigm implies a somewhat static response period when actual occurrences may be episodic, incurred by a steady dismantling of resources that erode the capacity to react to stress or cope in a constructive manner. As a result, the person may experience a series of new traumas that are as devastating as the layoff itself. For example, the job hunt may generate its own stress-induced reactions that leave the jobless worker and family to cope not just with the economic casualties and grieflike stages

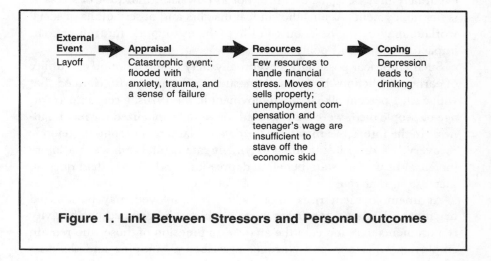

Figure 1. Link Between Stressors and Personal Outcomes

in response to the job loss but with entirely new social, emotional, and economic states.

To complicate matters, each behavioral and emotional response to the assaults and scars of joblessness may set in motion a chain of maladaptive behaviors and outcomes that further impair the functioning of the jobless worker, family, and other social support systems. As Figure 1 suggests, depression may lead to drinking. Drinking may lead to hostile and abusive interactions that then may precipitate the runaway behavior of an adolescent, flight by an abused spouse and at-risk children, or placement of an at-risk or abused child in foster care.

Indexes of Stress in a Restructured Economy

Research on the human costs of unemployment portrays grim pictures of the stresses endured by the long-term jobless, particularly when the unemployment rate is high. When the unemployment rate drops, one would expect a decline in many of the indexes of stress. However, studies on distressed economies and communities have suggested that the unemployment rate alone may no longer be the sole measure of distress or well-being.[33] Because of the unprecedented restructuring of the economy in recent years (especially since 1981), it is possible that unemployment rates may drop while poverty and the utilization of welfare grants may increase. Despite the difficulty in measuring it, underemployment eventually may be an as useful, if not as powerful, indicator of stress as is unemployment. Again, the clinical insights and observations of social workers may be the best source of hypotheses to guide future research, impact analysis, and policies.

Such empirical possibilities eventually may even confound the utility of earlier predictions by researchers such as Brenner, who claimed that with each 1 percent hike in unemployment in the 1970s, a certain percentage of people died, were incarcerated, or were hospitalized for mental illness. In the future, we may have the data to claim that despite "economic recovery," a drop in the unemployment rate actually may signal more increases in welfare state benefits, depression, and suicide than does an increase in that rate.

As unemployment rises, those who are employed may be affected negatively. Reduced resources to do a job and heightened productivity requirements may increase the anxiety and tension of those who remain employed.[34] Ferman and Gardner described a bumping and skidding phenomenon in the workplace and in the labor market in which underemployment rises as jobs shrink.[35]

Underemployment produces many of the same symptoms as does unemployment. Some experts who work with the jobless and underemployed believe that underemployment may even intensify symptoms because workers feel trapped and angry and all the attendant spillover effects hurt their personal functioning and family life.[36] Despite the fact that more people are working in the United States than ever before, the growth of low-paying jobs erodes the standard of living and plunges more workers and families into economic decline.[37]

The fiscal impact of the human costs of unemployment and underemployment have not been well documented. The costs for the nation of the use of social services, institutionalization, lost productivity, tax revenues, morbidity, and mortality have not been well delineated. What exists are beginning estimates of only partial costs. For example, Brenner claimed that the effect of unemployment and changes in income in the mid-1970s resulted in mortality that cost the nation $26 billion.[38]

Myth of Stress-Free Joblessness

Despite the great variance in the reactions, resources, and coping styles of jobless persons, the greatest determinant of their stress may be the economic conditions they face when they seek reemployment. Thus, for example, although the outcomes of joblessness range from little or no mental health problems to suicidal outcomes, the degree of harm the jobless endure may be tied to the duration of unemployment and the degree of support and resources they can claim, along with the difficulties they face as the compounding effects take their toll.[39]

Debates continue over whether workers in higher or lower socio-economic brackets are more impaired by a spell of joblessness. Some researchers claim that those workers in high-income brackets have more to lose and therefore may have more stress, while others may derive their conclusions from the stresses incurred by low-wage-earning workers who, when jobless, immediately skid into the ranks of the poor and even the homeless.

Much of the research on the human costs of unemployment is based on white male cohorts who experienced a single episode of unemployment. Clearly, more research is needed to differentiate outcomes based on ethnicity, sexual affiliation, gender, level of disability, age, and union–nonunion status. Moreover, because many jobless people experience several temporary or part-time jobs while they seek permanent reemployment and may endure more joblessness in the future, research is needed to document the outcomes of several episodes of underemployment and joblessness so that the toll on the worker, family, and community may be understood more fully.

Because research on the human costs of unemployment has been limited to the reactions of workers and their families rather than to those of their communities, the human costs ledger is incomplete. With entire communities losing the hub of community and family life through plant closures and the demise of livelihoods, the toll on all facets of community life needs to be better documented. Like families, some communities may reveal not only an impaired capacity to provide services but may begin to reject and blame the unemployed while absolving themselves of the responsibility for addressing the needs of the jobless. If this pattern is widespread and persistent, many of the dynamics that rip jobless families apart may be at work in communities (and even nations) that are affected greatly by job loss and economic decline.

The initiatives taken by some families who actually grow stronger during a jobless siege and by communities that provide positive countercyclical services and supports deserve further research and replication. The discovery of these exemplars, in addition to some of the shared negative dynamics that workers, families, and communities endure, may be accomplished more readily by social workers who encounter daily the functional and dysfunctional responses to the trauma of unemployment and economic decline.

Call for Action

Social work has a legacy of taking action when others have not. Rather than sitting on the sidelines, social workers have striven to combat some of the dynamics of helplessness and impairment, despite the laissez-faire inclinations of policymakers and political leaders around them. Although the profession has been chastised for "incomplete" interventions, it nonetheless can draw strength from its heritage of enablement and empowerment. The urgency for social work action is heightened by the fact that by the year 2008, workers may be forced to change careers at least four times in their lifetime.[40]

As the nation undergoes an unprecedented economic restructuring that will cause a loss of livelihood and stress among workers, many social workers will be undercut in their capacity to intervene. Nonetheless, the chapters that follow suggest the array of beginning steps that may be pursued to address, if not reverse, the cataclysmic harms to human well-being that will be wrought by an intensification of the same economic and labor market problems that gave rise to the Poor Law and to the profession itself.

Among its other attributes, power implies the ability to act. Much of the profession's roots and continuing mission as it discovers and confronts "new evils" offer reminders of its strength, capacity, and responsibility to take action when others are immobilized, incapacitated, or irreconcilably opposed.

Addressing unemployment and underemployment involves more than embracing new techniques or theories. Occupational problem solving may involve a fundamental reframing of presenting problems and their solutions, as well as expanded domains of practice—not just to improve the functioning of people and communities but to restructure the economy and its allocation of work roles and income. Whether the primary form of occupational problem solving is the treatment of an individual or advocacy for a full employment policy, new problem-solving resources and practice paradigms may emerge. Such changes may, in turn, shape job descriptions, agency programs, and collaborative undertakings with unions, businesses, legislators, churches, and many advocacy groups.

To take action on behalf of the jobless and underemployed may involve innovations in policies that affect not just corporate practices in the United States but the accountability of corporations for workers, families, and communities in the United States and throughout the world. The increasing domination of the global economy on the structure, location, investment, and production and labor practices of U.S. corporations means that actions taken on behalf of workers in local communities in the United States may have an impact on the well-being of workers elsewhere in the world. Thus, social workers in the United States have a critical role to play in documenting harms and engineering and mobilizing more effective action strategies, services, and delivery systems. "Technologies" in the profession that address only the symptoms related to job stress and not the precipitants must be expanded in ways that fully utilize the talents of practitioners and ensure more effective, durable outcomes for those people who are served.

Debates have raged over the centuries as to whether the system or the individual is responsible for such problems as joblessness and poverty. Although the profession has an ideological and empirical heritage that should support changes in the system, many practice technologies focus on the individual. Despite the reaffirmation by the profession of the ecological or ecosystems approach and of environmental and systemic causes or reinforcers of individual problems, practice paradigms have not been developed sufficiently to ensure that systemic and environmental explanations for problems result in systemic or multichange practice. Instead, many clinically oriented practice technologies address cognitive, behavioral, interpersonal, or familial attributes of problems and stop short of multimodal practice. This book offers suggestions for expanding social workers' practice repertoire and problem-solving resources so that the environmental and systemic shapers of problems stemming from unemployment and underemployment can be used as the next steps beyond psychological and interpersonal interventions.

In turning to some of the theoretical debates about the stresses of unemployment, we need to acknowledge that another source of the hesitation to address systemic conditions is some widely held beliefs and theories that focus on individual culpability and responsibility for problems and their remediation. The next section is a review of some of the theoretical, empirical, and practice implications of the debates about the stresses of unemployment and their causes.

Stress of Unemployment: Two Theoretical Perspectives

The unemployed always have been the clients of social workers. However, social work knowledge and practice have not been well informed by developing theories about the stresses of unemployment. Two dominant theoretical perspectives, which emerged in the past 30 years, attempt to account for some of the debilitation experienced by the jobless and may help to clarify the practice paradigms serving the unemployed. One theoretical perspective assumes that dysfunctional adaptations to unemployment are the result of "social selection"; this theory implies that the unemployed may have some mental health or health impairment that accounts for their marginal attachment to the work force and their frequent impoverishment.[41] Those who operate from this theory base assume that personal deficits are the causes of unemployment and that these must be addressed sometimes as a precondition for more effective employment and economic functioning.

The other theoretical perspective assumes there is a connection between changes in the economy or employment conditions and declining personal functioning. Adherents of this "social causation" or provocation theory may disagree over whether economic insecurity and unemployment cause such pathology as divorce, abuse, and depression or merely uncover it. Nevertheless, they would argue that the treatment of individual pathology, in the absence of employment resources, may exacerbate dysfunction.

That many social workers' repertoires are limited ot psychological interventions may imply inadvertently that much clinical practice reflects a social-selection thesis. Despite the absence of employment as a primary social work resource, social workers acknowledge the intricate interplay of such variables as an individual's personal attributes, inadequate participation in society because of structural barriers, and the consequent impoverishment that, in turn, may impair functioning further.

Sometimes jobless workers seek treatment when the link between their personal problems or symptoms and joblessness is explicit, in which case social causation or social selection theories are more obvious.[42] Others find their way to social service agencies after having passed through numerous critical coping stages that are associated with long-term unemployment. Unfortunately, these stages may blur the extent to which environmental sources such as a layoff or personal attributes such as poor physical health initially precipitated the chain of events that made them seek help. Susan's depression over her inability to find work, which led her to seek counseling, has a different linkage to unemployment than does Fred's theft from a liquor store to support his substance abuse that increased after he was forced to retire when his plant was sold.

Often clients are coping not so much with the immediate consequences of a layoff or their inability to find work but with other problems. In fact, the unemployment problems of many jobless clients who appear in the social service, health care, or criminal justice systems may be obscured by the complications and secondary consequences of joblessness. Thus, more research is needed to determine whether unemployed persons who have committed a crime, abused a child, are suicidal, or have had a heart attack have been so debilitated that they first need help with these problems before they can pursue reemployment or whether the best antidote is a good job, provided as swiftly as possible.

Regardless of causation, some presenting problems may be addressed effectively by using employment as a primary intervention. In Europe, the mental health treatment of some patients in psychiatric hospitals centers on employment as a precondition for the effective use of psychological resources.[43] In the United States, it increasingly has been demonstrated that jobs for workers with developmental disabilities, sometimes provided through sheltered workshops, are restorative and therapeutic and may be central to their ability to function outside of institutions.[44] A jail project showed that jobs are tools to prevent recidivism, regardless of the cause of criminal behavior.[45]

Several studies have illustrated the therapeutic benefits of employment for groups of jobless workers. For example, Kasl and Cobb noted that the blood pressure of workers, which was normal before the news of their layoff, became elevated with the notice of the layoff and stayed high until the workers were reemployed, at which point the blood pressure readings returned to their prelayoff levels.[46] A study of jobless teenagers and older workers who obtained jobs under the Comprehensive Employment and Training Act (CETA) found that employment reversed the symptoms associated with joblessness.[47] For the teenagers, CETA jobs improved or eliminated conflict with parents, sleeping and eating problems, and substance abuse; among older workers, it brought an end to suicidal thoughts and blood pressure problems. Wiesman, Pincus, and Redding suggested that employment may be an effective treatment for depression in women.[48] Furthermore, regardless of income supports, deficits, or caregiving responsibilities at home, employment has been shown to enhance the well-being, self-image, and parental functioning of women.[49]

Some jobs may be therapeutic, but underemployment usually is not. For example, one study found that jobs taken to tide workers over until more desirable work could be found left many workers more depressed than ever. Thus, the symptoms of teenagers and older workers who were placed in CETA jobs but disliked their working conditions were not reversed.[50]

Clearly, social workers are in a prime position to clarify not only whether unemployment is a cause or correlate of dysfunctional symptoms but the extent to which jobs may be antidotes to or an exacerbation of a pathology, regardless of its cause. Moreover, the absence of employment as a primary social work resource or practice strategy may impede the refinement of theories of the causes and treatment of some types of dysfunctioning and the consequent development of effective practice. In addition, employment increasingly is being recognized as not just central to the functioning of such groups as women; racial, ethnic, and sexual minorities; youths; persons with disabilities; and the aged, but as a right that they should be able to claim to participate fully in society. Therefore, it is imperative that social work be at the forefront in testing, advocating, developing, and implementing appropriate work opportunities for those who have been denied equitable access to such key societal resources.

Notes and References

1. K. H. Briar, *The Effect of Long-Term Unemployment on Workers and Their Families* (San Francisco: R & E Pubs., 1978); K. Briar et al., "The Impact of Unemployment on Young, Middle-Aged and Older Workers," *Journal of Sociology and Social Welfare,* 7 (November 1980), pp. 907–915; M. H. Brenner, *Estimating the Social Costs of National Economic Policy* (Washington, D.C.: Joint Economic Committee, U.S. Congress, 1976); J. P. Gordus, *Economic Change, Physical Illness, Mental Illness and Social Change* (Washington, D.C.: Congressional Research Service, 1984); S. K. Steinmetz and M. Strauss, "General Introduction: Social Myth and Social System in the Study of Intra-familial Violence," in Steinmetz and Strauss, eds., *Violence in the Family* (New York: Harper & Row, 1974), p. 9; R. J. Light, "Abused and Neglected Children in America: A Study of Alternative Policies," *Harvard Educational Review,* 43 (November 1973), pp. 556–598; I. Sawhill and H. Ross, *Time of Transition: The Growth of Families Headed by Women* (Washington, D.C.: The Urban Institute, 1975); J. A. Califano, "American Families: Trends, Pressures and Recommendations." Report to President Jimmy Carter (Washington, D.C.: U.S. Department of Health, Education & Welfare, 1976); T. Keefe, "The Stresses of Unemployment," *Social Work,* 29 (May 1984), pp. 264–268; D. G. Gil, *Violence Against Children: Physical Child Abuse in the United States* (Cambridge, Mass.: Harvard University Press, 1970); M. Sherraden, "Treating Unemployed Adolescents," *Social Casework,* 66 (October 1985), pp. 467–474; L. Margolis and D. Farran, "Unemployment and Children," *International Journal of Mental Health,* 13 (1984), pp. 107–124; J. Madonia, "The Trauma of Unemployment and Its Consequences,"

Social Casework, 64 (October 1983), pp. 482–488; M. I. Borrero "Psychological and Emotional Impact of Unemployment," *Journal of Sociology and Social Welfare,* 7 (1980), pp. 916–934; M. I. Borrero and R. Hectora, "Toward a Meaning of Work," *Journal of Sociology and Social Welfare,* 7 (November 1980), pp. 880–894; K. Windschuttle *Unemployment* (Victoria, Australia: Penguin Books, 1981); P. Rayman and R. Liem, eds., "Unemployment, Mental Health and Social Policy," *International Journal of Mental Health,* 13 (Spring–Summer 1984), entire issue; K. Root, "The Human Response to Plant Closures," *Annals of the American Academy of Political and Social Service,* 475 (September 1984), pp. 52–65; R. Liem, "Beyond Economics: The Health Costs of Unemployment," *Health and Medicine,* 2 (Fall 1983), pp. 3–9; and J. Hayes and P. Nutman, *Understanding the Unemployed* (London: Tavistock Publications, 1981).

2. L. Ferman, *Health Consequences of Unemployment* (Ann Arbor: Institute of Labor and Industrial Relations, University of Michigan, 1982); and G. C. Curtis, " Psychophysiology of Stress," in L. A. Ferman and J. P. Gordus, eds., *Mental Health and the Economy* (Kalamazoo, Mich.: W. E. Upjohn Institute for Employment Research, 1979), pp. 235–254.

3. *See* G. R. Liem, J. H. Liem, and J. Hauser, "Social Support and Stress: Some General Issues and Their Application to the Problem of Unemployment," in L. A. Ferman and J. P. Gordus, eds., *Mental Health and the Economy* (Kalamazoo, Mich.: W. E. Upjohn Institute for Employment Research, 1979), pp. 347–378; and S. Gore, "The Effect of Social Support in Moderating the Health Consequences of Unemployment," *Journal of Health and Social Behavior,* 19 (June 1978), pp. 157–165. *See also* H. McAdoo, "Stress and Support Networks of Single Black Mothers," in E. Mathews, ed., *Black Working Women* (Berkeley: Center for the Study, Education, and Advancement of Women, University of California, 1983).

4. *See* Margolis and Farran, "Unemployment and Children"; and R. H. Goldsmith, "The Effects of Paternal Employment Status on Fathering Behaviors, Cognitive Stimulation and Confidence in the Child's Future." Unpublished PhD dissertation, University of Michigan School of Social Work, 1986.

5. M. Jahoda, P. F. Lazarfeld, and H. Zeisel, *Marienthal* (New York: Aldine-Atherton, 1971).

6. Briar, *The Effect of Long-Term Unemployment on Workers and Their Families.*

7. N. E. Amundson and W. A. Borgen, "The Dynamics of Unemployment: Job Loss and Job Search," *Personnel and Guidance Journal,* 61 (May 1982), pp. 562–564.

8. W. Vroman, testimony before the U.S. House of Representatives, Committee on Government Operations, Subcommittee on Employment and Housing, May 22, 1986. *See also* Center on Budget and Policy Priorities, "The Plight of Jobless Workers in 1986," *Washington Social Legislation Bulletin*, 30 (March 23, 1987).

9. *For a more thorough discussion, see* Gordus, *Economic Change, Physical Illness, Mental Illness and Social Change.*

10. K. H. Briar, "Social Work Intervention and Layoffs," *Urban and Social Change*, 16 (Summer 1983), pp. 9–14. *See also* M. Johnson, J. Walsh, and M. Sugarman, *Help Wanted: Case Studies of Classified Ads* (Salt Lake City, Utah: Olympus Publishing Co., 1976).

11. K. B. Brooks, "Home to Roost," *Seattle Times–Post Intelligencer*, December 7, 1986, Sec. K, pp. 4–5.

12. M. H. Brenner, *Estimating the Effects of Economic Change on National Health and Social Wellbeing* (Washington, D.C.: Joint Economic Committee, U. S. Congress, 1984).

13. *See* J. Dewart, ed., *State of Black America, 1987* (Washington, D.C.: National Urban League, 1987).

14. *Report of the National Advisory Commission on Civil Disorders* (New York: Bantam Books, 1968).

15. U.S. Commission on Civil Rights, *Unemployment and Underemployment Among Blacks, Hispanics and Women* (Washington, D.C.: U.S. Government Printing Office, November 1982); D. G. Glasgow, *The Black Underclass: Poverty, Unemployment and Entrapment of Ghetto Youth* (San Francisco: Jossey-Bass, 1980); A. Sun and M. C. Johnson, "Declining Earnings of Young Men: Their Relation to Poverty, Teen Pregnancy and Family Formation" (Washington, D.C.: Adolescent Clearinghouse, Children's Defense Fund, 1987); and E. Seck, "Unemployment and Social Well-Being," *Urban League Review*, 10 (Summer 1986), pp. 86–97.

16. S. T. Martinez, "The Impact of Economic Insecurity: Children and Families in Rural Communities." Paper presented at the annual conference of the Alliance for Children, Youth and Families, Seattle, Wash., June 6, 1986; R. L. Goldfarb, *A Caste of Despair: Migrant Farm Workers* (Ames: Iowa State University Press, 1981); and A. C. Montoya, "Hispanic Workforce: Growth and Inequality," AFL–CIO *American Federationist* (April 1979).

17. "Hispanic Poverty Rises in 1985, Sets Several New Records; Likely to Surpass Black Poverty in 1990, New Study Finds" (Washington, D.C.: Center on Budget and Policy Priorities, September 2, 1986). *See also*

"Hispanics in the Workforce, part I" (Washington, D.C.: National Council of La Raza, 1987).

18. *See* C. C. Geisler et al., eds., *Indian SIA: The Social Impact Assessment of Rapid Resource Development on Native Peoples* (Ann Arbor: Natural Resources Sociology Lab, University of Michigan, 1982); and A. L. Sorkin, *American Indians and Federal Aid* (Washington, D.C.: The Brookings Institution, 1971).

19. S. A. Levitan and U. B. Johnston, *Indiangiving, Federal Programs and Native Americans* (Baltimore, Md.: Johns Hopkins University Press, 1975).

20. Brenner, *Estimating the Social Costs of National Economic Policy.*

21. B. L. Sung, *A Survey of Chinese-American Manpower and Employment* (New York: Praeger Publishers, 1976).

22. B. L. Sung, *Transplanted Chinese Children* (Washington, D.C.: U.S. Department of Health, Education & Welfare, 1979).

23. *See* B. Choy, *Koreans in America* (Chicago: Nelson-Hall, 1979); and D. Montero, *Vietnamese Americans: Patterns of Resettlement and Socioeconomic Adaptation in the United States* (Boulder, Colo.: Western Press, 1979).

24. R. T. Walls, "Disincentives in Vocational Rehabilitation: Cash and In-kind Benefits from Other Programs," *Rehabilitation Counseling Bulletin,* 26 (1982), pp. 37–46.

25. R. V. Burkhauser and R. H. Haveman, *Disability and Work* (Baltimore, Md.: Johns Hopkins University Press, 1982).

26. A. G. Watts, *Education, Unemployment and the Future of Work* (Milton Keyes, England: Open University Press, 1984).

27. Briar et al., "The Impact of Unemployment on Young, Middle-Aged and Older Workers."

28. "Report Will Point to Waste of Older Workers," *Socio-Economic Newsletter* (Institute of Socioeconomic Studies, White Plains, N.Y.), 11 (March–April 1986).

29. K. A. Snyder and T. Nowak, "Job Loss and Demoralization: Do Women Fare Better Than Men?" *International Journal of Mental Health,* 16 (1987), pp. 92–106; M. Abramovitz, "Blaming Women for Unemployment: Refuting a Myth," *Social Casework,* 65 (November 1984), pp. 547–553; L. Rosenman, "Unemployment and Women: A Social Policy Issue" *Social Work,* 24 (January 1979), pp. 20–25; and K. H. Briar, K. Knighton, and A. Van Ry, "Human Costs of Unemployment and Poverty for Women." Paper presented at the Annual Program Meeting, Council on Social Work Education, St. Louis, Mo., 1978.

30. M. P. Levine, "Employment Discrimination Against Gay Men," in J. Harry and M. S. Das, eds., *Homosexuality in International Perspective*

(New Delhi, India: Vikas, 1980), pp. 18–30; and L. M. Poverny and W. A. Finch, "Job Discrimination Against Gay and Lesbian Workers," *Social Work Papers,* 19 (1985), pp. 35–45.

31. *For a discussion of the mobility barriers facing children of low-income parents, see* R. H. DeLone, *Small Futures* (New York: Harcourt Brace Jovanovich, 1979). *See also* R. Sennett and J. Cobb, *The Hidden Injuries of Class* (New York: Vintage Books, 1973).

32. This section is an adaptation of the work of G. Davis and M. Rappley, trainers for the Department of Social and Health Services, Adult Service Workers, State of Washington, 1984–1985. *For a similar adaptation of the stress and coping paradigm, see* M. P. Van Hook, "Harvest of Despair: Using the ABCX Model for Farm Families in Crisis," *Social Casework,* 68 (May 1987), pp. 273–278.

33. *Report to Governor Booth Gardner and the Legislature* (Olympia, Wash.: Joint Select Committee on Unemployment Insurance and Compensation, December 1986); and K. H. Briar et al., *Dynamics of Economic Distress in Mason, Clallam and Stevens Counties: Report to the Governor* (Olympia, Wash.: Office of the Governor, 1987).

34. Personal communication from Jim Francek, former director of the Health Advisory Committee, Exxon Corporation, and currently, chair, Watershed Corporate Health Services, Westport, Conn.

35. L. A. Ferman and J. Gardner, "Economic Deprivation, Social Mobility and Mental Health," in L. A. Ferman and J. P. Gordus, eds., *Mental Health and the Economy* (Kalamazoo, Mich.: W. E. Upjohn Institute for Employment Research, 1979), pp. 193–224.

36. *See, for example,* L. Wasowicz, "Underemployed Suffer Much Like Unemployed," *Seattle Times,* November 10, 1983; and S. Winokur, "Workers Blame Themselves for Boring Jobs," *Seattle Post-Intelligencer,* May 20, 1985, p. C5.

37. B. Bluestone and B. Harrison, *The Great American Job Machine: The Proliferation of Low Wage Employment in the U.S. Economy* (Washington, D.C.: Joint Economic Committee, U.S. Congress, 1986).

38. Brenner, *Estimating the Effects of Economic Change on National Health and Social Wellbeing.*

39. H. G. Kaufman, *Professionals in Search of Work* (New York: John Wiley & Sons, 1982).

40. "Work Changes Seen in 2008," *Socioeconomic Newsletter* (Institute for Socioeconomic Studies, White Plains, N.Y.), 3 (June 1978).

41. Gordus, *Economic Change, Physical Illness, Mental Illness and Social Change.*

42. Some family service agencies, in attempting to respond more effectively to the jobless, found that a number of their clients were unemployed. Personal communication with Nikki Nelson, United Charities of Chicago, Employee Counseling Service. *See also* R. Sunley and G. W. Sheek, *Serving the Unemployed and Their Families* (Milwaukee, Wisc.: Family Service America, 1986). The Seattle Crisis Clinic, which established a category for recording data on the unemployed, found that in 1983, 33,000 calls for help came from the jobless, one-third of whom suffered emotional problems and had no place to turn for help and led to the development of the NASW-sponsored Counseling Referral Service for the Unemployed. Personal communication from P. O'Hara, Crisis Clinic, Seattle, Wash., 1984.

43. S. Olshansky and H. Untergerger, "The Meaning of Work and Its Implications for the Ex-Mental Patient," *Mental Hygiene,* 47 (January 1963), pp. 139–149.

44. K. H. Briar, "The Meaning of Work and Its Implications for Social Work Education." Paper presented at the Annual Program Meeting, Council on Social Work Education, New Orleans, 1978.

45. K. H. Briar, "Crime, Unemployment and the Therapeutic Benefits of Jobs." Paper presented at the Crime Prevention Conference, City University of New York, New York City, May 22, 1982. *See also* U.S. Department of Justice, Bureau of Labor Statistics, *Profile of Jail Inmates* (Washington, D.C.: U.S. Government Printing Office, 1980), p. 6.

46. S. U. Kasl and S. Cobb, "Blood Pressure Changes in Men Undergoing Job Loss: A Preliminary Report," *Psychosomatic Medicine,* 32 (January–February 1970), pp. 19–38.

47. Briar et al., "The Impact of Unemployment on Young, Middle-Aged and Older Workers."

48. M. Weissman, C. Pincus, and N. Redding, "The Educated Housewife: Mild Depression and the Search for Work," *American Journal of Orthopsychiatry,* 43 (July 1973), pp. 565–573.

49. P. Warr and G. Parry, "Paid Employment and Women's Psychological Well-Being," *Psychological Bulletin,* 91 (1982), pp. 498–516.

50. Briar et al., "The Impact of Unemployment on Young, Middle-Aged and Older Workers. *See also Start-up* (Seattle, Wash.: United Way of King County, 1974).

2

Dynamics of Unemployment

Employment is a pillar in the lives of many workers, their families, and their communities. Therefore, the loss of employment may lead to a decline in social, emotional, physical, economic, health, family, political, and occupational functioning. How workers, their families, and communities cope with the mounting consequences of employment and economic loss and insecurity may bring about their recovery or set them further astray. Interventions to aid the jobless, their families, and communities not only must be well timed to reverse or prevent more unraveling, but must address some of the critical coping thresholds that may be turning points that lead either to restorative or debilitating outcomes. This chapter presents frameworks to illustrate the types of phase-specific interventions that are needed to aid the jobless and reduce the hardships that they, their families, and their communities experience. Implications will be delineated not only for prevention, but for multimodal approaches to communities as well as the jobless and their families. Such frameworks and their implications for practice suggest the kinds of innovations that social workers may seek to promote through changes in policies, services, and clinical initiatives.

Ideally, a full employment economy in which jobs are more equitably distributed and compensated might negate the need for many, if not most, of the interventions that are presented to illustrate the kind of work that lies ahead for social workers and their allies. The painful realities in social workers' caseloads and communities require social workers to bring relief immediately while working for full and equitable employment rights. Thus, this chapter on dynamics, thresholds, and interventions is intended to promote local initiatives and empowerment strategies that may reinforce and impel the nationwide mandate for preventive and redistributive strategies discussed in chapter 9.

Uncertain Pathways to Economic and Employment Stability

Despite the undercutting effects of the loss of work roles and salaries, much of the problem solving done by the jobless, their families, and communities is strikingly adaptive, positive, and effective in stabilizing functioning. For example, jobless workers may land new and better jobs, start new businesses that thrive, cope with the human dimensions of unemployment in a positive way, and treat the job hunt as a numbers game in a gambling process so they do not personalize their rejections.[1] On another positive note, communities may diversify with employee-owned businesses that build an infrastructure for long-term community stability to buffer fluctuations in the larger economy.

Such reactions and responses reflect a significant level of empowerment in that the locus of control clearly remains in the victims, who demonstrate their adaptability, resilience, and creativity. However, such positive outcomes are random and hence are not predictable. Moreover, just because millions of the jobless move relatively easily into jobs each year, such jobs may not necessarily make their work careers or economic status durable. However, the provision of universal services to the jobless would be the framework for systematic intervention that would make it possible to disseminate tips and resources to enhance positive coping styles and outcomes so that models of successful adaptation and innovation could be diffused and replicated. The two scenarios that follow suggest different coping responses that might have been aided by a problem-solving framework in which the difficulties that Joe and Jason experienced might have been anticipated and reduced:

> Joe comes from a five-generation family of farmers whose crop failure and high-interest loans threaten to end his family's heritage of farming as a livelihood. Joe's desperation has made him irritable and sometimes irrational. Fights with his wife and neighbors have intensified and recently he began to contemplate suicide. Yesterday, after an argument with the loan officer at the bank, he returned to threaten the officer and bank president at gunpoint and promised to shoot them if they did not reconsider deferring his payments. He now faces charges of criminal behavior, and his despondency has intensified.

Jason sold some of his new farm equipment when he first began to have difficulty making payments. He since has become trained in machine repair work
and soon will open a repair shop at his farm. Although this newly diversified
livelihood may not produce a secure economic future, given the uncertainty
of small businesses, Jason nonetheless believes he has met the challenge of changing times in farming by trying to find new options. His ideas about small
machine repairs came from his brother, who visited a year before for a family
reunion and gave Jason some of the tips and suggestions for training so he could
get started.

Unlike Jason, Joe has no one in his family or community network who
can show him new avenues for either sustaining or diversifying his livelihood.
Joe is not an isolated example of desperation among workers who are losing their livelihoods.[2] His problems are consistent with those of many family
farmers in the United States, and his desperation may be shared by them,
even if it is not expressed in the same violent terms. Joe feels he has no
options left; his threats of suicide and homicide reflect his hopelessness.

A framework for social welfare intervention would have introduced
preventive mechanisms long before Joe's default on the loan so that his
farm and other family farms would remain viable or the farmers would
more easily find diverse pathways for earning their living. These options
might have been coupled with the provision of resources for retraining and
relocation or advice or loans for small businesses.

Despite the destructive forces of joblessness and economic decline, the
survival and stability of workers, families, and communities may be aided
by the bonding within occupational communities. Many workers are
enmeshed in networks that are linked by shared livelihoods. These ties are
deep affiliative relationships. Some workers are bound by a single industry
or resource-based community that geographically may further isolate,
demarcate, and circumscribe their network.[3] Occupational communities
may be found among automobile and steel workers, as well as those in
fishing, farming, mining, timber, and textile communities. The livelihood
may shape the identity of all family members and affect the multigenerational heritage, norms, values, and occupational expectations of the
offspring.

When the family's lineage is intertwined with the occupation, the
worker's readiness to shift livelihoods may be as severely diminished by
the fear of betrayal and loss of tradition as by the absence of information
about alternatives. Workers and their families may feel stuck not only
because they seem to have no options, but because by changing occupations, they would be rejecting or abandoning their life-style, their family's

heritage, and their livelihood all tied into one. They also may be unresponsive to some economic development schemes because they may be more interested in economic gains than in maintaining their social networks and community cohesion.[4]

Geographic isolation exacerbates the access to other occupations. Thus, a shift in occupation to ensure reemployment and survival at a previous standard of living may warrant relocation for some workers, but it may not be emotionally, economically, or socially feasible. The Jeffries family is a case in point:

Pat and Paul Jeffries and their five children have spent a lifetime fishing, as had their parents and grandparents. Although the salmon runs were plentiful for many years, they have been declining for the past eight years. Now trolling for salmon is more dangerous, and the fishing fleet must go farther off shore to make a minimally acceptable catch. Increasingly, fishing families with larger vessels have had to give up their boats because they could not make payments on their loans.

As far back as they can remember, the Jeffries have been a seafaring family. As members of a coastal native American tribe, their cultural identity and heritage is intertwined with fishing. A few cousins tried to make a living by boat building, but most have fished. Furthermore, it has been a matter of pride that they have not had to seek work in the city, to punch a time clock, and to have a boss "riding" them.

Like many fishing families, the Jeffries hope that if they hold on long enough, the fishing runs will recover. But no one knows for sure when that will be. They try to hang on, but the truck has been repossessed, and soon they will have to sell either the boat or their home to make ends meet (if they can do so, because property values have plunged so low that the likelihood of such a sale, especially of their home, is remote). However, the Jeffries do not feel alone because most people in their tribe have the same problems.

The Jeffries cannot relocate; Paul's mother is nearby and needs constant attention so she can avoid going into a nursing home. Three of their sons want to buy their own fishing vessel. The few families who left town in search of work have returned because they could not find jobs in the city. Even if Pat or Paul were to seek a new line of work, it would be difficult because Paul does not read or write well.

The Jeffries face not only the terror of an uncertain future of more losses but the consequences of laissez-faire practices. Moreover, multicultural communities of native American, Hispanic, black, or Asian families may be disproportionately afflicted by their loss of livelihood that has been caused by the rupturing of such industries as farming, timber, and fishing because they may have been more slowly absorbed into diversified industries than have their white counterparts. Because they hold victims of economic decline responsible for their own economic revitalization, they assume that they should have the resources, knowledge, skills, and, most of all, capacity to embark on a new livelihood. Such assumptions belie the incapacitation that may be rendering families like the Jeffries immobilized, rather than well positioned for launching a new livelihood.

Unemployment and the Economic Decline of Communities

Despite variations in adaptions to unemployment, communities, families, and individual workers may follow similar coping patterns. An examination of such patterns and the dynamics of unemployment and economic loss is necessary for developing a framework for intervention. For example, research on the consequences of long-term unemployment suggests that the jobless are victims of disproportionately high rates of mortality and morbidity—in effect, that they die earlier and are prone to stress-related diseases.[5] Destructive, deteriorating forces also are seen in families and communities; marriages may terminate and family members may be expelled or placed in institutions or in substitute care arrangements like foster homes.[6] Similarly, some communities, especially those that depend on a single industry or that are based on the extraction of resources, like mining (hereafter called *resource-based communities*), may become ''ghost towns'' because of mass outmigration and further economic deterioration.[7] Destruction and death, whether real or symbolic, as in the case of a ghost town, strike at the core of the caregiving functions of social work and social welfare.

The foregoing suggests that unemployment is neither a static nor episodic state but, rather, a continuously compounding condition that cannot be understood solely by examining its human consequences. The dynamics of the unraveling of the capacity of workers, families, and communities to function effectively may involve the corrosive effects of declining resources, the discounting by policymakers of their problems and needs, and their consequent self-recrimination and immobilization. Workers may be optimistic about the marketability of their skills until they encounter rejection or blame from the community. Thus, they may question not only their own skills but whether they even have a future. Families may be committed collectively to endure the ravages of economic insecurity until their financial resources are so depleted that they can no longer hold their creditors at bay. At some critical point, they then may determine that their marriage or family life has no future. Community leaders may be optimistic when they face the loss of a major industry, but when their lack of legal and fiscal resources prevents them from stemming the bankruptcy of shopkeepers, they may become despondent or resigned to their community's continuing demise. Common to these direct or indirect victims is a declining ability to solve problems that is reinforced by the loss of resources and the consequent discrediting that accompanies these losses.[8] Thus, without the power to solve problems that comes, in part, from a sense of having options, resources, and alternative recourses, the victims may sink into passive despair.

Figures 1 through 6 delineate multithreshold and multimodal interventions; they are not blueprints for action, just samples of the kind of multiimpact strategies that must be considered to enhance functioning and to counter the degradation of those afflicted by win–lose economic policies.[9] Such frameworks also may illustrate the ineffectiveness of some interventions to counter permanent damage or to restore the losses that already have begun to corrode the functioning of victims. For example, an excellent workshop on job seeking may be timed poorly and may be ineffective if it is provided to jobless persons who are unable to look for work because their need for housing, food, transportation, and clothing has taken precedence over looking for a job. That is, sometimes it is the timing of the intervention, rather than the intervention itself, that is deficient. Furthermore, although single interventions, such as food, health care, mortgage aid, Aid to Families with Dependent Children, or small business loans may be essential to the partial stabilization of workers, families, and communities, they may be insufficient to stave off the compounding losses and negative effects of long-term unemployment.

As the jobless, their families, and their communities attempt to cope with prolonged stress, they may pass through critical thresholds in which some of the losses and impairments are irreversible. For individuals, critical thresholds may involve such incidents as the denial of benefits, foreclosure, repossession, evictions, and divorce. At the community level, such thresholds involve tax breaks to new businesses that result in the loss of revenues and the gain of few new jobs, the termination of social service programs that are critical to the survival of the jobless, and the closure of shops and small businesses that further debilitate the functioning of individuals, families, and the community. For individuals, families, and communities, these events are not just part of an irreversible unraveling process; they may trigger new challenges, such as coping with homelessness

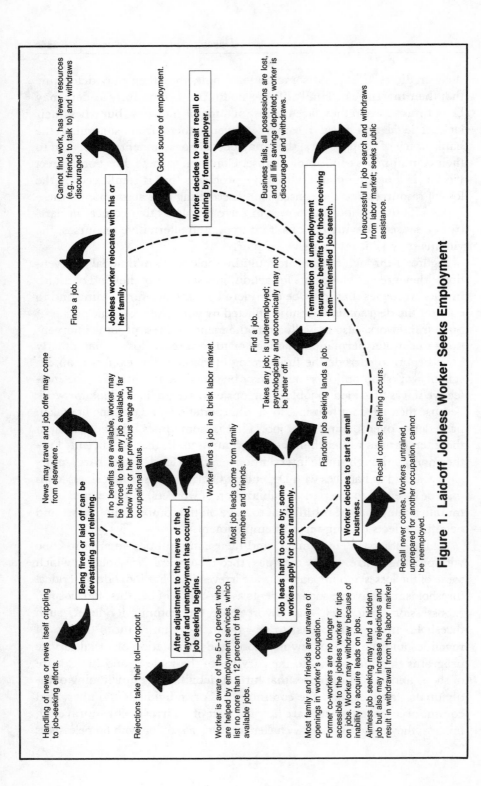

Figure 1. Laid-off Jobless Worker Seeks Employment

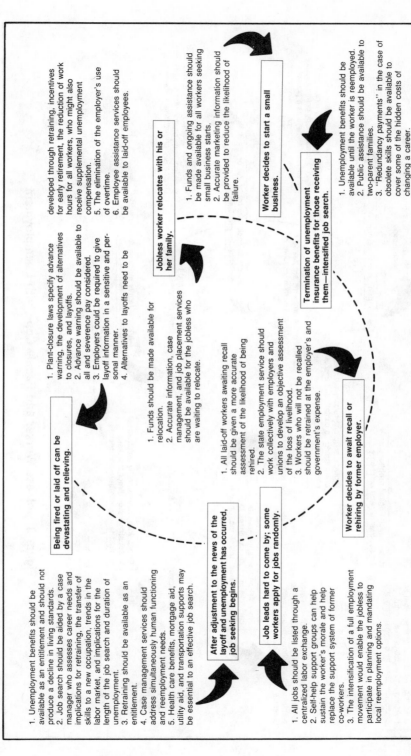

Figure 2. Interventions to Help the Laid-Off Jobless Worker Seek Employment

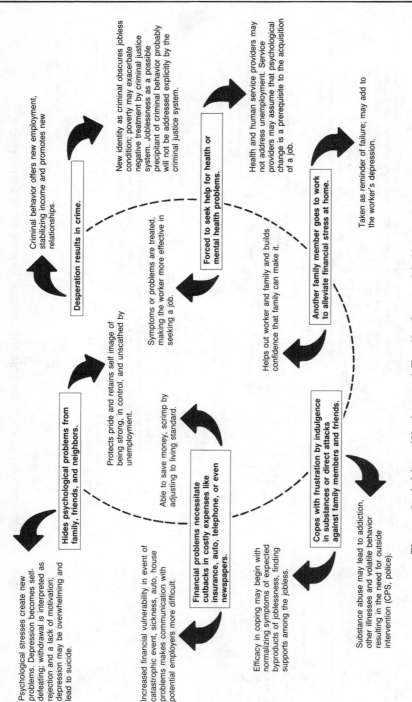

Figure 3. Jobless Worker and Family Cope with Unemployment

Psychological stresses create new problems. Depression becomes self-defeating; withdrawal is interpreted as rejection and a lack of motivation; depression may be overwhelming and lead to suicide.

Increased financial vulnerability in event of catastrophic event, sickness, auto, house problems makes communication with potential employers more difficult.

Efficacy in coping may begin with normalizing symptoms of expected byproducts of joblessness, finding supports among the jobless.

Substance abuse may lead to addiction, other illnesses and volatile behavior resulting in the need for outside intervention (CPS, police).

Financial problems necessitate cutbacks in costly expenses like insurance, auto, telephone, or even newspapers.

Copes with frustration by indulgence in substances or direct attacks against family members and friends.

Criminal behavior offers new employment, stabilizing income and promotes new relationships.

New identity as criminal obscures jobless condition; poverty may exacerbate negative treatment by criminal justice system. Joblessness as a possible precipitant of criminal behavior probably will not be addressed explicitly by the criminal justice system.

Health and human service providers may not address unemployment. Service providers may assume that psychological change is a prerequisite to the acquisition of a job.

Taken as reminder of failure; may add to the worker's depression.

Desperation results in crime.

Hides psychological problems from family, friends, and neighbors.

Protects pride and retains self image of being strong, in control, and unscathed by unemployment.

Able to save money, scrimp by adjusting to living standard.

Symptoms or problems are treated, making the worker more effective in seeking a job.

Forced to seek help for health or mental health problems.

Helps out worker and family and builds confidence that family can make it.

Another family member goes to work to alleviate financial stress at home.

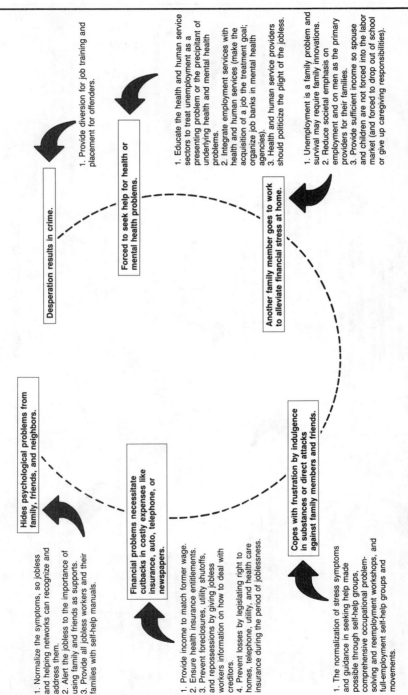

1. Normalize the symptoms, so jobless and helping networks can recognize and address them.
2. Alert the jobless to the importance of using family and friends as supports.
3. Provide all jobless workers and their families with self-help manuals.

Hides psychological problems from family, friends, and neighbors.

1. Provide income to match former wage.
2. Ensure health insurance entitlements.
3. Prevent foreclosures, utility shutoffs, and repossessions by giving jobless workers information on how to deal with creditors.
4. Prevent losses by legislating right to homes, telephone, utility, and health care insurance during the period of joblessness.

Financial problems necessitate cutbacks in costly expenses like insurance, auto, telephone, or newspapers.

1. The normalization of stress symptoms and guidance in seeking help made possible through self-help groups, comprehensive occupational problem-solving and reemployment workshops, and full-employment self-help groups and movements.

Copes with frustration by indulgence in substances or direct attacks against family members and friends.

Another family member goes to work to alleviate financial stress at home.

1. Unemployment is a family problem and survival may require family innovations.
2. Reduce societal emphasis on employment and on men as the primary providers for their families.
3. Provide sufficient income so spouse and children are not forced into the labor market (and forced out of school or give up caregiving responsibilities).

Forced to seek help for health or mental health problems.

1. Educate the health and human service sectors to treat unemployment as a presenting problem or the precipitant of underlying health and mental health problems.
2. Integrate employment services with health and human services (make the acquisition of a job the treatment goal; organize job banks in mental health agencies).
3. Health and human service providers should politicize the plight of the jobless.

Desperation results in crime.

1. Provide diversion for job training and placement for offenders.

Figure 4. Interventions to Help the Jobless Worker and Family Cope with Unemployment

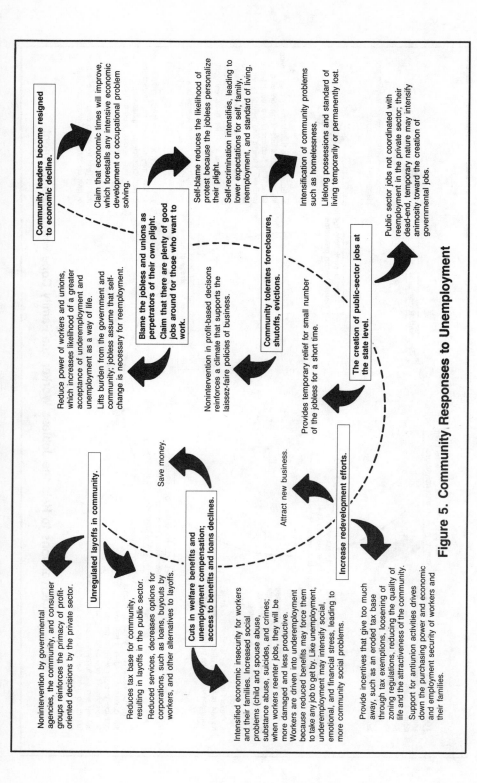

Figure 5. Community Responses to Unemployment

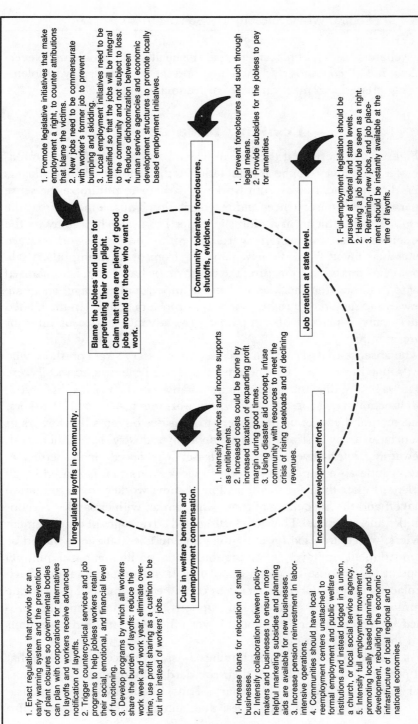

1. Enact regulations that provide for an early warning system and the prevention of plant closures so governmental bodies can plan with corporations for alternatives to layoffs and workers receive advanced notification of layoffs.
2. Trigger countercyclical services and job programs to help jobless workers retain their social, emotional, and financial level of functioning.
3. Develop programs by which all workers share the burden of layoffs: reduce the work week and work year, eliminate over-time, use profit sharing as a cushion to be cut into instead of workers' jobs.

Unregulated layoffs in community.

Blame the jobless and unions for perpetrating their own plight.
Claim that there are plenty of good jobs around for those who want to work.

1. Promote legislative initiatives that make employment a right, to counter attributions that blame the victims.
2. New jobs need to be commensurate with worker's former job to prevent bumping and skidding.
3. Local employment initiatives need to be intensified so that the jobs will be integral to the community and not subject to loss.
4. Reduce dichotomization between human service agencies and economic development structures to promote locally based employment initiatives.

Community tolerates foreclosures, shutoffs, evictions.

1. Prevent foreclosures and such through legal means.
2. Provide subsidies for the jobless to pay for amenities.

Cuts in welfare benefits and unemployment compensation.

1. Intensify services and income supports as entitlements.
2. Increased costs could be borne by increased taxation of expanding profit margin during good times.
3. Using disaster aid concept, infuse community with resources to meet the crisis of rising caseloads and of declining revenues.

Job creation at state level.

1. Full-employment legislation should be pursued at federal and state levels.
2. Having a job should be seen as a right.
3. Retraining, new jobs, and job place-ment should be instantly available at the time of layoffs.

Increase redevelopment efforts.

1. Increase loans for relocation of small businesses.
2. Intensify collaboration between policy-makers and businesses to ensure more helpful marketing subsidies and planning aids are available for new businesses.
3. Increase pension reinvestment in labor-intensive operations.
4. Communities should have local reemployment centers unattached to formal employment and public welfare institutions and instead lodged in a union, a church, or local social service agency.
5. Intensify full employment movement promoting locally based planning and job development, rebuilding the economic infrastructure of local regional and national economies.

Figure 6. Interventions to Enhance Community Responses to Unemployment

the welfare state, child placement, jail, or health care problems. Nevertheless, not all coping is dysfunctional, and the jobless display problemsolving strengths to meet an array of traumas.

Looking for a Job

Figure 1, suggests that the way in which news of a layoff or termination of a job is given can be as debilitating as the action itself.[10] Employers often distance themselves from workers, perhaps to minimize the sense of personalized consequences and responsibility. Thus, a memo from the personnel department on a pink slip clipped to a paycheck may be the sole source of communication regarding termination. Some workers learn about their layoff from the newspaper or from overhearing others talk about it. At this critical juncture, the news can be handled in a humanized way to minimize the shock as well as the impersonal message; adequate forewarning should be a right, as it is in European nations. (In the United States, only 9 percent of companies give advance notice of three or more months.[11])

The absence of early warning places unnecessary stress on those who are dropped from their jobs because they have little time to recoil from the news before they must make major changes in their plans, life-styles, and functioning. Moreover, an early warning may enable workers, managers, and economic developers to consider buyouts by workers or others or an array of strategies to aid an ailing industry. In addition, with forewarning, alternatives to mass layoffs can be reviewed. Such alternatives may include an equitable reduction in work hours that is shared by all workers, rather than the victimization of some workers by termination or layoff and the burdening of those who remain with expanded responsibilities and overtime. The well-documented advantages of outplacement services, which are used for executives and middle managers, should be extended to all employees as an organizational entitlement and minimal cooperative response to the trauma of a layoff or termination. Such outplacement–job placement services could be integral to the corporate or union employee assistance plan. Options for retraining that are provided by the employer also should govern the selection of interventions used to aid jobless workers.

All jobless workers and their families must have access to income that will prevent a sharp decline in their standard of living and may forestall their return to work at a lower salary. Thus, unemployment compensation, available in recent years to less than half and currently to one-third of the jobless, and an extension of medical benefits are foundations for sustaining the financial well-being of workers and their families and may prove critical to their reentry into the labor market (Figure 2).

Despite well-documented rationales for the layoffs or the termination of jobs, such as a decline in contracts or consumer demand, many jobless workers and their families wonder why they were not retained if they were performing well. Some may have experienced such rejection only during a love relationship. Nevertheless, despite the impact of rejection, the news actually may be a temporary relief to some because they no longer have to wonder when or if they will be laid off or fired (anticipatory worry may, in itself, be devastating and affect one's physiological functioning).[12]

After the layoff or termination, family members and friends, as well as the workers themselves, may have sufficient emotional resources to be supportive, which mitigates some of the effects of the loss. The amount and type of the workers' financial base may determine the degree of job seeking that ensues. Workers who are awaiting a recall may try to tide themselves over on unemployment benefits if they are covered. Without an economic cushion, such as an employed spouse, benefits, or savings, workers and their families may plummet financially. Thus, workers often are forced to take any job to tide them and their families over. Research suggests that such jobs may be stopgaps at best and, because of the effects of underemployment, may leave workers who take them more demoralized than their counterparts who remain jobless.

Workers, their families, and friends frequently retain an optimism in the early phases of the job search. It may be only after a new round of losses and rejections ensue from unsuccessful job applications that diminished coping occurs. Despite the probability of a prolonged job search, some workers immediately get jobs that are, in some cases, preferable to the lost jobs. Nevertheless, many workers do not land a good job right away, either because there are no openings in their line of work or because many qualified persons are applying for the few jobs that are available.

Because job seekers are uninformed about the probability of being hired, they may not be prepared to cope with seemingly fruitless job applications. Their often random approach to job seeking, coupled with the use of newspaper advertisements or employment services as sources of available jobs, inadvertently may undercut their success because most job leads come from friends and relatives (the "hidden" job market). Ideally, all jobs would be listed in a central labor exchange, as often is required in several European countries.

Many job seekers become like lost travelers who set themselves further astray as they attempt to reach a destination. Moreover, the very conduits to jobs, namely, relatives and friends, may become unapproachable because of interpersonal stress. Some friends see the jobless as a liability in that the jobless may ask for loans, make them feel at a loss as to ways to help, and make them feel guilty for the jobs they hold.

Family members, friends, and community residents may misinterpret the worker's failure to look for a job, recoiling, and resignation as signs of not caring and of not trying hard enough; such misinterpretations trigger a reaction by them that the jobless worker perceives as rejection and punishment, as in the following example:

Juan has been withdrawn, staring blankly at the television for hours. The curtains are drawn, and he seems immobile. His wife Maria, arriving home from her part-time job, questions whether he called the employers who had jobs listed and whether he went to talk to several old friends who might know of job leads. Juan explains that he just did not get to it today. Maria then accuses him of not caring about the family and of reneging on his promise to her to keep trying. She even begins to view him as a liability and asks him how long he thinks her meager income is going to keep them and their two children going.

Misinterpreting mortification that is associated with the multiple rejections as a sign of indolence or lack of motivation, Maria begins to distance herself from Juan. She no longer is prepared to discuss problems with him. Instead, she begins to figure out how she can protect their two children and herself from the economic chaos that his immobility is bringing them. This distancing and reframing causes her to view Juan no longer as a collaborator in solving the family crisis, but as a perpetrator.

At times, Maria gives Juan tips on how to approach employers, how to sound more self-confident on the telephone, and where he should try to look. Each time she makes a suggestion, he interprets it as a criticism, rather than a supportive gesture. His defensive reaction makes her more frustrated because she wants to help in a supportive, coaching role but is repelled by his hypersensitivity to feedback and suggestions. As is indicated in chapter 4, Maria and Juan's experiences reflect a normal dynamic in some families with a jobless member. Maria and Juan are Hispanic; they may be buffered by the support system of their family and community so that what might involve the total disintegration of a non-Hispanic family may be mitigated by their special Hispanic problem-solving networks.

Few are immune from the stress, uncertainty, and risks that are inherent in the prolonged search for a job. Thus, family supports, such as coaching and feedback, while essential, inadvertently may not only prove to be additional stressors, but may be misinterpreted as disapproval and rejection. Caught up in the emotional tensions of a job search, many are unable to step back and realize that their negative interactions are part of the predictable chain of family communication patterns during the crisis of unemployment. If families and their unemployed members were informed about the nature of miscommunication and the misunderstandings that ensue, as well as the facets of a good job search, they would have new frameworks for giving support, praise, and advice. Moreover, there would be less of a debate about the ''right'' way to get a job because empirically derived knowledge would provide an additional reference point for refocusing the means and goals of each day's activities. The reactions of the job seeker and families might be focused less on each other and more on the tasks of the job-seeking process.

When unemployment benefits, trade-adjustment assistance (provided to workers who are displaced by foreign competition), or other entitlements are terminated, jobless workers and their families face another major crisis: intensive, sometimes desperate, job seeking. The corrosive effects of prolonged unemployment, created by a decline in income and mourning of their multiple losses, may impede their job search and cause them to withdraw. Consequently, an array of psychosocial problems may ensue that may result in hospitalization or divorce. Some workers are strung along by their work organization on a recall status, which leads them to believe that they will be rehired when the demand for the organization's product increases and the organization's resources improve. Because many workers were recalled in the past, they may assume that they will be recalled in the future. Unfortunately, few sources of objective assessments have been developed and are offered to help workers determine whether they should be looking for a new job or planning to change the way they earn their livelihood. The recall status places workers and their families into limbo, often preventing them from planning for alternative forms of employment and plunging the workers into a deeper crisis than their jobless counterparts who have not been strung along. Clearly, a ready-made surplus of labor is beneficial to businesses but potentially harmful to workers, their families, and communities.

Some jobless workers, who still have resources and remain optimistic, but are frustrated by their job search, may strike out on their own by relocating or starting a small business. Despite the rejuvenating effects of assuming some modicum of control over one's situation, self-employment may not always be a route to economic security. Two-thirds of small businesses fail in the first five years, in part because they are undercapitalized, are ignorant of fiscal and marketing strategies, and place their owners and families in further debt.[13]

Some workers and their families attempt to relocate to other communities, where they hope to have greater access to jobs. However, without a network of family and friends to generate information on job leads and labor market trends, relocation may be yet another assault on one's dwindling resources and emotional stamina. Relocation assistance, often provided systematically in other industrialized nations, is minimal at best in this country. Although a few churches have attempted to provide assistance, such aid should be available as an entitlement and as part of a more efficient and humane labor–market exchange system.[14]

Coping with Unemployment

The stigma attached to joblessness in the American culture often impedes self-disclosure and help seeking through networks of friends and relatives (Figure 3). Some workers are unable to share the news of their firing or layoff with relatives and close friends. Thus, just when emotional support may be critical to their functioning, the likelihood of seeking it may diminish. Such reticence may seem functional to jobless workers, perhaps protecting their pride and sense of control. Nevertheless, as financial problems ensue, new stresses may be triggered that are compounded by the absence of any systematically provided information on how to cope effectively with the stresses of unemployment. Workers may impair their ability to find a job by cutting back on telephone calls, newspapers, insurance, and transportation, all of which are key conduits to employers and to sources of information about the labor market. Such cutbacks may render workers and their families more vulnerable to more debilitated family functioning; these compounding losses may set in motion new social, psychological, occupational, family, and health problems that further impede reemployment. Ideally, comprehensive services and entitlements for jobless workers and their families should ensure that no damage is done to their well-being as a result of joblessness; therefore, in addition to unemployment benefits, jobless workers should receive entitlements to health, dental, mortgage, and utility aid, along with transportation supports. Instead, it is up to the jobless to muster effective coping and problem-solving skills to deal with the human costs of their condition.

Despite the efficacy of the jobless worker and family in handling everyday problems, family members, nevertheless, may inadvertently place themselves at greater risk through arguments, agitation, and aggressive behavior. Children, who are less able to interpret events and who may imagine the worst possible scenario, may show their stress in physical ailments, which increases their need for health care, while adults may use and abuse substances or self-medicating devices to deal with their losses and uncertain future.[15] At any time, a new job may be landed, thereby forestalling the downward economic skid and less functional coping responses. But many workers may not be so fortunate and may be so harmed by the losses and their feelings of powerlessness that their adaptations may be dysfunctional and may involve substance abuse and violence against their families. Sometimes these dysfunctional responses will be directed at a child's acting out behavior or at the anger of a spouse. This type of abuse reflects a "victim's victimization" of others that instigates a new set of dynamics and catastrophic events with which workers, their families, and the community must cope. Moreover, the victim status of a perpetrator may be overlooked when the deviant behavior becomes the overriding issue for the family or friendship network. Self-protective maneuvers by the spouse and children, such as flight from the home or pressing criminal charges for the deviant behavior, further complicate the dynamics and reemployment outcome of the already high-risk situation.

Whether abuse is present or not, other family members may seek employment. Some families, recognizing their ability to mobilize resources, then may be strengthened by the successes of these members. The jobless worker who is a father and husband may interpret his wife's or teenager's employment as a sign of his failure and a threat to his role as provider. Ideally, the family can be a foundation for emotional support and a conduit to job leads. Without accurate information about occupational problem solving, however, such family supports may be impeded by doubts and debates about the effectiveness of the jobless worker's approach to the job search.

At any one of these junctures, the jobless worker or family members may be driven to seek help (Figures 3 and 4). Sometimes the stomachaches of the school-aged child may be brought to the attention of a teacher, a school nurse, or social worker, who then may seek to address some of the family's unmet needs. In other cases, the jobless worker or spouse may seek counseling. But counseling may be an uncertain route to reemployment if it is not infused with occupational problem-solving resources and techniques. Work on symptoms may bring relief to the worker and family, but the tools and pathways to reemployment necessitate more than the traditional psychological counseling available in many social service agencies.

Some jobless workers may find solace or relief in new identities that, while experienced in a negative sense, nonetheless give another explanation for or focus to their ensuing problems. Perceiving themselves to be sick and thus in need of health care, as alcoholics in the care of addiction experts, or as offenders coping with the criminal justice system may supplant the trauma of aimless job-seeking. Retraining or more schooling also may help jobless workers shift to a more acceptable identity. Unfortunately, few criminal justice, health care, or even educational personnel are prepared to address the occupational needs and rights of victims; rather, they often limit their services to the presenting problem at hand. Even so, such services may be new launching grounds for the worker's eventual reemployment.

Community Responses to Unemployment

Numerous distressed communities throughout the United States reflect the demise of manufacturing and resource-based enterprises and industries. (In 1986, 31 governors reported that the economies of their states were in a slump.[16]) Often with little control over their fate, community-based economies may be microcosms of nationwide responses to unemployment. Community policymakers, service providers, civic and church groups, on the one hand, may become victims and, on the other hand, may be held responsible for the paucity of problem-solving responses initiated to aid the jobless and the economy. Most interventions focus on the economy, through economic development initiatives, such as replacing lost industries with new ones. These interventions occur after the demise of jobs and industries, not as preventive measures.

Community agencies have major roles to play in the identification of high-risk industries and livelihoods, such as farming and fishing, and in developing problem-solving capacities to prevent their closure or to help workers who are at risk of being laid off.[17] Those industries that are not at high risk because of budgetary problems but that are planning to close because of factors that are unrelated to the profitability of the local plant can be scrutinized, and political pressure mobilized by mayors, governors, and others. In some cases, plants close that are well functioning but that serve the corporation's national or multinational need for consolidation or the maximization of profits by opening in another region of the country or another part of the world.[18] To this end, the needs of the jobless, while tied to their community's future economic base, nonetheless may be seen as secondary to economic initiatives.

As Figure 5 indicates, critical benefits and services to aid the jobless, such as unemployment compensation, public assistance, and police and social services, may be cut back to save costs, and tax revenues may be on the decline; some counties may even be forced to declare bankruptcy. Despite higher caseloads, the capacity of social service agencies to respond may be impaired, and there may be fewer service providers to respond to the rising demand for services. Jail and prison populations may also undergo unprecedented increases. Ideally, increased resources should be available in such times of loss and heightened risk to workers, their families, and their community. The damage done to a community's well-being because of unmitigated social problems and economic decline may be so great that the community becomes a ghost town.[19] The multiple assaults on the integrity of the families and neighborhoods that try to survive and sustain the community may become overwhelming. Thus, communities require disaster aid to counter their demise and their inability to meet the rising demands for help from the by-products of economic stress. However, wages from underemployment to cope with unemployment may not reduce the symptoms even though they may relieve the economic stress.

Credit once offered by grocery and general-purpose stores may no longer be extended, especially to the jobless, not because the jobless are seen as risky credits, but because shopkeepers also may be facing bankruptcy. Assets may plummet in value; thus, the sale of such possessions as a fishing boat or a house in a declining community may be impeded by the declining demand for them. The responses of a community may be based on short-run initiatives that result in tax giveaways to attract new business.[20] Rather than rebuilding the eroded tax base, tax giveaways may undercut the community's future revenue base while serving as ineffective incentives for attracting new business. Antiunion sentiments may accompany such tax giveaways, thereby further diminishing the capacity of workers and families to obtain adequate wages and working conditions.

Although there may be some attempts to create public jobs, such initiatives unfortunately may be seen as secondary to institutionalized jobs in the public or private sector. As utility shutoffs, foreclosures, and repossessions mount, there may be few publicly sponsored initiatives to counter these assaults on workers, families, and friends. Policymakers may not see any alternative but to tolerate and, in some cases, facilitate these practices.

Rumors may increase about jobs going unfilled, which encourages the belief that the jobless have little motivation to find work. Blame may intensify, especially when the problem-solving and coping efforts of the jobless are ineffective. Drunkenness, thefts, and accidents by uninsured jobless drivers may alienate heretofore sympathetic policymakers.

Countercyclical resources and strategies may reduce the community's subjection to the vagaries of the economy (Figure 6). Countercyclical resources in the form of unspent taxes and other revenue resources, including loans, money for services, and venture capital, are essential for hard times. Communities and regions have experimented increasingly with countercyclical funds to stabilize industries and employment.

More responsible partnerships need to be established between businesses and governmental structures to determine who is responsible for the consequences of layoff decisions. Such partnerships may encourage alternatives to closure and layoffs and even may promote the takeover and ownership of plants by employees.

The absence of full employment policies at the local, state, and federal levels intensifies not only social Darwinian practices, but the ease with which policymakers and job holders can rationalize few or no interventions beyond minimal supports. Community development can occur when resources, technical assistance, and intensive support are provided by federal and state bodies. The separation of human services from economic development initiatives may be inefficient and run counter to the ability of local agencies to empower workers and generate new jobs.

Entry and Reentry into the Labor Market

Although research has been conducted on worker's adaptations to unemployment after a layoff, little is known about the effects of reentering the labor market after a disabling condition, caregiving episode, schooling, long vacation, or institutionalization. Because the dynamics of reentry in these instances are different from those after a layoff or after a worker has quit his or her job, it is necessary to be clear about some of the distinctive problems associated with the kind of unemployment a worker is experiencing. Some incorrectly assume that these types of reentering workers have enjoyed the luxury of being out of the labor market and hence that their needs are not as great as laid-off workers. However, the needs of such workers are just as great because they are not eligible for unemployment compensation or for other benefits associated with layoffs, such as job-search support classes, outplacement services, or union benefits. Furthermore, such workers may lack not only experience but the knowledge about networking that is essential for a job search.

Some reentering workers may be operating by assumptions and tactics that were effective in earlier years but are not applicable in a changing job market. For example, mailing resumes to employers when there are few jobs may produce fewer interviews than hand delivering resumes.

These workers often strike out with a positive outlook about their ability to find a good job. It is not so much that their efforts prove futile, but the mortification experienced from rejections and other losses may corrode their reservoir of problem-solving skills. Moreover, this type of reentry can be traumatic because employers discount persons who lack experience or whose experiences have not been derived from working. Persons who have successfully completed a training program, college, or high school may be buoyed by their recent achievements and imbued with a sense of optimism. Such experiences, although empowering, may set the stage for greater emotional letdowns when these persons are confronted by disinterested employers.

Youths often have the most difficulty coping with the harsh realities of the labor market. Whether school performance is used as a gauge of success in the labor market, the multiple rejections encountered in job seeking may have profound effects for years to come, as the experience of Kim shows:

> Kim, an A student, is a young recent immigrant to the United States. She wants greatly to help her family by getting a part-time job after school. However, her language barrier and her lack of previous work experience, along with insufficient job openings, impede her. She becomes depressed and feels worthless. The fact that she is not alone in such rejections brings her little solace. She contemplates suicide.

Youths are vulnerable particularly to the dynamics of exclusion from the labor market because they may interpret an unsuccessful job hunt as an indication of their future lack of success in life. Moreover, they may feel betrayed, having complied with societal and family expectations of staying in school, only to be betrayed by their first encounter with the labor market.

Some new entrants may be missing the loss of their friends, the routines and structure of their prior situations, and earlier pursuits of schooling, caregiving, travel, and other leisure activities. As they separate from a major activity on which they centered their time and energy, any void that ensues may aggravate their sense of loss. Some may feel bereaved and mildly depressed solely because of the nature of the loss, which, unlike the grief experienced by previously employed workers, nonetheless may involve similar symptoms.

Women caregivers are not free from the sense of loss, for even though they may continue their caregiving responsibilities during the job search, they nonetheless may view caregiving as their primary responsibility, because it is too costly or impossible to delegate or share with others. Having been outside the labor market for a long time makes reemployment more uncertain and unpredictable.

Some reentering workers, such as high school graduates or high school dropouts, may be unprepared for a rough job search. The less skilled, knowledgeable, and prepared they are for work and for a job search, the more betrayed, confused, and frustrated they may feel. Women who are family caregivers also may face reentry problems not just because of their absence from the labor market but because they, as well as employers, are sometimes less likely to recognize the competencies they have acquired in household management, family caregiving, and civic roles. Women who are displaced from their homemaking roles by separation, divorce, death, or the joblessness of their husbands may be pressed into taking any available job; thus, their prospects for obtaining a job that could lead to a career are limited.

Reentering workers with disabilities, especially those who have been receiving disability benefits, may experience tortuous routes to jobs because of the discrimination they face, because they may not be able to regain their previous job or occupational status, and because disability benefits may be providing more secure supports than the uncertainty of wages and employment.[21] Threats of curtailed disability benefits make it difficult for such workers to weigh carefully the merits of various work roles, wages, and benefits. For some, ambivalence and even misinformation about whether their disability makes them unemployable or whether they are ready to work may aggravate their reentry problems. Lawson's research suggested that victims of disabling conditions, especially those that stem from work, may suffer some of the symptoms of posttraumatic stress syndrome.[22] Thus, a job search may intensify some of these traumatic memories even if they are not applicable to the current cast of potential employers or workplaces and hence, these memories must be understood as interfering with the workers' effectiveness in acquiring a job.

Dynamics of Underemployment

Just as workers, their families, and communities suffer from the erosion of jobs and livelihoods, so, too, they may be devastated by the effects of the underutilization of skills and wasted talent and resources. It may seem ironic that the effects of underemployment may parallel those of unemployment, but research is beginning to find remarkable similarities in some of the outcomes of these two conditions. Underemployment is linked to violence, substance abuse, marital conflict, and divorce.[23] It also is linked to depression and stress-related disease in workers whose aspirations exceed the available opportunities because they must start fresh in a new line of work, are unable to acquire a job commensurate with their training and skills, and face constraints on their work contributions owing to the limitations of the job.

Although workers may be relieved to be working because of the financial support and the organization of their time and functioning, the underutilization or misuse of their skills may breed resentment and a sense of futility. When co-workers and supervisors do not recognize that job descriptions may entrap workers or change the work system to accommodate and use the talents of these new workers, resentment may turn to self-denigration. Like a self-fulfilling prophecy, some workers even may begin to believe that they are capable only of performing the job they now have. As the workers' self-esteem plummets, so, too, may their social and psychological functioning. Lerner documented the mental illness, episodes of violence, withdrawal, and substance abuse to which underemployed and powerless workers are prone.[24] Some workers who are trapped in jobs that are not commensurate with their skills and prior experiences may continue to work full or part time while they search for the job they hope eventually to acquire. The search often is rendered more difficult when the workers' supervisors and co-workers sense their frustrations and ostracize them. "Occupational stress" workshops, undertaken by Shore and Lerner, have demonstrated the need to normalize and deal with the anger that underlies many of the symptoms as a precondition for problem solving and for empowerment.[25]

Underemployment may be a much more difficult phenomenon to detect than is joblessness because job titles, pay, and the social contributions of one's work may camouflage the underutilization of skills. Few workers may consciously recognize the need to find improved opportunities to use their skills in a different line of work. Such expectations may be limited only to those with a sense of entitlement and hope that alternative work opportunities exist. Many workers, such as women who have been homemakers, may be less likely to perceive their right to an alternative livelihood because there is no one else to whom they can delegate their job and because of norms that make occupational development as an entitlement less accessible to women. Underemployment disproportionately afflicts multiethnic groups, many physically handicapped workers, and young and older workers who often are relegated to jobs that others will not take; yet these jobs are equally incommensurate with the talents and skills of these often marginalized groups.

Notes and References

1. H. G. Kaufman, *White Collar Professionals in Search of Work* (New York: John Wiley & Sons, 1982); and K. H. Briar, *The Effect of Long-Term Unemployment on Workers and Their Families* (San Francisco: R & E Pubs., 1978).

2. *See* J. Loh, "Kansas Farmer Offers Ray of Hope in Gloomy Economy," *Lawrence Journal World,* June 1, 1986, p. A12; J. Loh, "Hope Springs Eternal at Planting Time in Kansas Town," *Lawrence Journal World,* May 25, 1986, p. D8; J. Mermelstein and P. A. Sundet, "Rural Community Mental Health Centers' Responses to the Farm Crisis," *Human Services in the Rural Environment,* 10, No. 1 (1986), pp. 21–26; "Farm Communities Dig in for Long Haul," *NASW News,* February 1987, p. 3; and A. S. Kahn and N. Hashenzadeh, "Small Farmers Going Under," *Socioeconomic Journal* (Institute for Socioeconomic Studies, White Plains, N.Y.), 8 (Autumn 1983), pp. 15–25.

3. M. Carroll, "Community and the Northwestern Logger." Unpublished dissertation, University of Washington, Seattle, 1984.

4. Personal communication from R. Lee, College of Forestry, University of Washington, Seattle, 1987.

5. M. H. Brenner, *Estimating the Effects of Economic Change on National Health and Wellbeing* (Washington, D.C.: Joint Economic Committee, U.S. Congress, 1984).

6. J. P. Gordus, *Economic Change, Physical Illness, Mental Illness and Social Change* (Washington, D.C.: Congressional Research Service, 1984).

7. J. A. Young and J. M. Newton, *Capitalism and Human Obsolescence* (Montclair, N.J.: Allanheld, Osmun & Co., Publishers, 1980). *See also Hard Times, Communities in Transition* (Corvallis, Oreg.: Western Rural Development Center, 1984); and K. P. Wilkinson, "Consequences of Decline and Social Adjustment to It," *Communities Left Behind: Alternatives for Development* (Ames, Iowa: Iowa State University Press, 1974), pp. 43–81.

8. As Dee Wilson noted, some of these dynamics may be similar to a form of "learned helplessness." D. Wilson, personal communication, Department of Social and Health Services, Olympia, Wash., 1980.

9. These figures were first presented at the workshop "Clinical, Programmatic and Policy Responses to Unemployment," held at the Annual Program Meeting, Council on Social Work Education, Detroit, 1983. The author wishes to thank Louis E. Ferman for his review of them and Bertram Gross for his suggestion to add full-employment activism as an intervention.

10. *For an excellent analysis of the causes, points, and stages of unemployment, see* L. Schore et al., *Starting Over (Surviving a Plant Closure)* (Oakland, Calif.: Center for Working Life, 1987). *See also* J. Hayes and F. Nutman, *Understanding the Unemployed* (London: Tavistock Publications, 1981).

11. National Committee for Full Employment, "GAO Report Finds Little Notice," *Jobs Impact Bulletin*, 6 (May 23, 1986), p. 2.

12. S. Kasl and S. Cobb, "The Experience of Losing a Job: Reported Changes in Health Symptoms and Illness Behavior," *Psychosomatic Medicine*, 37 (March–April 1975), pp. 106–122.

13. K. H. Briar, "Social Work Interventions and Layoffs," *Urban and Social Change*, 16 (Summer 1983), pp. 9–14.

14. C. Isenhart, "Churches Try to Ease the Farm Crisis," *National Catholic Register*, February 16, 1986, p. 1.

15. Like social service providers, few health care providers or hospitals respond to the jobless condition of their patients; they treat the physical symptoms instead. *See* R. Liem, "Beyond Economics: The Health Costs of Unemployment," *Health and Medicine*, 2 (Fall 1983), pp. 5–9. This phenomenon is true in England and perhaps throughout the world. *See* J. Popay and Y. Dhooge, *Unemployment and Health: What Role for Health and Social Services?* (London: Polytechnic of the South Bank, Department of Social Sciences, July 1985). There are exceptions, however; *see* T. L. Selby, "RN Helps Unemployed Find Health Services that are Affordable," *American Nurse*, 16 (June 1984), p. 1. Also, physicians in various communities have banded together to aid the jobless with reduced or free services. However, like some social service providers, the emphasis is on low-cost services, not employment-related problem solving.

16. R. Batra, *The Great Depression of 1990* (New York: Simon & Schuster, 1987).

17. J. M. Herrick, "Farmer's Revolt! Contemporary Farmers' Protests in Historical Perspective: Implications for Social Work Practice," *Human Services with Rural Environment*, 10 (July 1986), pp. 6–11; "Church Helps Jobless Relocate," *Socioeconomic Newsletter* (Institute for Socioeconomic Studies, White Plains, N.Y.), 10 (May–June 1985), p. 3; H. Kilbanoff, "Farm Economy Ailments Put Rural Hospitals in

a Tailspin," *Seattle Times,* May 7, 1987, p. B5; and D. Feeley, "Unemployment Grows, A New Movement Stirs," *Monthly Review,* 35 (December 1983), pp. 14–27.

18. G. Haas, *Plant Closures: Myths, Realities and Responses* (Boston: South End Press, 1985); S. Bowles, D. M. Gordon, and T. E. Weisskopf, *Beyond the Wasteland* (Garden City, N.Y.: Doubleday Anchor Books, 1983); B. Bluestone and B. Harrison, *The Deindustrialization of America* (New York: Basic Books, 1982); and Center for Popular Economics, *Economic Report of the People* (Boston: South End Press, 1986).

19. Young and Newton, *Capitalism and Human Obsolescence.*

20. A. Kotlowitz and D. D. Buss, "Localities' Give-Aways to Lure Corporations Cause Growing Outcry," *Wall Street Journal,* September 26, 1986, p. 1.

21. V. Jane Deneberg and W. H. Tullis, "Delayed Recovery in the Patient with a Work Compensable Injury," *Journal of Occupational Medicine,* 25 (November 1983), pp. 829–835.

22. B. Z. Lawson, "Work-Related Posttraumatic Stress Reactions: The Hidden Dimension," *Health and Social Work,* 12 (Fall 1987), pp. 250–258.

23. *See* M. Lerner, *Surplus Powerlessness* (Oakland, Calif.: Institute for Labor & Mental Health, 1986). *See also* K. Briar, K. Knighton, and A. Van Ry, "The Human Costs of Unemployment and Poverty on Women." Paper presented at the Annual Program Meeting, Council on Social Work Education, St. Louis, Missouri 1987.

24. Ibid.

25. *See* L. Schore et al., *Starting Over;* and Lerner, *Surplus Powerlessness.*

3

Clinical Practice with the Unemployed and Underemployed

 **E**ven though many causes of joblessness and underemployment are systemic, the consequences warrant effective clinical intervention. This chapter presents several strategies that not only contribute to a multimodal repertoire of services for social workers but can be undertaken by families, friends, and the jobless themselves. The effectiveness of direct one-to-one services for jobless and underemployed workers can be maximized when these services are combined with some of the multidimensional interventions delineated in the successive chapters.

The clinical assessment of the functioning of jobless and underemployed workers requires knowledge of their preparedness to tackle one of the most demanding jobs of all—the job search or the job-development process. Often, a person who has been grappling with economic, emotional, family, and health stresses may be unable to take on a full-fledged job search, let alone consider the promotion of a new product or service. Thus, this chapter will address the evaluation of occupational stress by delineating appropriate assessment and phase-specific interventions. In addition, strategies for aiding workers in the job search and with job mobility and job development are discussed.

Because valued social roles and occupational contributions are so critical to a person's identity, self-esteem, and life functioning, it is imperative that social workers acquire skills to help reduce occupational stress. Occupational problem-solving skills expand the repertoire of social workers with some new tools for addressing traditional presenting problems. This occupational problem-solving schema is intended to support a developmental approach to the achievement of short- and long-term goals. It should be noted that the schema is more comprehensive than are traditional employment counseling approaches. The holistic practices that social workers can bring to such problems as unemployment and underemployment underscore the importance of social work services and should help to empower the profession to intensify its leadership in delivering services.

The steps involved in occupational problem solving are not limited to but may involve the following two parallel processes:

The Assessment and Stabilization of Symptoms
1. Assessing and addressing symptoms.
2. Normalizing the symptoms of job problems.
3. Assessing and addressing loss.
4. Assessing strengths and social supports.
5. Developing an interim stabilization plan.

Acquisition of a Job
1. Promoting self-assessment for short- and long-term job goals.
2. Promoting an assessment of the labor market.
3. Capacity building for self-promotion.

Assessment and Stabilization of Symptoms

The assessment and stabilization processes draw on traditional social work skills. However, unlike previous practice, occupational problem solving may reframe presenting problems when warranted into normalized by-products of unemployment and underemployment. Rather than viewing presenting problems and symptoms as the sole issues to be addressed, the social worker uses them as starting points for giving help. Thus, the practitioner deals with the conditions that cause the symptoms while staving off more dysfunctional consequences.

Assessing and Addressing Symptoms

It is understandable that, in the past, clinical practice may have focused on the consequences of unemployment, such as depression and interpersonal conflict, rather than on employment problems themselves. Moreover, because the by-products of such problems may not seem immediately connected to some of the stresses that precipitate them, the need to address work-related issues may have seemed remote. For example, a jobless worker's distress may have resulted in a chain of deficits in resources and adaptations that leave him or her penniless, on the streets, and defined as a homeless person. Clearly, the need for housing and for other survival resources, including food, income, and health care, initially will take precedence over the need for a job.

Assessment becomes more complicated when psychological or behavioral dysfunctioning, such as depression or sleeping or eating disorders, is evident. In some cases, the provision of treatment for such dysfunctions may be a prerequisite to the acquisition of a job. In other situations, occupational problem solving, including the provision of a job through, for example, public service employment, may be the more effective way of treating symptoms, because research suggests that such symptoms even may be eliminated when a good job is found.[1]

No matter how well informed a worker may be regarding the skills and techniques needed to find a job, a job search may exacerbate the symptoms of unemployment by aggravating stress because unemployment is more than just a series of losses. The often costly and excruciating pain of rejections of job seekers may create new conditions, including phobias, anxiety attacks, aggression, and withdrawal. Thus, the social worker must be attuned not just to the by-products of a strained job search, but to the need to strike a balance between search behavior and the potential consequences of aggravated, sometimes life-threatening, symptoms. Some clients may need to take time out from the search to address other problems (housing, depression, and interpersonal conflict). During these times, contingency plans must be put into operation for coping financially and emotionally with a prolonged search, along with survival options, such as moving in with relatives or friends or pursuing less desirable lines of work.

The chaotic consequences of economic insecurity and unemployment should influence diagnostic judgments. As relief comes, in the form of a new job; supports for the job search; financial support (Aid to Families with Dependent Children); or a new adaptation to the situation like returning to school, symptoms may subside rapidly. It may be tempting to infer from the impaired social and psychological functioning that is associated with joblessness that some workers are unemployable until they acquire long-term counseling. Nevertheless, such judgments need to be tempered because it has been found that the provision of occupational resources during counseling indeed may cause the symptoms to subside.

Practice that simultaneously addresses symptoms as well as a more successful job search may involve cognitive interventions. It is important to know what jobless workers think when they receive a rejection letter, when the telephone is disconnected, or when they tell their children that they cannot afford to give them a second glass of milk. This self-talk does not just affect feelings and behavior; it may be one of the most critical factors in the chain of maladaptive or creative and functional responses to prolonged joblessness.[2] Role expectations, such as being an effective provider or caregiver or remaining independent of parents, heighten the automatic negative thoughts that jobless workers may have when daily events impair or impede their success.

According to Rappley, cognitive functioning may be one of the most critical factors in employability.[3] Cognitive reactions to stressors such as the loss of a job, rejections by prospective employers, or interpersonal conflict may trigger maladaptive thoughts and behaviors. These thoughts and behaviors may set in motion more of the dysfunctional dynamics of unemployment. Reframing, visualization, and the rehearsal of automatic positive thoughts and images may reduce some of the undercutting consequences of unemployment. The same cognitive improvements that reduce some of the psychological and interpersonal stress of unemployment also may make the job search or job-development process more successful.

Normalization of Symptoms

The normalization of symptoms may be helpful in showing jobless workers how their presenting problems are tied to job-related stress. In so doing, it helps to destigmatize workers who feel like "failures" or "deviants" because it reassures them that they and their families are right on schedule with the predictable by-products of unemployment or underemployment.

The normalization of symptoms, however, is not the same thing as the approval of symptoms. Thus, although some symptoms, such as increased abuse of people or substances or depressive behaviors, deserve empathic and contextual explanations, social workers must be sure they have distinguished between approval and normalization. Some jobless workers, fearing that they will not regain their stability or sense of mental well-being or imagining they are "going crazy," experience great relief and even a reduction of symptoms when their reactions are normalized. Because such stresses actually may impair their functioning, workers may believe that they are losing their grip on their occupational future and that they will not get a job. Again, normalizing these worries as predictable may bring relief while strengthening the workers' readiness to work on the symptoms and to search for a job. Helping workers to recognize and verbalize their anger and to shift the blame to the external environment may be therapeutic.[4]

Assessing and Addressing Loss

Given the major assaults on the occupational, economic, emotional, social, and interpersonal repertoire of jobless workers, assessing and addressing loss is central to the healing process and may need to accompany or to precede the job search. When the attachment to former work roles, work groups, life possessions, or social identity is ruptured by the loss of a job and income insecurity, bereavement may ensue. Because bereavement mimics depression, it may be difficult to differentiate between the two.[5] Nonetheless, helping jobless workers disclose their feelings about past and future cumulative losses is essential to some of the necessary grief work. Although research on separation and loss suggests that the bereavement process may take two years, jobless workers usually cannot afford a hiatus in the job search or in their roles as providers to undergo the necessary prolonged grief work. Nevertheless, the acknowledgment of loss, accompanied by cognitive reframing, may begin the healing process so that workers gain emotional strength and a new perspective on the immediate past and their future occupational problem-solving endeavors are enhanced.

Workers may surprise themselves as well as their families and friends in their enduring attachment to previous jobs, as Schore pointed out.[6] Such dynamics are not limited to but are prevalent especially in occupational communities that are undergoing occupational shifts; for example, fishing or farming families may yearn to return to their occupation "to try their hand just one more season," and former workers in textile mills may still hope that, despite their acquisition of a new job, the mill will recall them. Because a new job may not replace a multigenerational livelihood, occupational problem solving may be thwarted by attempts to return to the lost occupation despite the probability of failure. The more some workers are removed from their former source of a livelihood, the greater is its luster and lure. Thus, whether workers lose their jobs or their livelihood, grief work and support for the bereavement process may be an essential part of occupational problem solving.

Some of the healing symbols and resources that society uses to mark and cushion the loss of a loved one, such as a funeral or memorial service, do not exist for the loss of a job or livelihood. Retirement parties, which are one of the few formal kinds of recognition of one's transition to a new phase of life, generally are presented in a hopeful and even positive light and thus do not serve the same function as a funeral, despite their symbolization of change and loss. Although a funeral for a job might overstate the emotionality of the loss, some more appropriate counterpart would be helpful.

The massive restructuring of the resource-based and manufacturing sectors of the economy increases the likelihood that some jobless help seekers will require assistance in recognizing their degree of attachment to an irretrievable livelihood or job. Consequently, some approaches to locating a new job may reflect not just a search for a replacement for the job, but for all its extrinsic and intrinsic attributes. For this reason, unrealistic and even inappropriate job plans may be made in an attempt to recapture the lost work or content of the job. Therefore, social work with the job seeker should not only address grieving and loss, but should offer a form of continuity via a plan to find a job that has some of the attributes of the former livelihood. For example, a fishing family might work on the repair of radar in boats or a displaced farm family might continue to raise a few animals or crops while working in other industries.

Recognition of the losses entailed in the termination of a livelihood or job may help jobless workers to build a job-search plan around an occupational–diversification strategy (which allows them to maintain their identity with a livelihood but to work in some new capacity or to transfer skills to a new venture that still is linked to the old livelihood), rather than solely a replacement strategy. In this way, the losses may be reduced partially, because, after all, some of the threads of the job or livelihood may be reweavable into more diversified or expanded lines of work.

In some cases, job development may be the preferred course of action, especially in communities that lack jobs. Thus, job diversification may depend on community economic development. Community economic development is predicated on the notion that economic development should provide the maximum good for the maximum number. By assisting neighborhoods, minority groups, women, and the poor to be more in control, rather than passive members of economic processes, it can catalyze in consumers new visions for diverting the outflow of consumer funds, new visions in investing in otherwise "surplused populations," and new ways to respond to the community's need for services and products.[7]

Jobless workers whose outlook remains optimistic, whose interpersonal relationships are intact and unimpaired, whose ability to structure each day in a reinforcing way for themselves and their families, and whose "self-talk" still is positive have exemplary strengths that must be explicitly acknowledged and fortified. Furthermore, they may be useful models for other jobless workers and may need to be tapped for the help they could bring to support groups, buddy systems, or self-help workshops for the jobless.

Jobless workers whose stress-reducing habits include such healthy behaviors as exercise or other recreational pursuits must be acknowledged for their creative and functional adaptations. Such affirmation is significant, in part, because family and friends may be more critical of such "nonworking" behaviors. Thus, social workers can play an important role in building the esteem of and helping jobless workers interpret to others how important self-care may be to their survival and to their effectiveness in the job search.

Because studies have found that social supports may mediate and buffer the effects of unemployment, special attention must be paid to the intensity and types of social supports on which jobless workers draw.[8] Such supports include families who remain intact and perhaps feel stronger than ever, and friendships that grow despite occupational stress and the loss of roles. Social workers may want to address the strengths available in the assistance and advice-giving functions of neighbors, landlords, distant relatives, and former co-workers who come forward to provide job leads, loans, credit, and social support.

Interim Stabilization

Although stabilization of job seekers and their families may be a prerequisite to the job search, jobless workers may be reluctant to spend time on stabilization activities when they know a job may be their best remedy. Nevertheless, the assessment of financial, social, health, and emotional problems must shape stabilization interventions. Such an assessment may flag the need to prevent any additional disruptive effects of unemployment or to plan for them in a more anticipatory and organized manner. Living day to day in the hope that a job will be acquired impedes a more planful orientation to what, for some, inevitably will be a prolonged job search. Thus, social workers must help jobless workers and their families make contingency plans to deal with ensuing crises to stem the tide of economic loss and dysfunctional emotional and social adaptations.

Social workers also may promote the development of resources to sustain such fundamental amenities as housing, utilities, transportation, and a telephone. Worsening medical (and sometimes dental) problems must be assessed and dealt with. In addition, child care services, a prerequisite for the job search, and services to ameliorate other social and economic problems especially for women, may need to be arranged. A plan for dealing with creditors can be established and negotiated (involving the payment of as little as a dollar a month on some bills) until a job is acquired.[9] The development of resources through in-kind supports also may need to be encouraged. For example, a relative might move in with a single mother to provide child care while the mother looks for a job. A review of financial assets may yield plans to borrow money, to sell property and possessions, to use food banks, or to apply for benefits, such as food stamps.

Even though symptoms and resources at least are stabilized partially while the loss is being addressed, job seekers may be anxious to find a job. Therefore, occupational problem solving must involve a dual focus of supports for the job search and ongoing personal assessment and stabilization. Thus, for some jobless workers, the personal and job-search coping phases of occupational problem solving may occur simultaneously. For others, these phases may be sequential and developmental as the social worker enhances the workers' capacity to engage in a demanding job search.

It may be difficult to detect initially whether to promote job acquisition or to work exclusively on symptoms such as the reduction of substance abuse or depression. Sometimes the best test of whether a jobless worker can handle the potential aggravation of a job search is to approximate it through labor market research and a "pilot" job search.

Jobless workers and their families can be helped greatly by permission and a sense of empowerment that social workers can offer in the use of entitlement programs such as unemployment benefits, food stamps, and welfare and disability benefits. Because any job search or job-development initiative in hard times is fraught with burnout and more destabilizing consequences, workers need to feel justified in their use of an even long-term dependence on benefits until they are economically and occupationally afloat. They need to see benefits as a source of protection and investment in themselves so they can reemerge intact and healthy enough to acquire a job or even create their own.

Promoting the sense of justice, and investment in themselves and in the community in workers and families using entitlement programs to tide them over also is critical to the locally based economic development process. Many communities now depend on locally based development to forestall their decline. Some countries like Germany offer jobless workers the right to collect all their unemployment benefits in a lump sum to be used as venture capital for a small business or for retraining. Thus, for some workers and their families, unemployment and public assistance entitlement programs must be reframed as investments in their short- and long-term occupational problem solving, job search, and job development. Without such "investment" resources, locally based reemployment initiatives in the form of home-based businesses or services might not develop. Given that many jobless workers are faced with a jobless community, such entitlement programs may be the sole bridging resource that enables them to become economic developers for their localities. Because some ventures may take several years to become solvent, entitlement benefits may prove to be critical stabilizers and long-term investment resources on which communities and workers depend for revitalization.

The next section describes several steps that could be intertwined with symptom-stabilizing activities without overwhelming the worker with the potential reactions and hardships that could ensue with a premature or uniformed job search.

It also is assumed that many social workers are aiding workers and their families in communities and regions that are undergoing a decline. Thus, some of the previous techniques of job hunting may not be as relevant to rural areas or to communities that do not have jobs. Instead, what is needed may be assistance in promoting locally based employment initiatives in which the jobless take the lead in job-creation activities, often in groups and sometimes as individuals.

Such locally based economic initiatives are not substitutes for publicly provided jobs or full employment mandates and resources. However, they offer alternative ways for practitioners to aid communities and jobless workers so that workers and their families begin to rebuild their decimated economy rather than relocate. The outpouring of interest in recent years in locally based economic initiatives, especially in some progressive circles here and abroad, gives social workers new support and tools to combat unemployment in jobless regions. Such locally based economic development may prove critical not only to revitalizing declining communities, but to building a better economic foundation for historically underdeveloped areas and underemployed populations, such as native American tribes, especially those who live on reservations; multiethnic neighborhoods; central areas in cities; and entire regions of the United States. Economic development activities that are designed and controlled by local residents, rather than large corporations that may have no accountability to a region or community, offer alternative methods for replacing one kind of capitalistic institution with another that may be more responsive to human needs and community concerns.[10]

Job-Acquisition Phase

The job-acquisition phase of occupational problem solving involves more than resume writing and a job search.[11] According to Gentry, as well as many standard job-search programs, its components include the setting of short- and long-term goals, research on the labor market, and self-promotion.[12] Determining which line of work best fits one's interests and developmental needs and rights often is an overlooked facet of the job search. A period of joblessness can be a stepping stone to some unclaimed dreams of earlier years or the opportunity to diversify one's employment future. For this reason, for some people, unemployment actually may stimulate a positive and creative reassessment of their lives and plans for the future.

Restructured labor markets not only make occupational diversification mandatory, but they intensify the human consequences of a potentially fruitless job search for workers who are caught unaware when their field is in a decline. Many job seekers may believe themselves to be employable in their former line of work. Thus, a careful appraisal of their objectives is essential not only to an effective search but to expanding the developmental options of jobless and underemployed workers. Even disliked past jobs yield clues to the selection of new jobs and livelihoods. If not the job content itself, such jobs suggest preferences for working conditions, working relationships, and so on. Ideally, the objective should fit into a developmental framework, perhaps involving a short- and long-term goal. Otherwise workers may be constrained unnecessarily by their focus on finding a job. Thus, even the short-term job target, which may mean underemployment, must be framed against some long-term work goals that then can be used to ensure that the worker does not get stuck in a short-term stabilizing job.

Self-Assessment: Multidimensional Perspectives

Expectations that workers bring to their occupational lives may be shaped by previous training, experiences in the labor market, class, ethnicity, gender, age, and related variables. Some workers see work history as a true progression, representing unfolding earning power (through promotions and wage-related union negotiations), possibly complemented by an increased use of their talents, skills, and resources. The loss of work feels like a major setback, not just in financial functioning but in their occupational development. The loss of a job may be misconstrued not only as failure but as failure that brings the punishment of having to begin again. Jobless workers' assessments of their occupational setbacks may impair their ability to see other talents that have emerged in their previous work lives. Moreover, some may lack the ability to recognize which of their transferable competencies are applicable to other lines of work.

For example, the jobless worker whose previous job was billing and filing may have acquired excellent interpersonal skills with creditors and with consumers who owed money. This billing and filing clerk may be able to transfer such interpersonal competencies into jobs that involve public relations, consumer relations, or a related focus. Socialized by society to approach their jobs in narrow and often linear terms, many workers perceive their work history as a series of links between job titles rather than as a vast array of competencies that may be transferable across many classes of jobs and fields.

The older the worker, the greater the likelihood that competencies are derived from an array of life events. A scanning of their family, friendship, and community roles as well as of their previous work, will present a more variegated picture of the multiplicity of their abilities than will a job history alone. The evaluation of clusters of competence may be effective in pulling together threads from many life spheres, including prior education and training, work as a volunteer in the community, travel, hospitalization, institutionalization, and so forth.

As Figure 1 indicates, many of these clusters of competence can be converted into an array of job titles and functions. As these configurations are generated with job-seeking or underemployed individuals, they may form a kaleidoscope (as one turns the wheel, new connections and patterns emerge). There are many ways to guide job seekers to the job classifications and work environments that best fit their talents and abilities. Unfortunately, few jobs use all one's talents and abilities. Thus, the choice of different lines of work also means clarifying which skills will not be used. Although the aforementioned billing clerk has excellent interpersonal skills, he or she also may be equipped with sufficient bookkeeping skills to try to move competitively into a bookkeeping job. Jackson estimated that 70 percent of the jobs draw on similar basic skills of communication, obtaining feedback, taking corrective action, monitoring results, targeting, budgeting, and managing time.[13] Crosscutting most jobs and underlying the skills an individual brings to a job are such skills as planning, feedback, correction, verbal and written communication, evaluation, selling, persuading, presenting, delegating, and organizing. Jackson further claimed that workers use the technical skills for which they were hired only 20 to 25 percent of the time.[14]

These multidimensional perspectives on self-assessment help to broaden the visions and possibilities for future work roles. Most importantly, however, may be the reframing of the job search into priorities as well as contingency plans, or short- and long-term goals. The job searcher may

Activities, Skills, Competencies

	Neighborhood	Hobbies	Paid Work	Family Work Roles	Prior Education and Training Conferences
1987	Organized block mom program; recruitment, network support	Neighborhood gardening; reading; organizing, negotiating analysis	None	Care of elderly mother; home nursing skills	None
1986	Testified before city council against a developer; research, speech writing	Reading; sewing; analytical skills and manual dexterity	None	Reconstructed basement; carpentry, construction	Took community college course on home repairs
1985	Sold subscriptions for benefit; sales marketing	Sewing for class pro-jects at local school; design and construction	None	Supervise home health care aids attending to mother	Attended caregivers conference

Figure 1. A Sample Cluster of Competencies

continue to pursue a previous line of work while refocusing his or her sights on an interim or long-term work objective.

All these decisions and steps may seem cumbersome, given the pragmatic need for a job. However, occupational problem solving needs to parallel psychological and interpersonal problem solving by reframing problems into a series of baby steps toward a goal. Doing so may make the process more promising and manageable.

Just as short- and long-term goal assessments may pinpoint the dreams that are unclaimed, such assessments also should clarify the qualitative and value-congruent needs that workers have for their paid work. Some value analysis may suggest that some workers do not want to be in jobs involving products that have no social utility or in work organizations that are organized hierarchically. Value analysis also may suggest new paradigms for organizing paid work. In fact, in some communities in the United States and in other western industrialized countries, dislocated workers may seek cooperative forms of work organizations. In other cases, such visions for long-term job goals may necessitate locally based economic development schemes that put groups of jobless workers at the forefront of testing new routes to building their community's economic infrastructure.

Some goal assessment can be conducted best in a support group in which the sense of efficacy in starting a new business venture may be associated with the need for promoting innovative structures in the emergent work organization. Like feminists, newly dislocated workers increasingly are using economic and employment problem solving as routes for testing new work organizations that are more process oriented and are concerned with the equitable allocation of good and bad tasks and the democratization of decision making in the workplace.

Such assessment can be grounded in the natural helping networks of groups of jobless workers who are members of unions, victims of the same plant closure, or jobless members of a community undergoing economic demise. Group-based assessment of short- and long-term occupational goals thus can fortify the sense of collective capacity for trying new ventures that an individual assessment might not tap.

Research on the Labor Market

Perhaps as important as defining short- and long-term occupational goals is the labor-market research that must be conducted to ensure employability. Many workers seek jobs when job openings are infrequent or when a glutted labor market reduces the probability of landing a job in the near future. It is ironic indeed and seemingly unjust that some of the skills required to do an effective job search and even labor-market research may seem more demanding than those being offered to an employer. Nevertheless, researching the labor market not only can be revealing but can serve as an antidote to the rejections and isolation that are inherent in actual self-promotion activities. It is a less-threatening and more productive means of building job leads, networks, and sources of support than is making all contacts for prospective job openings.

Labor-market research provides information on where the jobs are located and which types of employers to contact, the availability of jobs, how many contenders are vying for these jobs, short- and long-term trends in the field, and contacts in the field who may give advice on particular employers, issues, and problems. Such knowledge also helps the job seeker calculate the time required for a successful job search and determine whether another line of work would prove more promising. Sometimes an assessment of the labor market will suggest when a temporary job is needed to tide the job seeker over until a more desirable job is open. For example, if only three computer operator jobs have become available in the community in the past year and new graduates are flooding the market annually from a local training program, the probability of a newcomer to the community being hired will be slim unless he or she is experienced or willing to take a substantial cut in pay. Such a probability is based on the number of openings versus the number of job seekers, as rough as they may be, and helps job seekers focus their short- and long-term financial and occupational plans.

Locating the key informants on trends in hiring may require multiple research strategies. A systematic inventory of the persons the job seeker already knows who might have job leads, including his or her family and friends, is often a fruitful beginning. Key employers also can be located through the business section of newspapers, the yellow pages, business publications, and directories of businesses and other types of employers. Reference librarians in public libraries are excellent sources of information about such publications and others that may cover the work organizations in the occupations of interest to the job seeker.[15]

All this research points to the need for job seekers to generate a roster of jobs and informants who can give helpful advice on possible jobs, as well as provide referrals to persons who may be hiring or who may know of actual jobs that are opening up. Such contacts may help to reduce the random nature of the job search and focus the job seekers' energy so that they will present themselves at the right place and time just as their skills may be needed. Labor market informants also may help job seekers seem like members of a network, not strangers to future hiring personnel. For example, in the initial contact or during an interview, the job seeker could mention the informant who referred him or her to the hiring personnel or the advice that was given. This networking may help to reduce the "outsider" phenomenon, because hiring personnel usually do not hire "strangers" but those who have requisite skills and who fit into the work "family."

Job seekers may not realize the extent to which knowledge of the labor market resides within some of their own social support systems. An ecomap, which lays out—through boxes or circles with connecting lines— all those in the job seeker's reference group who may be conduits to information on the labor market, may display quickly the pathways to information that exist.[16] Sometimes by focusing on several possible job targets, job seekers may identify an array of different key informants in their personal networks; therefore, with several job targets, they may want to create an ecomap for each type of job they are seeking.

Labor market informants often are not the hiring personnel in work organizations. To acquire an appointment with such personnel, Jackson suggested that it is important not to mention to the receptionist or to the personnel expert that one is looking for a job but instead to stress that the goal of such an interview is to obtain information on the key organizations, trends, and future directions in a specific job line or field.[17] Thus, acquiring the name of key personnel (even those who do the hiring) may prove to be less difficult, because receptionists will not think they must shield their employers from a job seeker. Remarkably, many of these key informants enjoy talking about trends and lending their expertise to the occupational development of the job seeker.

Research has shown that most successful job searchers are fostered through personal networks and that jobs usually are not acquired through such formal routes as advertisements in newspapers, state employment offices, or private employment agencies.[18] This research is consistent with the privatized practices of U.S. employers who, unless they are receiving federal funding, are not compelled even to list job openings with the state employment services. It is precisely because so few jobs are listed that plying the hidden networks is critical. These networks may simulate a form of occupational kinship for job seekers who otherwise are isolated from the pathways to employment and the key personnel who are the gatekeepers on these pathways.

Research also has suggested that want ads in newspapers, which policymakers often cite as evidence that plenty of good jobs are available if the jobless would be willing to take them, are often misrepresentations of the actual work that is available.[19] These advertisements may be listed in such a way as to embellish the jobs so that job seekers are encouraged to pursue them. Because there are no systematic controls on jobs that are listed in the want ads, such practices may render jobless workers all the more vulnerable, given their often desperate need for employment. As they become increasingly knowledgeable about labor market trends, however, job seekers may become skilled at spotting which advertisements misrepresent jobs.

Some labor market research may involve a feasibility analysis for developing a new product or service. Technical assistance in feasibility and marketing analysis may be available in the form of brochures or personal consultation from the Small Business Administration, the local Chamber of Commerce, or an Economic Development Council. Nevertheless, much of this research falls onto the jobless or underemployed worker, family members, or other members of a support network. The failure of a small business is attributable, in part, to the relatively unsupported and unsubsidized feasibility analyses that fall on the shoulders of the hopeful inventor or entrepreneur. It is not due necessarily to the product or service that is being marketed.

Simultaneously, data on venture loans and ways to collectivize the risks of small-business failure are poorly communicated tips and tools that rarely trickle down to community-based enterprises. Therefore, it is incumbent on social workers, although social workers may lack some of the feasibility analysis and business development tools or experience themselves, to help mobilize and support consultative activities and locally based revolving loan funds.

In addition to determining if a business strategy is likely to be successful, a feasibility study is based on an analysis of the skills that a worker or network of workers brings, what resources are needed and are available, and whether there is a sufficient need and demand for a product or service. The feasibility study may address not only the need for the product but the competition; what type of organization, auspices, and structure can best deliver the product; and the level as well as the type of financing available.

Because financing is critical not just to the feasibility of a new enterprise or service but its long-term durability, various loan-fund sources must be researched. It is possible that gaps in the financing of locally based initiatives may lead to the development of resources by social service agencies to ensure that revolving loans are available to promising new ventures.

Self-Promotion

Clarified job goals as well as knowledge of specific hiring trends and actual job openings must be complemented by self-promotional activities. The idea of "selling oneself" may seem crass, not only to social workers but to workers who may see the acquisition of a job as solely a match between the vacant job and the baseline skills and knowledge they bring. This view of the hiring process might be appropriate when there are more jobs than qualified workers and hence hiring practices are far less selective. However, few workers in the United States today have the freedom to rely solely on their skills to find jobs. Despite employers' attempts to be objective about their needs, they often select personnel on the basis of personal attributes as well as skills; hence, nonverbal messages may be as important as what job seekers convey verbally. Forging a fit between the employer's needs and the capabilities of the job seeker is thus another essential component of acquiring a job.

The work organization is a social–political–economic entity, and new employees may be selected on the basis of their fit with the work organization and work group, not just on their skills. Therefore, prospective applicants must convince employers that they have the desired skills and work habits, interactional behaviors, and motivational attributes that make them extra special and durable employees.

Self-promotion may be understood best as

■ Articulating the skills that make the job seeker right for the job.

■ Presenting some evidence of being a hard worker and being committed to getting the job done.

■ Conveying the ability to solve special problems that may fit the employer's needs or special interests (such as wanting to develop additional skills to help with a new contract or emerging market).

■ Displaying knowledge of and interest in the employer, including past and current trends. (This information is especially hard to come by without intensive research on the labor market and the specific employer.)

Resumes and job applications. Resumes and job applications are the first screening tools that employers use for hiring and often are revealing statements about the effectiveness of the job seeker's self-promotion. Many resumes are modest or straightforward statements (or understatements) of previous jobs and attributes. Lists of past job titles may cloak the array of skills a worker has acquired, and employers cannot be expected to infer an applicant's attributes from these job titles. Thus, a resume must be a thoughtful reflection of competencies and attributes, rather than an inventory of previous work experiences. An in-depth review of competencies may be the culmination of the self-discovery and reframing process that emerges from the self-assessment, labor market assessment, and self-promotion processes.

In labor markets with an abundance of job seekers, employers may use resumes to screen out otherwise qualified applicants. Unless they actually are hiring for specific positions, employers simply may throw resumes away. Their uncertainty about hiring jobless workers can be heightened if they learn that a specific applicant had experienced conflict on a previous job or even that the applicant and not others was laid off by a particular employer. Thus, the social worker needs to help job seekers reframe their prior experiences so their confidence is not undercut and they can reclaim any lost pride in the quality of work they do and in their ability to function effectively with supervisors and work groups. Doing so may mean that the social worker helps the job seeker minimize rather than dwell on what still may be a major emotional and occupational setback (being fired) so that it is not a barrier to acquiring a job.

Studies have found that job seekers who have frequent interviews receive more job offers than those who do not. According to Jackson and Azrin and Besalel, among others, the more rejections one has, the closer one comes to getting a job.[20] Thus, the goal of an effective job search is to maximize the number of interviews one has, while gearing oneself up for numerous rejections. This goal is best achieved by considering the job search to be a ''game.''

One main tool in the game is the resume, which can be used as a conduit for an interview by hand delivering and by including applications filled out on the job site followed by a request to discuss the job in more detail with the hiring person. Job seekers may be poorly prepared for the amount of intensive work required to obtain a face-to-face interview with an employer to discuss the job or some attribute of the work organization. Their feelings of inadequacy or uncertainty about asserting their rights to learn more about jobs through direct contact with employers come, in part, from their respect for ''channels of command,'' their uneasiness in imposing their needs on persons with authority, and the unempowering nature of hierarchical relationships. Consequently, social workers can provide much support, rehearsal, and ongoing feedback to help job seekers develop or strengthen the interactional skills necessary to obtain such face-to-face interviews. Most job search handbooks include examples of the kinds of questions asked in interviews; these guides can be used as a self-help tool by job seekers, who can role play these interviews with friends or relatives. It is useful to audiotape or videotape these mock interviews so that job seekers can pinpoint the responses they would like to have handled differently; that is, they can see or hear for themselves when their answers were weak and the points at which they need to be more assertive, more direct, or more positive about themselves. The use of audio- and videotapes minimizes the need for the social worker, family member, or friend to be the primary source of constructive feedback.

Job-seeking tips. Some may question the appropriateness and even the ethics of giving job seekers tips that may put them at an added advantage over others in being hired. Such questions are important reminders of the win–lose nature of the U.S. economic system and a labor market that conveys one set of messages to job seekers (by looking hard, one will land a job), while abiding by another set of rules (ensuring that there always will be some people without a job). In a full employment society, job seekers would not have to rely on competitive and convoluted mechanisms to give themselves an advantage over others because skills, not marketability, would be the overriding basis for matching workers and jobs.

Nevertheless, job seekers who are seen by social workers usually need an extra boost to compete for jobs. Millions of jobs change hands each day. Many of them are filled by persons who have the special advantage of already being employed. Moreover, the employment services of a social worker, like high-quality jobs themselves, should be available to all persons as a right. Thus, as social workers intensify their services to the jobless, it is not to give compensatory services but to demonstrate and test the significance of more universal employment rights and services.

Self-promotion actually may come more easily to some persons when they are marketing a product or service in which they believe. Workers who seek alternative work organization structures and home- or community-based economic ventures may fare as well if not better in promoting their own product than in fitting into a labor market that they believe may underemploy them or repeat old negative experiences of hierarchical decision making and the exploitation of workers. Social work supports to the pioneering individual or group who is testing some enterprise activity may shift from coaching and feedback around interviewing for a job to coaching for the effective marketing of a product to loan officers as well as to potential consumers. Similar techniques used in preparing for job interviews, such as rehearsal, coaching, demonstration, and feedback, may fortify the locally based economic development benefits that jobless workers bring to their communities, families, and future livelihoods.

Network-Based Occupational Problem Solving

Family members and friends who constitute the job seeker's natural support networks may help the jobless worker especially when they are given the tools for group-based occupational problem solving. By combining individualized occupational problem solving with network-based job search supports, the social worker can increase the likelihood that the jobless worker's search for employment will be effective. Applying some of the occupational problem-solving tools just discussed, Ron, a social worker in a multiservice center, attempts to promote reemployment in a region that has been affected greatly by the loss of jobs in the mills and mines:

Julia is a 30-year-old single mother who recently has been laid off from a local mill. Unable to make mortgage payments or to care adequately for her two school-age children, she appealed to her minister for help, who referred her to the local multiservice agency. Julia has spent the last few weeks receiving social work services from Ron. Ron first helped Julia analyze all the spheres of her family life that were affected by unemployment so that he and Julia could pinpoint which problems seemed pressing or were imminent.

Ron was quick to reassure Julia that her sleeplessness, lethargy, and dissatisfaction with her parenting indeed were attributable to her unemployment and might be remedied by a good job. Julia related her battle with headaches and increased food intake, which she attributed to the stress of an uncertain and dangerous future. Her negative feelings about her inadequacy as a provider and caregiver seemed to heighten her behavioral problems. Thus, through normalizing her symptoms and helping her reframe negative thoughts about her role functioning, Ron was able to help Julia begin to display a more positive outlook. Ron also pinpointed the possibility of foreclosure on her house if her finances were not put in order. By helping her plan for future financial crises, Ron was able to get Julia to mobilize some family resources that she otherwise might not have claimed. Sometime before, Julia had inherited jewelry, which she had left for safe keeping with her mother. She found that the value of the jewelry was sufficient to reduce the burden of utility, telephone, and car payment bills and was able to negotiate its successful sale and create new resources she had not realized would be so critical to her survival.

Both Julia and Ron were hard pressed to determine whether her recall to the mill was a realistic hope. In fact, there were sufficient indications that the mill eventually might close if new equipment was not purchased soon. Unfortunately, it was not easy to gain access to information on the labor market.

Helping Julia scan all her life dreams left Ron with a sense of the visions Julia had set aside when her education was ended abruptly by marriage and child rearing. It was only when her husband moved away several years ago that she became dependent on the mill as her source of a livelihood. The mine where her husband worked had so many closures because of accidents that tensions became great at home and they divorced. Since the divorce, Julia had lived close to economic crisis even when she was working. With her lay off, she figured the house would be one of the first resources to go on her list of cutbacks. Julia's sense of economic vulnerability has been reduced with the sale of her jewelry, which temporarily stabilized her at an income that would allow her to maintain her house for three more months. In the meantime, she considered a job search in a new line of work. Initially, the thought of a radical shift, including relocation, terrorized her. Now diversifying and expanding her options made sense because she was becoming more and more convinced that the mill would not rehire her.

Ron's skillful acknowledgment of Julia's grief over the loss of a livelihood that was so intertwined with her friends and family in the community even got her to evaluate the idea of relocating. As Ron helped Julia recognize pathways to jobs that she might find through her multigenerational family located nearby, he helped her develop an ecosystem evaluation of those to whom she could turn for help or who were stressors. This ecomap revealed six possible sources of information about jobs, as well as occupational pathways to new careers. Julia also included in her ecomap 10 other key support persons in her life who could be conduits to leads about new jobs.

Occupational options revealed in her "reclaimed dream" assessment included design and graphics work, writing, and establishing a child care center. Julia's sense of urgency about finding a job made her reluctant to explore the writing and child care center goals that both require more education. Nevertheless, she asked an uncle who owns a printing shop in a nearby town for advice about jobs in graphics. In her research on the labor market, she discovered that design work also required more schooling, especially if she were to have any mobility. Despite this limitation, her uncle encouraged her to consider applying for a design job with a regional publisher that had just opened its offices and was hiring entry-level assistants. Unfortunately, there were few design jobs, even at the assistant level, so Ron helped Julia calculate the odds of her being hired in the field. As Ron helped Julia build on the leads generated by her network of friends and family, they identified six possible sources of employment in the region where she might pursue her design interests and developed contingency plans to counteract the consequences of her failure to find a design job. Furthermore, Julia's decision to sell her house if she acquired a design job in an outlying community gave her the chance to probe new job possibilities in other communities.

Ron instituted a job-search support group (job club) to which he referred Julia because he believed that Julia's chances to find a job would increase through such group-based supports. Now that she had identified several different job goals, Julia was prepared to use the encouragement, feedback, and support of these fellow job seekers. Had she entered the group without the individual planning time with Ron, she might have had less of a chance to rethink her new job focus because she would have been swept up quickly by the dynamics of the job search when she still was at the self-assessment and goal-planning stages.

Ron's decision to develop a job club was based on Azrin and Besalel's well-documented group-based behavioral approaches to the job search.[21] As chapter 5 discusses in more detail, the job club offers additional resources to the job seeker and social worker that not only may maximize success but may generate multimodal interventions on behalf of the unemployed. Job clubs assume that success is intensified when social support, feedback, encouragement, and information exchange are provided. They reduce the isolation of the job search by using a network of peers or "buddies" to increase skills, motivation, and problem solving. The group-support dynamics of job clubs may help a job seeker compile the best inventory of his or her skills and competencies, which, working in isolation, he or she might not systematically discover. Group-based supports are essential for keeping the job seeker's motivation and courage high enough to sustain the continual arrangement of interviews, debriefing of employer contacts, and rejections. In addition, members of job clubs can share rides, information, child care responsibilities, haircuts, housing, and countless other resources.

Job clubs are exceptional forums for addressing deficits in skills in a nonstigmatizing way. About one-third of the adult population is estimated to be illiterate.[22] With the demise of industries and livelihoods, the illiterate dislocated person is severely handicapped. Many jobs once were acquired without any requisite skills in reading or writing. Now, some job seekers must reveal their illiteracy to their families and friends for the first time. In some cases, their deficits will prompt a spouse or friend to fill out job applications for them. In other cases, the illiteracy will result in a return to school to adult basic education courses.

Literacy problems often can be supported most effectively in the context of a job club, where it is likely that others also may share the problems. Thus, the support and destigmatization made possible in job clubs or other support groups for the jobless can offer immeasurable benefits to workers with this critical problem.

As chapter 5 suggests, when jobless workers form job clubs, their successes lie not just in finding jobs at rates that are 40 to 60 percent higher than those who are not in job clubs, but their self-image and value to others increase and their self-recrimination decreases.[23] Sometimes job clubs are antidotes to accusations at home that the job seeker is at fault for not getting a good job because they may demonstrate new ways to conduct a job search, to organize one's day, and to frame the job-search experience. Few social workers have the time to supply all the emotional reinforcements that the job seeker needs and that may be best fortified by a peer group or buddy system. Thus, organizing self-help, group-based supports for one's jobless clients either through one's agency or through referral to ongoing job clubs sponsored by a state employment service or elsewhere may be an effective complement to the clinical service approach described.

Group-based dynamics may be so prevalent in unions and in occupational communities that affiliative relationships provide an excellent base for the infusion of tools for occupational survival and diversification. Social workers may be surprised by the absence of help seeking among members of these support networks. Because members of these networks constitute caregiving resource systems for one another, to some extent, the idea of help seeking may seem alien, artificial, and unnecessary to them. Nevertheless, these networks have the same right and need for information about survival that is provided by social service agencies. Thus, clinical responses to joblessness may need to include outreach, self-help, and capacity-building strategies with these self-contained support networks. Such outreach and capacity building may forge new help-seeking pathways at appropriate junctures to prevent some of the dysfunctional coping responses to joblessness.

Notes and References

1. K. Briar et al., "The Impact of Unemployment on Young, Middle Aged and Older Workers," *Journal of Sociology and Social Welfare,* 7 (November 1980), pp. 907–915; and S. Kasl and S. Cobb, "The Experience of Losing a Job: Reported Changes in Health Symptoms and Illness Behavior," *Psychosomatic Medicine,* 37 (March–April 1975), pp. 106–122.

2. M. Rappley, "Barriers to Employability." Lecture presented at a workshop for the Department of Social and Health Services, School of Continuing Education, University of Washington, Seattle, 1984–1985.

3. Ibid.

4. *See* L. Schore, "Social Work with Dislocated Workers: A Non-Traditional Clinical Model." Paper presented at the Workshop on Unemployment, Regional Symposium of the International Council on

Social Welfare, Rome, Italy, 1987. *See also* R. Liem, "Beyond Economics: The Health Costs of Unemployment," *Health and Medicine,* 2 (Fall 1983), pp. 3–9.

5. C. Norton and E. K. Rynearson, "Separation and Loss." Symposium lecture presented by the Separation and Loss Institute, Virginia Mason Hospital, Seattle, Wash., September 15, 1984.

6. L. Schore, "Empowering Dislocated Workers through Union-Based Counseling Programs." Paper presented at the conference of the American Psychological Association, Washington, D.C., August 1986.

7. *See* D. P. Ross and P. J. Usher, *From the Roots Up* (Toronto, Canada: James Lorimer & Co., Publishers, 1986). *See also* M. K. Sanyika, "Minorities and CED: Preliminary Issues," *Economic Development and Law Center Report* (Berkeley, Calif.: National Economic Development and Law Center, May–August 1984), pp. 64–67.

8. G. R. Liem, J. H. Liem, and J. Hauser, "Social Support and Stress: Some General Issues and Their Application to the Problem of Unemployment," in L. A. Ferman and J. P. Gordus, eds., *Mental Health and the Economy* (Kalamazoo, Mich.: W. E. Upjohn Institute for Employment Research, 1979), pp. 347–378.

9. One useful resource is L. Feldman, *The Family in Today's Money World* (2d ed.; New York: Family Service Association of America, 1976). *See also* J. May, "Conquering Your Financial Fears," *Public Welfare,* 40, No. 4 (1982), pp. 11–17.

10. *See, for example,* S. M. Chandler, "The Hidden Feminist Agenda in Social Development," in N. Van Den Berg and L. B. Cooper, eds., *Feminist Visions for Social Work* (Silver Spring, Md.: National Association of Social Workers, Inc., 1986), pp. 12–19; S. Haberfeld, "Economic Planning in Economically Distressed Communities: The Need to Take a Partisan Perspective," *Economic Development and Law Center Report* (Berkeley, Calif.: National Economic Development and Law Center, October–December 1981), pp. 7–16; and S. Gould, "Women in Poverty: A Challenge to CED," *Economic Development and Law Center Report* (Berkeley, Calif.: Economic Development and Law Center, Spring 1986), pp. 2–4.

11. Much of the conceptualization of the job-acquisition processes was made possible by my work with M. Gentry, M. Vinet, and M. Rappley, trainers for the Department of Social and Health Services, In-service Employment Training, Olympia, Wash., 1985–1986.

12. M. Gentry, "Job Search Techniques." In-service training lecture presented to the Washington State Department of Social and Health Services, Olympia, Wash., 1985–1986.

13. T. Jackson, *Guerrilla Tactics in the Job Market* (New York: Bantam Books, 1981), p. 34.

14. Ibid., p. 173.

15. T. Jackson, "Developing Sources in the Hidden Job Market," *National Business Employment Weekly,* June 29, 1986, pp. 13–14. *See also,* N. H. Azrin and V. A. Besalel, *Finding a Job* (Berkeley, Calif.: Ten Speed Press, 1983).

16. A. Hartman, *Finding Families* (Beverly Hills, Calif.: Sage Publications, 1979).

17. Jackson, "Developing Sources in the Hidden Job Market."

18. Azrin and Besalel, *Finding a Job.*

19. M. Johnson, J. Walsh, and M. Sugarman, *Help Wanted: Case Studies of Classified Ads* (Salt Lake City, Utah: Olympus Publishing Co., 1976).

20. Jackson, *Guerilla Tactics in the Job Market;* and Azrin and Basalel, *Finding a Job.*

21. N. H. Azrin and V. A. Besalel, *Job Club Counselor's Manual* (Baltimore, Md.: University Park Press, 1981).

22. J. Kozol, *Illiterate America* (Garden City, N.Y.: Doubleday Anchor Books, 1985).

23. Azrin and Besalel, *Finding a Job;* and Azrin and Besalel, *Job Club Counselor's Manual.*

4

Family-Focused Approaches to Joblessness, Underemployment, and Work Problems

Because unemployment affects not only an individual but an entire family and perhaps even several generations of family members, family-based services must address not only the symptoms of joblessness and the job problems themselves but their multigenerational effects. Social workers have long been champions of family services and of practice approaches that address the ripple effects of a family member's problems on the functioning of the family unit. Thus, family-centered approaches with jobless and underemployed workers fit squarely within the tradition of social work services.

The impact of joblessness on the entire family unit or multigenerational family system still is being documented. However, it is known that parents' occupational obsolescence or exclusion may blunt their children's aspirations and self-identity and hinder the children's achievement in school and occupational development.[1] Parent–child relationships may be damaged irreparably—not just while the parent is unemployed—and thus relationship problems may persist for a lifetime. Child abuse and mortality have been linked to unemployment, as have children's behavioral problems, health, and school performance problems.[2] A spouse's symptoms may parallel those of the jobless worker, even though their onset may be later.[3] Divorce or permanent impairment of the family unit may occur.[4] Battering and other forms of spousal abuse also may follow in the wake of a spell of joblessness.[5] Substance abuse, another major by-product of unemployment, may set in motion a chain of dysfunctional or life-threatening outcomes for family members.[6] Thus, unemployment may be one of the most corrosive situations for the functioning of a family, triggering a series of maladaptations that not only dissolve the marital or family unit but that unravel its very ability to care for family members.

The challenge for social workers is to recast problems that once were considered endemic to the family system or interpersonal relationships into a framework of economic and employment problems. Refocusing attention on labor, economic, and occupational issues illuminates how work problems, as well as the problems involved in the loss of or search for a job, may be displaced onto all family members. It is possible that some family and marital disputes that now dominate family therapy sessions are labor-related issues that stem, for example, from the inequitable sharing of family work roles and power-based resources. An examination of the family through a labor-economic-occupational lens may point to the need for new dynamics and resources, as well as the need for full and equitable employment rights for all family members, not just the one who has lost a job or is underemployed.

This chapter builds on the previous chapter's discussions of clinical interventions by outlining family-based approaches that may prove useful to family members or to the entire family unit. Drawing on some of the dynamics of family functioning discussed in chapter 2, this chapter suggests some of the requirements for a family-based assessment and for the mobilization of services that may alleviate stress and promote reemployment. In addition, some of the displacement effects of joblessness on other family members will be discussed so that occupational problem solving may be understood as a family and even multigenerational issue.

Family-Based Assessment

In many cases, the spouse or child of the jobless member may seek help or come to the attention of social service agencies. Unemployment alone is not seen as the primary motivation for help seeking; rather, some by-product, like increased interpersonal friction between husband and wife or a child's acting-out behavior in school becomes the ''presenting problem.'' Practice that ignores the dynamics of the family system or responds solely to symptoms (such as bruises) will miss the dynamics that make the joblessness of one family member the original precipitant or reinforcer

of the problem behaviors of another family member. Few families are able
to articulate uniform perceptions of the problem; therefore, even when
all members are present, their disclosures involve their personalized ver-
sions of the consequences of one member's joblessness. The following case
example of the Storrow family illustrates the effects of the joblessness of
Jack, the husband and father:

> Jane, the wife of an unemployed worker and mother of two, seeks help from
> a private child and family welfare agency because of the possible abuse of her
> youngest child Ginny, age 3, who has bruises and welts and whose temper
> tantrums have increased since her father, Jack, has been out of work. Tom-
> my, the 10-year-old, is upset about not being able to go to Boy Scouts or to
> have friends visit. He has been skipping school and getting into altercations
> with his peers.
>
> Jack claims that he is doing the best he can to "keep the family going—to
> keep a roof over their heads and food on the table." The pain he experiences
> in not being an effective provider and in not being able to find a job is muted
> by his claims of becoming nothing more than a "caretaker" of the children.
> Although he talks about looking for work, he is averaging only about one job
> interview every three months.

Family-based assessment reveals that members often do not attribute their
problems to joblessness, as Figure 1 suggests. In the Storrow family, Jane
and Tommy, at least, think that Jack is a liability and that they may be safer
without his assuming child care responsibilities. The suspicion of child abuse
led the social worker at the private agency to make a referral to the child
protective services agency.

Initially, Jack's referral to the child protective services agency for abus-
ing Ginny did not lead to help with his job search. However, the fact that
Jack's occupational stress was addressed empathically by the child protective services worker made him more open in his disclosures about his episodes
of abusive behavior. Ideally, child welfare investigations, like any other
family-oriented service, would focus on ways to alleviate stress by dealing
with its precipitants. In isolated cases, some child welfare and related family-
service approaches pay explicit attention to employment problems. Yet most
forms of family intervention lack the tools to deal with such problems.
Families, too, may lack the cognitive scripts to reframe their interactional
problems in employment-related terms. Thus, of the most significant services that can be offered to a family are the occupational and job-placement
aids that not only relieve the problems of family functioning but may restore
and strengthen the vulnerable marital or family unit.

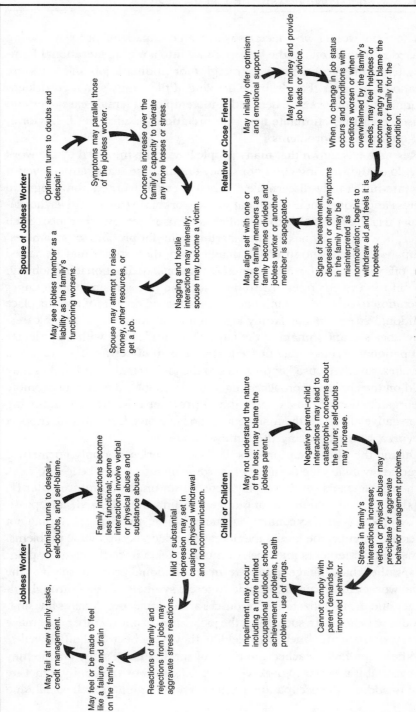

Figure 1. Family Dynamics and Coping Responses

Jobless Worker

May fail at new family tasks, credit management.

May feel or be made to feel like a failure and drain on the family.

Reactions of family and rejections from jobs may aggravate stress reactions.

Optimism turns to despair, self-doubts, and self-blame.

Family interactions become less functional; some interactions involve verbal or physical abuse and substance abuse.

Mild or substantial depression may set in causing physical withdrawal and noncommunication.

Child or Children

May not understand the nature of the loss; may blame the jobless parent.

Negative parent–child interactions may lead to catastrophic concerns about the future; self-doubts may increase.

Stress in family's interactions increase; verbal or physical abuse may precipitate or aggravate behavior management problems.

Cannot comply with parent demands for improved behavior.

Impairment may occur including a more limited occupational outlook, school achievement problems, health problems, use of drugs.

Spouse of Jobless Worker

Optimism turns to doubts and despair.

Symptoms may parallel those of the jobless worker.

Concerns increase over the family's capacity to tolerate any more losses or stress.

Nagging and hostile interactions may intensify; spouse may become a victim.

Spouse may attempt to raise money, other resources, or get a job.

May see jobless member as a liability as the family's functioning worsens.

Relative or Close Friend

May initially offer optimism and emotional support.

May lend money and provide job leads or advice.

When no change in job status occurs and conditions with creditors worsen or when overwhelmed by the family's needs, may feel helpless or become angry and blame the worker or family for the condition.

Signs of bereavement, depression or other symptoms in the family may be misinterpreted as nonmotivation; begins to withdraw aid and feels it is hopeless.

May align self with one or more family members as family becomes divided and jobless worker or another member is scapegoated.

The social worker who operates within an occupational problem-solving repertoire may be one of the first to infuse into a multigenerational family system some new tools and strategies for finding a job and assessing vocational interests. For example, looking at the family as a high-risk environment for an overstressed and underemployed female caregiver and housekeeper may stimulate new interpretations of affective, behavioral, and interactional problems.[7]

Research has shown that many people have been impaired by the work they do or the working conditions they endure; the scars remain even if they are not readily discernible.[8] When pressed, workers may begin to express anger over their treatment in the workplace (the caregiver/housekeeper usually is less able to verbalize her frustration over her job). Such anger, however, may be a normal starting point for probing some families' occupational needs and strains. If unaddressed, these strains may be passed onto offspring in the form of blunted aspirations, occupational immobility, or confusion about roles. In some cases, the pressures on the younger generation to succeed and to fulfill the unachieved dreams of parents place additional stress on the family's occupational morale. In other cases, a member's abandonment of the family's identification with a particular occupational heritage may be treated as a form of betrayal. As Figure 2 indicates, family-focused approaches to the jobless and their families may build on the clinical approaches suggested in chapter 3 and may promote a reorganization of the caregiving and provider roles while minimizing the negative effects on the many generations involved, mobilizing support networks, and addressing the family's finances.

During the assessment process, the social worker not only normalizes anger but evaluates the possibility that some members may be feeling stuck in their joblessness, underemployment, or an uncertain future. Clarifying the interconnections among anger, feeling immobilized, and possible by-products such as conflict, substance abuse, and depression may not necessarily compel the family members to work on occupational problems. Some family members may seek immediate relief from the crisis or pain; thus, rather than engage in long-term occupational problem solving, the social worker may have to provide concrete symbols of relief through advocacy and the mobilization of resources around such problems as housing, schools, or benefits. In such cases, the joblessness of one member may make the rest of the family members feel like they have been laid off as well.[9]

When they have reached the point of seeking help, some people may believe that it is easier to dissolve the marital unit or the family structure than to address the occupational deficits and their emotional, social, and

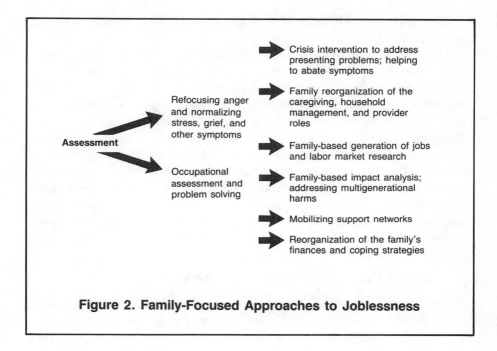

Figure 2. Family-Focused Approaches to Joblessness

financial consequences. In some cases, the risks of physical and emotional abuse may be too immediate to salvage the family unit until the abuse has stopped or the victim is protected by out-of-home arrangements, such as foster care for a child, a shelter for a woman and her children, or a boarding home for an aged or disabled member. As with occupational problem solving discussed in chapter 3, the abatement or stabilization of symptoms may be critical before long-term occupational needs can be addressed. Some family members will demonstrate improved functioning when given a reason to hope that their times together can and will improve; others may require immediate simultaneous work on symptoms as well as occupational problems. In certain cases, the higher the person's self-esteem, the greater the potential for self-motivated changes. Thus, focusing on Jack's employment problems as one stressor that has led to his attacks on Ginny may not only eliminate the attacks but may give him new tools for understanding his violent outbursts. Curbing these outbursts also may require some training in alternatives to excessive discipline. It may well be that Ginny's behavior has become less manageable since Jack lost his job and that it reflects the increased stress in the family and the reduced tolerance at least by Jack of the behavior and demands of a normal 3-year-old.[10]

In the sections that follow, expanded family-based practice with jobless and underemployed workers are discussed. All the members of a family with a jobless worker have the need and right to know the nature of the condition of joblessness, how normal it is, and how blameless all of them and especially the jobless worker may be; the potential trauma of the condition for all involved, including all immediate family members and often friends; the effects on individuals and on the family system; about occupational problem solving and diversification; and, the potential reoccurrence of another jobless episode. In addition, family members need reassurance when they are using all the appropriate survival resources and job search tactics that they are coping successfully even if they are losing ground.

Involving the Family in the Job Search

The family's capacity to engage in occupational problem solving may be hindered by few skills and little information about job-search strategies. This deficit may impair them not only because they cannot solve problems effectively, but as in the case of the Storrow family, they cannot confront Jack's joblessness with confidence that they have done everything possible to avert it or to get him reemployed. Even though they are not aided by society and are unempowered by the absence of information about how to search for a job, research nevertheless suggests that Jack's return to work may be fostered by job leads that come from the family and friendship networks with which he is having difficulty.[11] Thus, the social worker's role is to affirm the capacity of the family to aid the jobless member not only by normalizing occupational problems such as joblessness but by informing the family of the best job-search techniques and the routes to additional aid if the family needs them. Such information is both a preventive tool to minimize the effects of future occupational problems and an empowerment device that ensures that the family members are as informed as possible. Once workers and their families know that they are using the most desirable job-search techniques, accusations and self-doubts may begin to diminish, thereby freeing them to work on the critical by-products of unemployment, such as problems with credit.

Engaging family members in job-search strategies, in labor market research, and especially in identifying job leads may reverse some of their attacks on the jobless member. However, sometimes, in their desperation or enthusiasm to generate job leads and to help the jobless member get a job, they may intensify their "nagging." It is critical that all family members recognize that the jobless worker may be pursuing state-of-the-art strategies for getting a job and still remain jobless. Such a recognition can help to cushion the family members' ridicule or nagging and may help them understand and appreciate what the jobless member is encountering. Thus, a good class on the job search may include all family members for special, if not all, sessions and should specify explicitly their roles as natural helpers and as crucial developers of jobs. Family and friendship networks may account not only for the generation of job leads but for the identification of possible experts on hiring trends in a specific field. Clearly, the distancing and verbal and physical abuse that occur, given some of the dynamics of joblessness, run counter to the critical role that the family and support networks may play in getting the jobless member reemployed. Harnessing or rebuilding the capacity of families and friends to be conduits for jobs may require the social worker to reach out to them before the jobless or underemployed worker has been so isolated and blamed that their differences become irreconcilable. Thus, the family should be involved as early in the job-loss or underemployment situation as possible. Future stress then can be confronted more as a challenge to be encountered than as a trauma that will damage them permanently.

Reorganizing Caregiving and Provider Functions

The most overlooked facet of family life is the amount of work that is required, especially of women, to keep the family functioning as a unit, to address and coordinate individual members' needs, and to promote a caring environment for growth. Women who have chosen to work only in the home may be displaced from their round-the-clock caregiving roles when their husbands are underemployed or unemployed. The need to work outside the home forces them to delegate those roles to family members who are at home, regardless of these members' ability or preparedness to perform the tasks; to hire others to perform them; or to neglect them (leaving a child unattended). Although the caregiving roles may impede women's entry into the labor market and an outside career; they may, nonetheless, result in new role challenges for men. Furthermore, shifting caregiving responsibilities to older children, in some cases, also may result in undesirable outcomes for the family, for these children, and those for whom they are caring.

Most families facing the economic and employment crisis of the Storrows would consider multiple ways to generate income. For example, Jane might be a likely candidate for occupational development. Yet she cannot afford to pay for child care and she believes that Jack is too stressed to be given the responsibility of caring for their children, particularly because of his excessive discipline and its abusive consequences.

Normalizing the heightened stress that Jack feels because of his new caregiving responsibilities as well as his unemployment may make him more open to receiving help instead of defending himself. On the one hand, Jack needs to feel that he is competent as a provider, so intensifying his caregiving tasks may be inappropriate at a time when he is less emotionally and behaviorally equipped to handle them and when he should be using his energy to look for a job. On the other hand, helping him recognize how dysfunctional his yelling and threatening behavior has been and how it may trigger Ginny's increased demands for affection and tantrums will help him to see the need not only to get his anger under control but to refocus Ginny's as well.

Despite the hope that Jack might have fewer child care responsibilities, the family's economic crisis may warrant that Jane seek part-time employment. Moreover, Jane may begin to see the crisis as a chance for her to develop in the long run. Thus, she may welcome the opportunity to relieve the family's current economic stress and to bring long-term economic stability to the family through her efforts. In addition, because it is uncertain whether Jack's out-of-control behavior and aggression will recur, Jane may realize that she must be self-sufficient. Therefore, Jane's search for any part-time job she can find, ranging from work in a fast-food restaurant to secretarial work, may not just bolster the family's finances but may launch her in a gainful occupational role and avoid tension at home.

The family's economic and child care situation then may plunge Jack further into the caregiving role in which he already has fared poorly; the social worker's responsibility is to see the potential damage of this situation and to mobilize alternatives when warranted. For the first week of Jane's job search, the social worker arranged with the Storrows that Jane would schedule interviews in the afternoons so that Jack might use the mornings for his contacts. In the afternoons, Ginny napped, and Jack's mother often was available to care for the children. This temporary arrangement could be stabilized when Jane got a job. Nevertheless, just because Jack agreed to share the caregiving tasks during the afternoon did not mean that he had the emotional resources or skills to cope with Ginny's temper tantrums. Because he resented his caregiving responsibility and Ginny's acting-out behavior, he might be less likely to provide a nurturant yet structured atmosphere. In fact, Goldsmith found that jobless fathers may be less well equipped emotionally than their employed counterparts to be nurturing or to have positive interactions with their children, especially when their child care responsibilities increase.[12] The social work assessment may conclude that a preferable arrangement would be for Jack to share the responsibilities for caring for Ginny with his son, Tommy. In helping the family organize to meet the crisis of the joblessness of one member and its displacement effects on others, the social worker, by necessity, may help family members probe their capacity to perform adequately not just in their job-search role but in the substitute family caregiving role that may be emerging as well.

Multigenerational Impact of Joblessness

Substance abuse, child abuse, and spouse abuse are but a few of the multigenerational carryovers that may be precipitated by a single episode of unemployment. If the family members are to understand the differential consequences of the loss of a job and income for all of them, they must address the multigenerational impact of the loss. For example, while Tommy's substance abuse, declining school performance, and related behavioral problems may not have been triggered only by his father's joblessness, the stress and uncertainty regarding the family's future, his father's feelings about him, and his own worries about an occupational future may perhaps increase his risk of succumbing to the drug culture in his school. Furthermore, the verbal or physical abuse Tommy receives from his father, which perhaps started with Jack's jobless episode, nonetheless may set in motion undesirable habits that, if not addressed, may plague the family for generations to come. Moreover, Tommy's peers also may be experiencing doubts about their occupational futures if their parents also have been unemployed in recent years. Although Tommy may be unable to pinpoint the impact of his father's economic and occupational losses on him, he can be helped to talk about his previous jobs, which, like those of most children, involved working for neighbors.[13] Tommy also can be helped to discuss his occupational aspirations and the extent to which they may have been shaken by watching the stress of his parents and his friends' parents.

Despite Tommy's claim that his use of drugs has little to do with his blunted work aspirations that stem from his family situation and more to do with peer pressure, he will have a harder time controlling his use of drugs if he has few occupational incentives to induce him to do well in school. Thus, although Jack's joblessness may not have triggered fully Tommy's experimentation with drugs, it may have undercut Tommy's sense of purpose in trying to function in school and in attempting to build a positive occupational future. Hence, the social worker might attempt to build Tommy's sense of an occupational future and the steps he might take toward achieving it. Using some of the same approaches that have been discussed in chapter 3, the social worker might at least acknowledge Tommy's worries about his future and reassure him that knowledge about how to look for a job is critical for planning his future career. Tommy even may begin to consider occupational options when he seeks to use his time in more constructive ways than drug abuse.

Research suggests that Tommy's occupational confusion and possible drug addiction may lead him into permanent drug-using behaviors. Thus, even if he is helped to get a job, the job may help to better finance his drug habit rather than serve as a bridge to a career. Nevertheless, social workers are or should be as prepared to foster the treatment of an addiction as the promotion of an occupational future.[14]

One reason why Jack's response to his joblessness has been so dysfunctional is that it reminds him of the destructive consequences that ensued when his father, John, lost his job. Jack was beaten badly when John's drinking became severe and Jack ran away on several occasions. Jack swore he would never be like his father. Despite his father's early death, Jack never forgave him for the disruption brought on by his unemployment and subsequent deterioration. When Genevieve, Jack's mother, was forced into employment to support Jack and his two younger siblings, it was hard for Jack to tolerate his mother's mandate that he remain in school instead of go to work. Jack resolved that he would never let himself get into the circumstances he now faces, which makes his self-recriminations even more severe.

The social worker used a genogram to plot the occupational heritage of the family. By having the Storrows draw a family tree to guide a description and analysis of the multigenerational occupational stresses, strengths, and skills, Jack is able to talk more readily about his fears that he is becoming like his father. It also is clear that neither Jack nor John had been prepared for a permanent job loss and that each believed that the jobs they held had furnished a suitable livelihood. The occupational genogram enables Jack, Jane, and Tommy to wonder about how the stresses of Jack's job loss could be curbed before they set in motion some dysfunctional scripts for Tommy. In addition, Jane is able to come to terms with some of her anger over her lack of preparation to seek out-of-home employment since the genogram depicted few women in her heritage who were employed or even had aspirations to seek work out of the home.

The stress of unemployment may set in motion dysfunctional interactions or habits that may take on a life of their own, even after the jobless worker finds a job. Thus, although social workers can look to reemployment as an antidote for some of the human costs of joblessness such as depression, adaptations in some cases may persist. The social worker who is serving the Storrows is concerned that Jack's problems with Ginny may not necessarily subside just because he gets a job. Once the habit is in place, other stressors may trigger interactional problems and abuse even if they are not occupationally derived. For this reason, addressing interactional habits and problems is as essential as addressing unemployment if treatment outcomes are to be effective.

Mobilizing Support Networks

An assessment of the impact of joblessness will determine whether the family's coping resources can be fortified by the building of new roles and relationships that offer expressive outlets. Because joblessness often forces families to turn inward, which depletes their economic and emotional resources, intervention should rebuild or replace at least some of the relationships and roles that have been lost. Some of the isolation and withdrawal of workers and their families can be countered by self-help support networks. Some of these networks are fashioned through the job clubs and job-search support groups discussed in chapters 3, 5, and 7. Others may emerge naturally when jobless workers band together in teams or pairs to share job leads and to give each other emotional and concrete support.

Support networks also may be constructed through the natural helping pathways used by the jobless and their families. For example, while attending a meeting of Parents Anonymous, a jobless parent may seek occupational advice and support from the group. A teenager may find that in getting help with substance abuse from Narcotics Anonymous or Alcoholics Anonymous, additional guidance and support for new occupational possibilities may emerge. The wife of a jobless worker may gain new and valuable emotional sustenance from her fellow churchgoers.

Family members may be hard pressed to find new sources of assistance and emotional support. It is the social worker's responsibility to create a supportive group, network, or even buddy system to shore up some of the emotional and perhaps problem-solving resources so they can flow back to the family. The mobilization of networks is like the creation of a new family for a vulnerable family not only to help ensure that the vulnerable family weathers its joblessness but to counter the dynamics of withdrawal that may be at work. Because the jobless family may be forced to cut back on spending and affiliative relationships, an undue burden may be placed on the family system when it is least likely to have the emotional and social problem-solving resources to deal with the burden single-handedly.

Social workers inadvertently may worsen this situation when they focus exclusively on the family's internal dynamics, including the strengthening of parenting, communication, or supportive relationships. The family's need for regeneration may be fostered best by extending its base of resources or creating new ones, rather than exacting changes at a time when its emotional, social, and economic responses are depleted. By working on new roles that reduce their isolation and bolster their sense of purpose, family members often increase their ability to use parenting classes and other deficit-oriented services.

Addressing the Family's Finances

Because of changes in the family's labor base, the family undergoes financial disruption. Thus, the family may need systematic aid with analyzing and constructing a revised budget, dealing with creditors, and realigning living relationships. Many families are unable to anticipate that they might face repossession, foreclosure, and bankruptcy. Families may shift into a non-materialistic mode to cope with these losses and assaults on their credit and purchasing power. Some families may embrace holidays with exchanges of emotional and social support and with minimal exchanges of material gifts. The families' strength increases when they are helped to see how well they have stayed within the limits of their reduced budgets and have survived a potentially trying time in which the losses could have been more debilitating. Duncan indicated that, over a 10-year period, one out of four families may slide into poverty.[15] The precipitant of this slide may not always be unemployment as it is officially and traditionally defined; instead, the precipitant may be the displacement of women because of divorce, separation, or the death of a spouse.

Because plummeting resources affect not only the family's life-style and social identity but its ability to carry out societally allocated tasks, helping the family with its financial crisis must be a paramount social work intervention. Financial planning for the worst possible scenarios may give families a sense of control over the possible course of their joblessness. For example, families who know that if worst comes to worst, they can move in with relatives, sell their home and move into an apartment, or even split up temporarily, as depressing as such thoughts may be, may have a sense of being able to cope with their unraveling social and economic problems. Organizing the family as a team to examine these options and to treat their survival as a challenge to be met may help to fortify their sense of endurance and to counter the avoidance or wishful thinking that plagues many jobless families.

Because states have various laws about creditors and liability, it is important that the social worker be knowledgeable about these laws so that he or she can provide appropriate credit counseling to families.[16] It is possible, for example, that the creditors will be satisfied if the jobless family pays only the interest due on a loan. Sometimes, with sufficient lead time, even foreclosures can be negotiated because many banks and some loan companies do not want the responsibility for repossessed property. Some loan companies and banks even may forego repossession when an intermediary, like a social worker, advocates an alternative plan. Thus, early intervention in the form of a payment plan that is manageable for the family, may allow the family members to stretch themselves to hold onto their homes and property. In other cases, planning for a possible sale rather than hanging on until a house or car is repossessed may be desirable.

Many jobless workers have been creative in their desperate attempt to generate revenue. Those who seek retraining may take out guaranteed student loans to provide some relief to their families, as well as to support their education. Those who are reluctant to claim entitlements and feel too stigmatized to apply for food stamps, commodities at food banks, Medicaid, and related benefits must be helped to understand that they have contributed hard-earned taxes to pay for these benefits, which are theirs as a right. Some families, rather than exhausting all their resources to prove their eligibility for benefits, may wish to turn over their deeds for long-term investments, such as a house, to relatives instead of being forced to give them up during their financial crisis.

Notes and References

1. J. Ogbu, *Minority Education and Caste* (New York: Academic Press, 1978); and R. H. DeLone, *Small Futures* (New York: Harcourt Brace Jovanovich, 1979).

2. D. G. Gil, *Violence Against Children: Physical Child Abuse in the United States* (Cambridge, Mass.: Harvard University Press, 1970). *See also* R. J. Light, "Abused and Neglected Children in America: A Study of Alternative Policies," *Harvard Educational Review*, 43 (November 1973), pp. 556–598; L. Margolis and D. C. Farran, "Unemployment: The Health Consequence for Children," *North Carolina Medical Journal*, 42 (December 1981), pp. 849–850.

3. G. R. Liem, J. H. Liem, and J. Hauser, "Social Support and Stress: Some General Issues and Their Application to the Problem of Unemployment," in L. A. Ferman and J. P. Gordus, eds., *Mental Health and the Economy* (Kalamazoo, Mich.: W. E. Upjohn Institute for Employment Research, 1979), pp. 347–378.

4. K. Briar, *The Effect of Long-Term Unemployment on Workers and Their Families* (San Francisco: R & E Pubs., 1978).

5. S. K. Steinmetz and M. Strauss, "General Introduction: Social Myth and Social System in the Study of Intra-familial Violence," in Steinmetz and Strauss, eds., *Violence in the Family* (New York: Harper & Row, 1974), p. 9; and J. P. Gordus, *Economic Change, Physical Illness, Mental Illness and Social Change* (Washington, D.C.: Congressional Research Service, 1984).

6. T. F. Buss and F. S. Redburn, with J. Waldron, *Mass Unemployment, Plant Closings and Community Mental Health* (Beverly Hills, Calif.: Sage Publications, 1983).

7. *See* K. Briar and K. Knighton, "Family and Work." Paper presented at the Annual Program Meeting, Council on Social Work Education, Miami, Fla., 1986.

8. M. Lerner, *Surplus Powerlessness* (Oakland, Calif.: Institute for Labor & Mental Health, 1986).

9. L. Schore et al., *Starting Over (Surviving a Plant Closure)* (Oakland, Calif.: Oakland Center for Working Life, 1987).

10. R. H. Goldsmith, "The Effects of Paternal Employment Status on Fathering Behaviors, Cognitive Stimulation and Confidence in the Child's Future." Unpublished PhD dissertation, University of Michigan School of Social Work, 1986.

11. N. H. Azrin and V. A. Besalel, *Finding a Job* (Berkeley, Calif.: Ten Speed Press, 1983).

12. R. H. Goldsmith, "The Effects of Paternal Employment Status on Fathering Behaviors."

13. B. Goldstein and J. Oldham, *Children and Work* (New Brunswick, N.J.: Transaction, Inc., 1979).

14. E. Greenberger and L. Steinberg, *When Teenagers Work: The Psychological and Social Costs of Adolescent Employment* (New York: Basic Books, 1986).

15. G. Duncan, *Years of Plenty, Years of Poverty* (Ann Arbor: Institute for Social Research, University of Michigan, 1984).

16. *See* F. L. Feldman, *The Family in Today's Money World* (2d ed.; New York: Family Service Association of America, 1976).

5

Agency-Based Services for the Unemployed and Their Communities: Toward a Continuum of Care

Few conditions and their consequences are as preventable as is unemployment, few conditions undercut functioning as severely as does joblessness, and few conditions are as amenable to social service intervention as is joblessness and its outcomes. These facts, along with some of the unique dynamics of unemployment, should make the development of programs and outreach on behalf of the unemployed the central concerns of social service planners, community organizers, managers, and researchers. Furthermore, occupational problem-solving services should be integral to an array of social service modalities, rather than solely the responsibility of direct service practitioners.

Drawing on the dynamics of unemployment, in this chapter, a framework for developing services that are sensitive to the needs of the unemployed and underemployed and models of outreach, advocacy, and community development are presented. Because communities that are in an economic decline may depend on traditional social service agencies for preventive services and economic revitalization, the chapter also includes models of economic development for communities that have proved effective in other distressed areas.

Given that social workers and agency directors may feel strapped by the rising demand for services and as well as shrinking budgets, they may resent suggestions for new initiatives that might aggravate their workloads. However, the suggestions promoted in this chapter may help alleviate the sense of futility that arises when incomplete interventions impair the effectiveness of outcomes or when agencies cannot deal with the conditions that cause clients and communities to dysfunction in the first place. In effect, addressing employment and economic injustices may help to restructure services and programs so that these issues become fundamental to an agency's mission and to the effectiveness of services.

Assessing the Need for Services

Although poor jobs and working conditions may be deforming, a good job may be the foundation for successful human functioning. Therefore, agencies may benefit from attending to the occupational problems and needs of those they serve, including high-risk children, youths, and families; those with disabilities or mental health, health, and substance abuse problems; offenders; women; ethnic minorities; sexual minorities; the poor, hungry, and homeless; the aged; displaced homemakers; and migrants and immigrants.

Some might argue that the provision of employment services by different agencies in a community would constitute a duplication of resources. The fact that employment services may be lodged formally in the state employment service does not preempt the need for the infusion of an occupational framework into all areas of social work practice and all social service agencies because the social work repertoire cannot afford to overlook this critical approach to assessment and intervention. Moreover, counselors at the state employment service may lack some of the diagnostic and treatment skills of social workers that, when combined with employment strategies, may maximize the effectiveness of social work, especially with the long-term unemployed.

Before services are planned, the agency may need to generate basic data to document the unmet needs of its clients and community residents who are not being served. For example, it would be helpful to ascertain what percentage of individuals and family members being served have presenting problems that may be caused by occupational stress (especially joblessness and underemployment); have presenting problems that are not caused by occupational stress but that, nonetheless, are affected by it; could improve immeasurably if occupational problem-solving services were provided as an adjunct to or enrichment of current services; or would benefit more from traditional interventions, such as individual psychotherapy or life-skills counseling, if they were combined with job-search or job-strengthening interventions. Next, the agency should determine whether it or the service system is reaching the known victims of chronic unemployment, underemployment, or recent mass layoffs, given the unemployment conditions in the community. If not, then the agency should decide if it should increase its outreach services to prevent the negative consequences that new or chronic victims of joblessness experience when excluded by the system that should be serving them.

Pathways to Service

Seeking help from a social service agency is an anathema to many workers and their families. Thus, workers who need and are eligible for critical services may have to overcome cognitive, emotional, and social obstacles to using them.

The findings of studies on the responsiveness of social service programs and agencies to the needs of the jobless have been sharply mixed. Rayman poignantly depicted the inertia of social service agencies about aiding the jobless.[1] She found, for example, that several directors of mental health services were resistant to the development of services for the unemployed, despite the permanent loss of livelihoods in the communities they served. Studying health and social service programs in the United Kingdom, Popay and Dhooge found similar sentiments, which they attributed, in part, to a sense of powerlessness and to the conflicting missions and purposes of particular agencies.[2] Even social service agencies that serve jobless victims may experience variable rates of help seeking. Some may be flooded by the jobless, while others may prepare for an influx that never occurs.[3]

Brenner posited a lag of up to five or six years between the loss of a job and the consequent deterioration of functioning.[4] Other researchers have found the lag to be minimal; variations are attributable to local economic conditions. Uninformed by such findings about the lag and variance, agency managers may interpret incorrectly the absence of help seeking right after a mass layoff to an absence of needs among the jobless. Yet, the unemployed also may swamp caseloads, as has been the case in some state welfare agencies recently. Research by Sunley and Sheek showed that some family service agencies anticipated this hiatus in help seeking and conducted outreach activities in storefronts and unions to prevent some of the harms that could later ensue.[5]

Suggestions on ways to promote increased use of mental health, family counseling, and other similar services by the jobless are drawn from the implications of research on the dynamics of joblessness and on previous patterns of using services. Services to the jobless may need to address the fear that the jobless will be seen as more deviant than they already feel if they admit to more (especially psychosocial) problems than just their joblessness; the stigma associated with help seeking; and beliefs that such services are not job or income related and thus represent detours from their occupational goals. Workers may seek help only after they define themselves as more troubled than their cohorts (when most of their jobless colleagues return to work and they do not).

Outreach Services

As was suggested in chapter 2, the earlier the intervention is introduced and the more phase specific the outreach and type of service, the greater the likelihood of restored functioning. For example, helping workers to consolidate their debts and to plan for their financial survival right after they lose their jobs may be far more effective than waiting until creditors are no longer willing to negotiate because of tardiness in payments or miscommunication over payment plans.

Just as the timing of services is important, so, too, is the destigmatization of services. Because some jobless persons perceive the act of seeking help as the admission of a deficit, they may postpone seeking help until they either reach a major crisis in coping or become convinced that professional help will improve their functioning. Paradoxically, such persons often perceive that the positioning of traditional mental health or family services in places where they have easy access to them is a negative reflection of their already impossible situation. Social workers who operate agency-based employee assistance programs in such sites as community mental health centers have demonstrated the importance of changing the name of the service to dissociate it from the potentially stigmatizing name of the sponsoring agency.[6] Even services that are designed for jobless workers may be stigmatized by the name of the program and by the setting in which the services are provided; thus, for example, "job-search strategies," rather than "coping with unemployment," may be a preferable title for a workshop.

No matter how impaired in functioning are some long-term jobless workers, their focus on acquiring a job may make them loathe to seek social services, however needed, that seem unrelated to getting a job. Even a center for the jobless such as Start-up, a United Way-sponsored agency in Seattle, Washington, had difficulty reaching out to certain groups of the unemployed until it instituted job banks and job placement aid.[7]

For many jobless workers, help seeking may be similar to the psychological minefield inherent in the job hunt. Outreach information provided to the jobless may cite the stress signs that warrant help and normalize them as predictable by-products of unemployment. Models of outreach and self-help handbooks have been produced by the Center for Working Life, Oakland, California; the Policy Center of Adelphi University's School of Social Work, Garden City, New York; the University of Washington's School of Social Work project with the Central Area Motivation Program and the Seattle Worker Center, Seattle; and King County Family Services, Seattle. Outreach information is used to create a pathway for improved problem solving, especially when home remedies fail. Normalizing the onset and progression of problems may help the unemployed and their families feel more understood and less stigmatized but alert that if the conflict escalates, professional help may be warranted.

Agencies have innovative roles to play in promoting self-help materials and resources so that jobless workers and their families are empowered to enhance their natural ability to solve problems while preparing themselves to seek professional help if necessary. Traditional listings in "where-to-turn" directories may not thoroughly describe the kinds of symptoms that jobless persons may encounter or the risks of avoiding professional help. Moreover, such directories primarily describe social service, not employment-related, programs.

Videotape use with distressed farm families apparently has been successful, especially when no other outreach resource is available.[8] Ironically, some of the creative work by rural mental health centers depends on outreach and referrals by bank officers in farming communities.[9]

Outreach includes school- and church-based networking and collaboration with agricultural extension services or related organized service systems, such as the Department of Fisheries for the fishing industry. Outreach in rural areas also may include capacity building in hospitals and with the health care community, because many jobless or underemployed victims will not define their need for mental health or social services. Instead, they may first seek health care for psychosomatic or other stress-related symptoms.[10]

Assuming that the mission and resources of an agency make such innovations possible, the following outreach and self-help services could be instituted:

■ Advertisements on late-night television and radio of various services that are relevant to the jobless and their families.

■ Informational brochures that are disseminated in places where the jobless congregate, including bars, union hiring halls, billiard and video game parlors, employment services, large employers with job openings, food banks, blood banks, shelters for the homeless, welfare offices, and welfare rights offices.

■ Tips on coping that are broadcast on public and commercial radio and television stations, printed in newspapers and church bulletins, and inserted in grocery bags.

■ Handbooks and videotapes that normalize symptoms and help seeking and specify the risks to functioning that may require professional help, provide tips on how to cope, and promote occupational self-assessment tools that offer workers and their families an ''early warning system'' regarding occupational obsolescence and financial management strategies.

■ Specialized outreach to recovering alcoholics, to parolees, to persons on probation, and to children, youths, and families who are served by child protective service agencies.

Policy Diagnoses

Social workers and social service agencies are the primary repositories of knowledge about the series of assaults and losses that the jobless endure, given their dwindling economic, social, and emotional resources. Mortgage foreclosures, repossessions, and the lack of health care all signal not only profound damage to workers and their families but preventable calamities. To this end, managers, planners, and research staff of social service agencies can make a major contribution to strengthening the resources of the jobless and the practitioners who serve them by documenting the preventable costs of losing one's home, one's car, one's health care, and one's lifelong possessions and presenting this information to the legislatures and the courts.

Many presenting problems and their consequences, such as repossessions and income insecurity, can be reframed as evidence of deficits in policies and services. Therefore, an agency can initiate an ongoing dual assessment or policy-diagnosis process that reflects the services the agency is prepared to offer and the unmet need for services and the policies that are required to ameliorate the presenting problems and their causes.[11]

Berglind suggested an action theory for social work that posits that assessments are constricted by the skills and resources for intervention that are available.[12] Thus, if psychological skills and resources are the predominant basis for intervention, then problems most likely will be framed in psychologically treatable terms. An expanded action system, involving multimodal strategies to promote economic change and the acquisition of a job, may foster more helpful assessments of problems. Nevertheless, the reframing of clients' problems in a policy-diagnosis process not just to fit what services providers are prepared to offer but to document the deficits in services and policies expands clinical assessment to include the development of policies and services. Thus, rather than selectively addressing only those issues or symptoms that fit prevailing social service technologies, the agency is in a pivotal position to foster broader-based problem solving by choosing which problems it can address readily and which are beyond the purview of the social services. An abbreviated illustration of policy diagnosis is as follows:

Traditional Assessment. Timothy is a 32-year-old male who is partially disabled whose wife, Sally, is expecting a baby at the same time that the utilities are slated to be shut off. Neither he nor his wife has been working, and he is involved heavily in litigation to claim workers' compensation for an injury he suffered on the job. Timothy seeks help for their stress. His description of depressive symptoms and interpersonal conflict suggests that he can benefit appropriately from therapy. He claims that his wife will join him in therapy sessions once he has made contact with the multiservice agency.

Reframed Assessment. Timothy, a 32-year-old partially disabled victim of a workplace injury, is unable to claim workers' compensation because of restrictive coverage. Despite litigation, he has little hope of claiming benefits, short of whatever can be acquired from the company through legal advocacy. Excessive time spent on litigation (which may yield only a small sum of money, such as coverage for doctors' fees and physiotherapy) has preempted him from planning to reenter the labor market. As a result of cutbacks in workers' compensation, he is impaired in his ability to plan for the future beyond his hope of winning his claim through the courts. Depression and marital conflict might have been minimized had workers' compensation been available. The likelihood of utility shutoffs makes Timothy and Sally's home a high-risk environment for their baby, who is expected in the next three weeks. Therefore, an emergency fund, financed through state or local funds or private sources, to prevent a shutoff or a moratorium on shutoffs for all the jobless in the area might have reduced their worries and the risks to which they will soon be subjecting their baby. Uncompensated health care coverage also may have affected the degree of prenatal care that Sally has received and increased the risks of problems during childbirth. Unrestricted workers' compensation, adequate health care coverage, and a utility loan or entitlement program might ease some of Timothy and Sally's financial stress. Marital conflict and poor prenatal care, accompanied by prolonged joblessness, may have caused intractable damage to their marriage, their baby, and Timothy's ability to solve his occupational problems.

The policy-diagnosis process empowers social workers to promote the development of resources and problem-solving strategies by generating evidence or examples that can lead to change if presented to elected officials, the mass media, other agencies, or private-sector work institutions. Policy diagnosis also may minimize the coverup of clients' problems that stems from gaps in resources and entitlements while documenting the need for additional policies and services. Without documentation of the consequences of cutbacks and deficits in services and policies, policymakers in the public and private sector may be more inclined to overlook the human costs of decisions and to be removed from the consequences of and responsibility for outcomes.

Self-Help and Collective Action

Social service agencies and programs have exceptional resources to promote self-help activities by the jobless and their families. Data generated from policy diagnoses should not only inform a problem-solving process in the wider community but should help those who have been most harmed by the condition to advance their own needs and rights. After the clients' immediate needs are addressed and some degree of stabilization and occupational problem solving has occurred, agencies may be the conduits for multimodal self-help efforts. Agency personnel may promote opportunities for the jobless to testify, organize, and advocate on their own behalf, as well as to combine forces to share resources with others through brokering and the exchange of resources.

As part of its mission, an agency can offer many services that involve the self-education of clients, public education, and advocacy. At a minimum, the agency can feature self-help forums that present the jobless with positive coping models. Such forums can promote prevention, to normalize the predictability of symptoms, and outreach strategies for other jobless persons who might be less inclined to seek services if the services were not promulgated in part by the jobless themselves. The jobless also can speak poignantly about the gaps in services and entitlement programs and the painful consequences to them, their families, and the community. Public education panels or workshops for local, state, and nationally elected officials are excellent frameworks for advancing knowledge and ideas about necessary changes, especially because many elected officials assume that the jobless can weather their plight in a painless way because, in some areas of the country, officials rarely hear directly from the jobless on a sustained basis.

Some agency leaders may want to appoint official task forces to address the unmet needs and rights of the jobless. Or agencies may provide staff or office-related resources so that the jobless can establish their own community-wide program or agency-based task forces or committees. These task forces may focus on the distinct problems of specific groups of the unemployed, such as jobless workers who are victims of industrial accidents, youths who are facing uncertain work futures and have few opportunities for part-time jobs during their high school years, workers whose plants are planning to close, or farmers who are threatened with losing their farms.

Conferences that highlight the issues that the jobless face may not heighten only public awareness but may stimulate the development of specialized resources and activities by advocates in such organizations as churches, unions, the Parent–Teacher Association, and rotary clubs. Some conferences may be springboards to the development of more programs and to legislative advocacy, while serving as vehicles for agencies and social service providers to advance their professional practice.

Combating a Sense of Deviance and Hopelessness

As the managers and staff of agencies vie harder for funds during times of cutback, they may be reluctant to confront representatives of some of the very systems that support them financially (such as corporate foundations). Such hesitancy may be mitigated by evidence that prevention may be far less costly than services; such evidence also may empower line workers to document what earlier interventions might have generated in terms of restored functioning and the minimization of irretrievable losses. Some jobless workers may not only personalize their condition but may fear that any politicization of it may make others perceive them as more deviant and marginal.[13] Moreover, because individuals or agencies usually take risks when they feel secure, it is understandable that advocacy activities may be most impeded when they feel vulnerable. Therefore, advocacy activities may need to be reframed so that they fit within the agency's mission of setting the record straight.

Despite a history of organizing strikes and fostering class-action suits or grievances, it must be recognized that the capacity of many unemployed people to engage in activities to change the system may be blunted by the effects of unemployment. These effects may increase their uncertainty about the future and their reluctance to be associated with what they fear others will perceive as activist or deviant behavior that may impair their future livelihood. Others will be too preoccupied with the sheer survival tasks of the daily job search and of coping with the losses of unemployment.

Agencies and social service programs may need to seek opportunities to set the record straight, especially when aspersions are cast on the jobless. When union busting, lock-outs, and other strategies are used to achieve wage concessions and to break the negotiating power of labor unions and result in the economic decline and displacement of workers, such victim blaming may be on the rise. Moreover, blaming workers and their unions for corporate noncompetitiveness in obtaining contracts and for the resultant closures of plants because of bankruptcy camouflages some of the consequences of the unfettered economic restructuring that is occurring both nationally and internationally. Displaced workers and their families in resource-based economies also are blamed for their plight. For example, families in farm and fishing communities may be seen by detractors as having become financially overextended from obtaining loans for new equipment or as being motivated by greed and overproduction. Such criticisms attempt to mute not just the plight of these families but a public outcry for timely relief.

Public education—a long-time mission of social service agencies and programs—must be intensified during hard times to counter some of the growing intolerance for those in need. Some of this intolerance stems from the same "retreat" dynamic seen in communities in which leaders may become immobilized by economic downturns. Thus, when opinion leaders campaign against social services and aid for dislocated groups, they may play effectively on the economic uncertainty or insecurity that engulfs many people, both the employed and the unemployed, during an economic decline. At election time, the popular are often those who promise to respect the worries of the economically insecure by giving them tax relief rather than exacting higher taxes.

The devisive separation of those with a stake in holding onto their resources from those who have lost theirs not only perpetuates win–lose campaigns but does little to acknowledge and deal with the consequences for and toll on all of the economic insecurity of the few. It is possible, for example, that social service agencies can play a leading role in showing how aid to the jobless or poor is more of an investment than an expense, in light of the long-term costs of nonintervention, such as homelessness, crime, and institutionalization.

Fortifying Practice

To infuse work-related interventions into traditional practice requires acceptance not only that such interventions are relevant but that they produce more effective practice outcomes. Developing and strengthening of the work role may provide a more stable foundation for the use of psychological and interpersonal treatment techniques by enhancing the person's overall functioning and effectiveness. Phil and Laura's situations demonstrate this concept:

> For several months, Phil, age 67, has worked with Paul, his counselor, to mourn the loss of his wife, Linda, and to adjust to the loneliness and emptiness he feels. His retirement was intended to give back to both of them the years they were unable to be together because of all his traveling. Now, with Linda's death, Phil feels stripped of all meaningful roles and reasons for living. Paul is sensitive to the role trauma Phil has experienced. Moreover, Phil's reluctance to join groups at the senior center and to volunteer for civic activities makes the possibility of part-time work seem like a more acceptable antidote to the isolation and bereavement Phil is enduring. Because the work role is more familiar to Phil than are volunteer activities, he is more inclined to hunt for a job among colleagues he thinks might hire him. Thus, as Phil becomes a job seeker (something he has never done before), he is guided through all the goal setting, analyses of options, and anticipatory rejection reactions by his counselor, who finds that this focused activity helps reduce Phil's symptoms. With a job in hand, Phil is able to look again at the structure and meaning of his daily existence, and his preoccupation with suicide, as well as his abuse of substances, are reduced. Clearly, unemployment had little to do with Phil's help seeking, but a part-time job became the catalyst for more effective grief work and the reduction of symptoms.
>
> Paul was reluctant, at first, to use employment as an adjunct to treatment, especially with a retired senior citizen. His negative preconception of the harms of the world of work plus the consequences of the loss of role from yielding one's job made him judicious in his use of job clubs and job development with his clients. However, his agency had developed a job club and had posted job listings, so employment services were being infused slowly with traditional modes of practice. In addition, referrals were available for the retraining of older workers and for their employment in public agencies. These ancillary services formed a supportive framework that reinforced the clinically warranted use of employment with Phil. Had Phil not had a network of colleagues to whom he could turn for leads and interviews for jobs, Paul might have encouraged Phil to join the agency's job club, which seemed less foreign to Phil than venturing forth to a job club in another setting on less familiar territory.

Like Phil, Laura has had a series of losses, including a baby's death from sudden infant death syndrome, divorce, and poverty. Laura's mental health worker is treating her depression in part by helping her develop a more meaningful social role through her organization of a support group for parents whose babies died from sudden infant death syndrome. Although Laura would like to get a job, her severe anemic condition prohibits a search for as well as the strain of full-time work.

Capacity Building of Staff Members

The critical study by Popay and Dhooge regarding social workers' responses to the jobless in the United Kingdom reveals that many social workers do not even address the work history of those they serve. In addition, some practitioners may be confused as to whether unemployment is the cause or consequence of emotional problems.[14]

It is not uncommon for social workers and other professionals with whom they practice—planners, managers, researchers, and secretarial staff—to assume, as does the wider general public, that individuals who are jobless must have some deficit that led them to be laid off. Training of the social service team and management staff may be helpful in ferreting out these beliefs and showing how they may bias assumptions about the cause of unemployment, the assessment of clients' problems, and the treatment strategies that are sought.

Research on client satisfaction in traditional social service settings frequently depicts a misfit between the clients' need for services and the reframing of the problem by social workers. The problems that are cited most frequently as the sources of dissatisfaction are "hard" services like jobs, housing, and income.[15] Thus, training may need to expose the stigma that is associated with the provision by practitioners of hard services. Moreover, training may help counter the idea that the development of services and resources is a nonprofessional task compared with the more "challenging" tasks of psychological assessment and treatment. Reminders that traditional assessments may be biased without a knowledge of employment is one component of training. Social workers may be assessing functioning that is induced situationally by joblessness or by the traumas of an unassisted job search yet attribute the symptoms to personality or interactional deficits. Moreover, some jobless clients and their families may be reluctant to work on presenting problems such as substance abuse or improved parenting until positive incentives and outcomes emerge. Occupational assistance and the hope of an improved job or escape from joblessness may encourage clients to follow through on other treatment plans for which they have less emotional energy. Thus, training may help to fortify practice and the effectiveness of services by giving practitioners a new framework that encapsulates traditional treatment techniques.

Another major training issue involves the development of knowledge about local job markets, resources, hiring trends, and key informants to be used in the vocational assessment process. Practitioners may vary in their ability to generate empowering resources with the individuals, families, and groups they serve. Often the jobless and underemployed become the most effective generators of knowledge about the labor market. Such capacity building, along with expertise in occupational forecasting and employment trends, may be enhanced by the presentation of frequent guest speakers from local employment agencies, as well as guidance departments of universities, community colleges, and high schools. The experts' knowledge then will need to be translated into a multimodal intervention framework to be used by the social worker. Moreover, because many professional public and private employment counselors work with individuals who may be less encumbered by some of the corrosive symptoms of unemployment, the content of their presentations may have to be adjusted to fit the clients of a specific agency or program.

One source of expertise may be employment caseworkers from local welfare departments, who, despite pressures to promote workfare programs, may have developed a sophisticated developmental, occupational, problem-solving framework. Also critical to knowledge about occupational problem solving will be the retraining, job-placement, and vocational rehabilitation funds that are available to groups of targeted clients who represent many of those served by social service agencies. In addition, agency staff should be familiar with community economic development resources and the steps involved in taking action.

Ideally, training should include some of the features and processes of various support groups, ranging from job clubs to advocacy systems. Books on job clubs and articles on movements of the unemployed may offer models for self-help initiatives that are initiated and supported by the agency.[16]

Job-Support Groups and Job Clubs

Although job-support group and job club models are not substitutes for the assessment of the goals of individual clients or the treatment of their symptoms, their group-based supports nevertheless offer resources to jobless workers and social service providers that cannot be acquired as easily in a casework relationship. In some settings, it may not be possible to initiate an ongoing support group or job club that continuously receives new members because groups form bonds that make them like a closed family system. Thus, the fostering of a job club or a support group may entail the rearrangement of the responsibilities of the social work staff to ensure that these groups are covered adequately. Job clubs may require two full-time social workers per week, especially if they operate on a strict 14-day timetable, as prescribed by Azrin.[17] The job-support group and job-seeking workshop may involve less staff time and may serve as more of a touchstone for self-directed activities than the concentrated two-week workshop format of the job club.

Because the traditional job club focuses primarily on the acquisition of jobs, many of the other developmental or psychosocial issues, such as dealing with depression and financial loss, are not addressed. For example, the job club assumes one will borrow the small amount of money needed for stationery supplies, record keeping, and transportation.

Because members of the job club may need a bank of telephones, as well as opportunities to demonstrate their interviewing abilities on videotape, a classic job club may require the purchase or lease of materials and equipment (in some cases, these resources may be donated).

The agenda for the job club will include resume development and tips on how to fill out applications, locate jobs, arrange transportation, use standard scripts for information gathering, seek interviews, correspond with prospective employers, use friends and acquaintances to help locate leads, and handle questions in an interview.

Complementing the formal job club is the variety of job-search support groups that may meet for three consecutive days (half a day each), one evening a week, or a whole day. These support groups, although they have not been evaluated as rigorously as have job clubs, contain many of the same attributes, but they can be tailored to the needs of the staff and volunteers of an agency and to the unemployed themselves.[18] The agency may conduct these groups at the agency or through a church, union, or community college. Some groups are convened solely for educational purposes—that is, to launch members in a systematic job search by providing them with materials and scripts. Other groups are designed to be ongoing (until every member has a job). These groups become tightly knit, almost like a family, and take on functions that meet their members' basic needs, such as housing, giving one another haircuts, and making or altering clothes, in addition to employment.

The degree of heterogeneity or homogeneity of the group may shape its recruitment procedures, its meeting place, and so forth. Thus, a group may consist of recovering alcoholics, ex-offenders, older or prematurely retired individuals, those whose unemployment stress is manifested in child abuse, displaced homemakers, or homeless men or women.

Job clubs or job-search support groups may be shared by agencies or by a consortium of programs. One or two practitioners in an agency may decide to specialize in employment and community economic development and serve as consultants to their practitioner colleagues. However, the inclusion of the occupational problem-solving framework is critical for many, if not most, persons who are served by a social service agency, regardless of whether the employment-related interventions are referred to others or are implemented by the practitioner. Employment supports may not only increase client satisfaction with services but may raise practitioners to new levels of competence and success. Practitioners who have included employment services, such as job clubs, in their repertoires describe their results as dramatic and note that their clients' ability to apply constructive problem solving to other life stresses, including future joblessness, has been maximized.[19] Social workers, who describe their breakthroughs with members of job clubs or persons who once were seen as unemployable, claim that the transformation in those they serve is the most rewarding aspect of their careers. One such client—a jobless, unskilled, and illiterate man who was also a chronic substance abuser and child abuser—was enrolled in a basic education program for adults. The sense of hope he felt from his progress impelled him to follow through on his substance abuse treatment and to control his angry behavior as a parent.

One reason why the practitioner and his or her social service program can be a good source of employment support is that not all clients find a job. Thus, the ongoing casework relationship may not only help to buffer the effects of failure but will pinpoint corrective strategies to be undertaken through the agency's advocacy role, through publicized data gathering on the gaps in jobs in the community, and through the empowerment of the jobless, along with practitioners, in their demands for full employment for their local community, state, region, or nation.

Developing a "One-Stop" Service System

Communities that lack a diverse social service base or those that are beset with a proliferation of agencies may need to pool their resources to create a "one-stop" service system for the jobless. A multiservice agency for the unemployed may be the hub of a service delivery system that can be the foundation for the employment initiatives that are spawned by local agencies. Its creation may depend on staff being lent by a few key social service agencies, like a crisis service center, a family service or mental health clinic, a food bank, and a public or private child and family welfare agency. Rather than serving solely as therapists, these staff may mobilize volunteers, grants, and resources (such as microfiche listings of jobs from the state employment service). In a sense, the multiservice agency also may function as a clearinghouse for information on innovations in serving the jobless, as well as initiatives in economic development and assessments of the viability of entering certain occupations and work organizations. In addition, it might serve as an intake system for various social service agencies so that persons with specialized needs can be referred to or provided with case management services.

Remembering that the economic policies that are prevalent in the United States have emphasized the creation of a surplus work force so that there are fewer jobs than there are workers, social workers should be aware that many of their clients, even those who have mastered the skills and used the supports of the job clubs, may not find jobs. The failure of individual and group-based occupational problem solving, especially because there are not enough good jobs, must fuel a far more intensive initiative that transcends individual social service programs and agencies. Thus, the multiservice agency can become the political fulcrum for demands for full employment, as well as extensions of unemployment compensation, early warning of impending layoffs by employers, and retraining programs. However, this ongoing advocacy for more jobs and resources for community-based economic development must accompany the individual and group-based employment strategies operating in other agencies.

This network of agencies may help social workers and the wider community unite the unemployed, not as clients of particular agencies but as workers who are unable to find work. Without the growth of movements of unemployed workers, the deliberate gap between the number of jobs and the number of workers will not be exposed and political pressure will not be brought to bear on its elimination.

Movements of Unemployed Workers

For decades the social work profession has sought ways to maintain multimodal practice strategies involving "case-to-cause" or "case-to-class" problem-solving paradigms.[20] Without practice formulations that address the cause of conditions and symptoms, the profession is used by society to cover up inequities in the system that should be changed. A rich heritage of reform and the capacity to foster progressive self-help movements places the profession in a prominent position to advance changes in the system.

One source of pressure has been organizations of the unemployed. Often developed by those who had been successful union organizers or other types of leaders in their former jobs, these organizations have been founded, at times, under the auspices of social service agencies, unions, or churches, and have gone on to become freestanding voices and social movements.

A pilot exploratory study of such groups on the East Coast found that the membership of these groups may reach 3,000.[21] Their funds come from grants from foundations, churches, and unions; community development block grants; donations from individuals; and dues. The services they provide include housing, legal advice, and counseling. They may have few staff members or many (organizations such as the Mon Valley Committee in McKeesport, Pennsylvania, may have as many as 25 to 30 staff members). Lobbying and community education through the mass media, lectures, and meetings with leaders of public opinion are critical roles for paid staff as well as volunteers. On the average, organizations have three paid staff members whose common functions include counseling, organizing, bookkeeping, operating a hotline, and coordinating activities. In many cases, their roles as volunteers are a bridge to new career possibilities for displaced workers from manufacturing industries. In some instances, the political work of these organizations' paid and volunteer staff members may be a stepping stone to an elected political office. Mobilizing the community against a foreclosure or an increase in utility rates is critical to the political success of their work, making the community so aware of the plight of the jobless that nonjobless members join them in advocacy.

It is remarkable that despite the task of full-time job seeking, some jobless persons are able to devote themselves to building a support movement. Although the leaders of these organizations admit that it is hard to hold onto members after they get jobs, new developments have occurred, especially on the East Coast, where a national network of organizations of the unemployed has emerged. The network unites the groups through newsletters, common policy goals, and the exchange of information.

These self-help advocacy groups have sought to reopen deserted steel plants. They helped to mobilize the Democratic party caucus of the House of Representatives to extend coverage of unemployment benefits. Additionally, they are well known for preventive strategies to forestall or end mortgage foreclosures, utility shutoffs, and exclusionary health care practices for the jobless who need medical attention. By harnessing the resources of foundations, and the support of local churches, politicians, and social service agencies, these self-help groups also provide a range of counseling and survival services to their members.

Although their techniques for successful organizing have yet to be evaluated systematically for the purposes of replication, the exploratory study revealed that the variables that are central to their success in mobilizing jobless workers are high unemployment rates, plant closures, the choice of specific targets around which members can rally, helpful politicians who validate the work of these groups, and group leaders who have been organizers in the past.

Linking Employment and Economic Development Initiatives

Some traditional social service agencies, especially the Urban League, family service agencies, and rural mental health centers, have been sponsors of innovative employment, retraining, and job placement services for the jobless and underemployed. Through the use of grants from public agencies and private foundations, they have developed demonstration projects to promote occupational problem solving and employment. Public grants may come from the U.S. Department of Labor or the U.S. Department of Commerce, state commissions on vocational education, state emergency job training programs, and public service agencies to support retraining and services for dislocated or unskilled workers, vocational assessment, preemployability services, the development of public service jobs, and job placement. In addition, public and private organizations have provided special grants for projects that link occupational problem solving to prevention and early intervention with high-risk populations.

These grants may not only facilitate the development of new services, but they may help to increase the visibility of traditional social service agencies in the employment service sector. The social service agency ultimately may be the cohesive building block in the community that reaches out to occupationally high-risk populations and then integrates economic development initiatives and funds into a collective problem-solving effort led by indigenous community groups. Thus, rather than supporting economic development by external firms and developers that may not ensure the long-term stability of a community or capital that stays in the community, the social service agency becomes a vehicle for the development of enterprises in the community by local groups and for reemployment initiatives for jobless individuals. Without the cohesiveness provided by the social service agency, the community and its employed and unemployed members may be preempted from using their talents, dreams, and expertise in activities that promote both economic and employment redevelopment.

It is appropriate for the social service agency to serve as the broker and stimulus for community-based economic initiatives. In fact, community action program agencies (CAPs), which were instituted during the War on Poverty to deliver services and to organize the poor and jobless, now are intensifying their economic development capacity as many communities undergo unprecedented economic distress. Departments of community development at the state and local levels use funds from the U.S. Department of Commerce and other federal departments. As the U.S. Department of Commerce's initiatives become linked to the capacity building of distressed communities and their residents through the work of the CAPs and community development corporations, economic and social welfare become integrated. No longer is economic development seen primarily as a vehicle to improve the tax base by raiding businesses from other regions through ill-advised tax giveaways. Rather, it becomes a new instrument for empowering and vitalizing impoverished groups and communities by giving them the tools and resources to establish their own economic ventures.

According to Windschuttle, who evaluated the effectiveness of local employment initiatives (LEIs) in various industrialized nations, the overriding contribution of LEIs is that they are created and controlled locally.[22] LEIs have experimented with a variety of systems for organizing work and human relationships. As Windschuttle noted, one survey found many European LEIs to be in the service rather than the manufacturing sector, involved in transportation, merchandising, housing repair, recycling, and caregiving and recreational services. LEIs may help workers buy out a company plant that has closed or relocated. Windschuttle stated that local intermediary organizations like social service agencies help the jobless not only connect to needed resources but interpret and build their entrepreneurial capacities. The staff of social service agencies helps to bridge the sociocultural gap and psychological isolation of the long-term unemployed from traditional leaders and related economic development officials. Some of these intermediary agencies offer help with product development, financing of feasibility studies, and start-up and development costs. Sometimes funds are deployed to develop incubators that function as multipurpose sites, which provide round-the-clock support for the design, testing, and initial marketing of products. Although many new community-based ventures fail, the aid and expertise of the intermediary organization in budgeting and controlling financial operations may reduce such failures.

Part of the mission of social service agencies, according to Windschuttle, is to ''animate'' or empower jobless workers with confidence, role models, and exemplars of the kind of initiatives they might undertake.[23]

Home-based industries, not like the exploitive cottage-based industries of the past, may be one of the fastest growing arenas in which women can start small businesses. Clearly, some of these businesses will fail, but the effort, excitement, and process of staying connected to a vision, rather than giving up emotionally in a defeatest adjustment to the dismal prospect of not finding a job, particularly in economically distressed rural areas, may make the difference in long-term outcomes for the worker, the family, and the community. The meaningful social role—the sense of self-development and reduced social isolation—that may accompany such an undertaking may be a critical but overlooked feature of these entrepreneurial activities.

Labonté-Roset cautions, however, that locally based initiatives may involve great exploitation of workers, given the many extra hours required to get a new initiative solvent.[24] Social service agencies that are well positioned to be brokers for groups of jobless clients and the economic development resources that might aid them are perhaps undercutting their own developmental role in revitalizing communities. More profound outcomes than entrepreneurial visions may occur. In fact, new movements of workers and new responses from policymakers can be forged best by the organizations closest to the isolated jobless and a community that needs their talents and contributions.

Notes and References

1. P. Rayman, "The World of Not Working: An Evaluation of Urban Social Service Response to Unemployment," *Journal of Health and Human Resources Administration,* 4 (Winter 1982), pp. 319–333.

2. J. Popay and Y. Dhooge, *Unemployment and Health: What Role for Social Services?* (London: Polytechnic of the South Bank, Department of Social Sciences, July 1985).

3. T. Buss and F. S. Redburn, with J. Waldron, *Mass Unemployment: Plant Closings and Community Mental Health* (Beverly Hills, Calif.: Sage Publications, 1983).

4. M. H. Brenner, *Estimating the Social Costs of National Economic Policy* (Washington, D.C.: Joint Economic Committee, U.S. Congress, 1976).

5. R. Sunley and G. W. Sheek, *Serving the Unemployed and Their Families* (Milwaukee, Wisc.: Family Service America, 1986).

6. *Initiating Social Work Services in Labor and Industry* (Silver Spring, Md.: National Association of Social Workers, Inc., 1984).

7. *Start-up* (Seattle, Wash.: United Way King County, 1974).

8. Conversations with farm families and their advocates, Decorah, Iowa, 1986.

9. J. Mermelstein and P. A. Sundet, "Rural Community Mental Health Centers' Responses to the Farm Crisis," *Human Services in the Rural Environment,* 10, No. 1 (1986), pp. 21–26.

10. Ibid.

11. The author thanks Art Emlen of the Regional Research Institute at Portland State University, Portland, Oreg., for coining the term "policy diagnosis" to describe the outcome of the dual assessment process.

12. H. Berglind, "An Action Theory for Social Work Practice." Unpublished paper, University of Stockholm, Sweden, 1986.

13. This phenomenon was first discovered by E. Bakke, *Citizens Without Work* (New Haven, Conn.: Yale University Press, 1940). It was found to be prevalent in the author's study; *see* K. Briar, *The Effect of Long-Term Unemployment on Workers and Their Families* (San Francisco: R & E Pubs., 1978).

14. Popay and Dhooge, *Unemployment and Health.*

15. *See* D. Fahs Beck and M. A. Jones, *Progress on Family Problems* (New York: Family Service Association of America, 1973).

16. *See* N. H. Azrin and V. A. Besalel, *Job Club Counselor's Manual* (Baltimore, Md.: University Park Press, 1981); N. H. Azrin and V. A. Besalel, *Finding a Job* (Berkeley, Calif.: Ten Speed Press, 1983); and D. Feely, "Unemployment Grows, A New Movement Stirs," *Monthly Review,* 35 (December 1983), pp. 14–27. *For examples of self-help activities, see* G. Haas *Plant Closures: Myths, Realities and Responses* (Boston: South End Press, 1985); and E. S. Keeler, "An Evaluation of the First Two Years of a Job Club Program Utilizing the Percham Model with a Two-Year Follow-Up." Unpublished PhD dissertation, Gonzaga University, Spokane, Washington, May 1987.

17. Azrin and Besalel, *Job Counselor's Manual.*

18. *Start-up.*

19. Personal communications with employment and training caseworkers during in-service training, Department of Social and Health Services, Olympia, Wash., 1984–1985.

20. Case-to-class was a paradigm used by R. R. Middleman and G. Goldberg, *Social Service Delivery: A Structural Approach to Social Work Practice* (New York: Columbia University Press, 1974); case-to-cause and cause versus function in social work are attributed to R. P. Lee, "Social Work: Cause and Function," in *Proceedings of the National Conference of Social Work* (Chicago: University of Chicago Press, 1930), pp. 3–20.

21. The author and Marie Hoff thank Paul Lodico of the Mon Valley Unemployed Organizing Committee and students Glen Loutey, Linda O'Neil, Mary Fickey, and Lydia Carol for their exploratory research efforts.

22. K. Windschuttle, "Local Employment Initiatives," *Society,* 24 (Spring 1986). *See also* M. Bendick, "Economic Change Redundancy and Worker Reemployment: The American Experience" (Washington, D.C.: Bendick and Egan Economic Consultants, Inc., 1984).

23. K. Windschuttle, "International Programs and Experience." Unpublished paper, New South Wales College, Kensington, Australia.

24. *See* C. Labonté-Roset, "Youth Unemployment in Europe and Political Responses to it," *INUSW Newsletter* (Stockholm) No. 5 (October 1986), pp. 2–6.

6

Measures of Distress: Social Welfare Implications

Mary is a recently divorced single black mother of three children who has been looking for a job as a computer programmer for the past eight months. She is in increasingly difficult financial straits. Unable to make her last two mortgage payments, she risks the possibility of foreclosure. Mary is faced with the dilemma of moving to another town or state to find work or taking any job to tide her over.

At the public policy level, Mary is one of the many million workers whose life crises that were created by joblessness have been camouflaged by numerical head counts of the jobless and then further disguised by abstract unemployment rates. When she hears that members of Congress are less interested in pursuing special aid for the unemployed because the unemployment rate continued to decline in the last quarter of the year, she gets angry. Why, she wonders, are decision makers guided by rates and percentages, rather than by the realities and needs of people?

This chapter probes beneath the statistics on unemployment to examine the implications of trends in unemployment for different groups of workers, their families, and their communities. It discusses how such data can better inform social work practice and help to predict the changing needs and problems of workers, families, and communities. Methods are suggested for recasting the current statistics into more meaningful indexes of risk and guides for practice and for generating data to support social welfare. Finally, the chapter suggests ways of publicizing the true conditions and problems of the jobless to influence the deliberations of policymakers and program planners.

How one defines and measures a social problem such as unemployment determines not just the public and political attitudes about its significance, but who is to blame for the problem, the nature and type of aid to be given, and whether aid is warranted in the first place. Although statistics on unemployment rates are generated routinely, interpretations of their implications vary. When Mary hears that the national unemployment rate has dipped to 7.5 percent, she may figure that there is still hope that she will find a job in computer programming. On hearing the same news, political leaders may be less inclined to promote direct aid for the unemployed because they think that the reduced rate implies that the economy is expanding and that the unemployed will be absorbed in time. An employer whose business is prospering may interpret the declining unemployment rate as a sign of a future shortage in labor, while a labor union representative may decry the absence of full employment, calling attention to the jobless who are left behind in the wake of the improved economy. Social workers' responses to such news may vary. Some may feel that it is irrelevant to the clients they see; others may be concerned about those who are still jobless and may challenge the policymakers to promote work opportunities for all jobless people. The declining unemployment rate is not necessarily an indicator of improved well-being through increased employment. It may be a sign that fewer jobless people are looking for jobs because they have become discouraged or impaired by the human costs of unemployment or have taken low-level or part-time jobs just to survive.

Counting or Discounting the Jobless?

Despite the obvious and gross inadequacies of the current formulations, official statistics on unemployment are a starting point for developing long-term problem-solving initiatives. Because policymakers and the business community persist in seeking data on the labor supply, monthly rates of unemployment are the primary statistics promulgated to the public. Moreover, definitions of the available labor supply are restricted to active job seekers. Social workers and social service programs would benefit from data that depict the severity of unemployment from profiles of the number of persons touched by unemployment throughout the year, especially because such prevalence or incidence rates tend to be 2.5 times the actual monthly rate or average rate for the year. In examining the extent of unemployment for 1981, for example, although the actual average rate was 7.6 percent, in reality, 19.5 percent, or 23,382,000 workers were affected throughout the year.[1] Moreover, by examining the statistics on the incidence of unemployment, one can see that there may have been as many people out of work in each year in the early 1980s as there were during any year in the depression era of the 1930s.

Data on unemployment are generated by the Current Population Survey introduced by the Bureau of Labor Statistics on a regular basis in 1940 to conduct monthly household interviews in sample communities in the United States. Households are asked if any person has been out of work in the past week and looking for work during the past four weeks. Those who have worked one hour or more during the previous week are considered to be employed. Extrapolated from these responses are national rates expressed as percentages, representing the ratio between the number of unemployed persons versus those in the labor force (unemployed and employed). The unemployment rate thus reflects one segment of the "immediate labor supply" by counting only those who are actively seeking work. The number of discouraged workers who have stopped looking and those who have not looked and do not think they can get a job are now estimated in a separate count. The monthly estimate for discouraged workers is between one million and two million workers.[2]

The National Committee for Full Employment publishes the jobs-deficit rate, which includes the number of unemployed, discouraged, and part-time workers who want to work full time. In June 1987, the job-deficit rate was 11.2 percent, rather than 6 percent promulgated in official statistics.[3] Similarly, for years, the National Urban League has included discouraged and part-time workers in its Hidden Unemployment Index.[4] Gross attacked the undercounting of the unemployed by suggesting that if the count of unmarried persons were taken, using the criteria for the jobless count, only those who were actively seeking a mate would be considered.[5]

Given the prevalence of unemployment and underemployment and their consequences for social work practice, it is important to examine some of the labor market concepts used to differentiate among types of unemployment. Economists and other labor market analysts have found it useful to specify the kinds and sources of joblessness to pinpoint possible interventions. *Cyclical joblessness,* for example, is attributed to downturns in the business cycle that cast new victims into the ranks of the jobless owing to layoffs generated from the declining demand for goods and services. *Seasonal joblessness* results from seasonal fluctuations in the demand for goods and services. *Frictional joblessness* refers to persons who are "between jobs." The *structurally unemployed* include persons whose joblessness is attributable to some systemic problem, such as discrimination, or personal characteristics, such as deficits in or the obsolesence of skills. Among those who are considered structurally unemployed are ethnic minorities, women, persons with disabilities, sexual minorities, and victims of automation, plant closures, divestitures, and the flight of capital. For example, although the unemployment rate dramatically dipped to 3.6 percent in 1968, joblessness among ethnic minorities was estimated to be 6.7 percent. In 1981, the jobless rates averaged 6.8 percent for women, 14.2 percent for ethnic minorities, and 19.6 percent for youths.[6] In the same year, unemployment rates among male "heads of households" were 4 to 5.2 percent, compared with 9.9 to 10.7 percent among female "heads of households."[7] Structurally unemployed workers increasingly are found in manufacturing industries in which unemployment rates jumped from 5.5 percent in 1978 to 12.3 percent in 1982.[8]

Underemployment connotes a variety of problems; official rates on underemployment are based on part-time workers who are seeking full-time jobs. For the purposes of this book, the definition of underemployment is expanded to include persons whose jobs do not tap their levels of skills or education and do not reflect their prior earnings. In addition, underemployment is a by-product of jobs in the "secondary labor market" that offer few promotional or developmental outcomes. It has been suggested that at least one-third of the jobs in the United States relegates workers to this dead-end employment involving poor working conditions and low wages. Temporary workers who receive no benefits and low pay constitute a sector of the emergent tertiary labor market that employs mainly minorities, women, and youths.

A historical perspective provides a useful basis for making sense of these seemingly illogical rationales for excluding discouraged, marginalized, and infrequently employed persons from the official count of the jobless. Social welfare history reminds us that the U.S. economy has depended on a surplus of labor. Moreover, in recent decades, full employment has been defined as a nonaccelerating rate of unemployment that does not increase inflation. The "full employment" rate was defined as 4.5 percent in the 1960s, 6 to 7 percent in the 1970s, and 8 percent in the 1980s.[9] Thus, it is predictable that current measures of unemployment will minimize the number of jobless workers who are readily available for work, while more elaborate mechanisms rationalize the exclusion of various groups of workers from the labor force. These factors further weaken the utility

of unemployment rates as indicators of the human costs of unemployment
with which the profession is concerned. Specifically, the undercounting
of those with a need and desire for work does a disservice not only to the
victims, their families, and communities but to social welfare planners who
are attempting to create and fund special programs for high-risk
populations.

The undercount of the jobless is exacerbated by the official view that
there are primary and secondary workers, which implies that some workers
need jobs more than other workers. Such a hierarchy undercuts the attention that is paid to various groups of jobless people. For example, despite
the growing number of women who are heads of households, the rate of
unemployment among married men, nonetheless, still is heralded by some
as the most sensitive indicator of the degree of dysfunction of the economy
and labor market.[10] However, some argue that the joblessness of male
versus female breadwinners should be given the greatest weight in the
counts of the unemployed. Another insidious distinction is made between
workers who, it is alleged, are attached casually to the labor force (for example, youths and women) and those who are firmly attached. This
distinction is used by some to argue that married men are the primary
wage earners and that other (''casual'') workers are not driven to work
out of necessity.[11]

Such inferences not only marginalize groups of workers but encourage
policies and practices that exclude them from the labor market. For example, some estimates of the impact of the increased participation of
teenagers and women in the labor force on unemployment rates have concluded that the exclusion of these two groups in the count of the jobless
would lower the unemployment rate by several percentage points.[12] These
calculations suggest that some analysts consider women and youths to be
less worthy labor force participants than are male heads of households.
Such thinking counters the values of social welfare that affirm that all people have the right to equal participation in this society.

Discouraged or Disaffiliated Workers?

It is important to understand the political context within which social
welfare measures might be advanced to improve the rights of workers and
of the jobless. Such a context makes all the more pressing the knowledge
derived from practitioners who deal with the human consequences of these
exclusionary, sometimes systematically discriminatory, policies.

In recent years, debates have been waged about whether discouraged
workers, given their growing prevalence, warrant more attention from

policymakers. Policymakers who have a business perspective may indeed view discouraged job seekers as casual workers whose need for work may be questioned because they have stopped looking for a job. Unfortunately, such policymakers and experts on unemployment may not comprehend the aversive nature of a fruitless job search and the self-recrimination that may grip a wounded job seeker. The absence of such knowledge, coupled with the belief that the jobless are responsible for their condition, reduces the attention given to discouraged workers. Nevertheless, rates of discouraged workers now are collected officially, although they are not promulgated widely.

It is possible that Mary's frustrated attempts to find work will cause her to stop looking for a job when the rejections mount and she is overcome with depression. Her response would not be atypical. Mary may surmise that it was one thing for her joblessness to persist in a deep recession, but joblessness during a period of economic recovery must reflect either some deficit in herself or racist or sexist hiring policies. Thus, her functioning may deteriorate just at the time that she might be designated statistically as a discouraged worker and discounted politically by some as not being as motivated or as ready for work as are others with a stronger attachment to the labor force.

Casual Attachment to the Labor Force

Centuries-old beliefs about the inherent tendencies of some workers to be idle and poorly motivated to work arise today in relation to the more than 30 percent of jobless workers who not only endure multiple spells of unemployment each year but are questioned about their motivations to work.[13] Empirically, little is known about the millions of workers whose lives may involve multiple and frequent spells of unemployment and only short spells of employment. Although seasonal work explains many such fluctuations in the duration of jobs, the absence of solid data on causation leaves some to question the "pathological instability of those who cannot hold jobs."[14] This phenomenon, sometimes described as *turnover unemployment* is attributed to a pattern of changing from one low-paying, unpleasant job to another several times a year. It is possible, given the deindustrialization of the U.S. economy and the increasing underemployment of workers, that the number of workers who experience multiple spells of unemployment will increase. Once these workers are blamed for the "instability" of their employment, systematic pressures to address their needs and to improve their opportunities to work may be blunted. Therefore, advocacy by social workers may be necessary to change these attitudes.

Several states view such casual attachment to the labor market as a reason for excluding these workers from unemployment compensation. Workers are penalized most in states that constrict eligibility on the basis of marginal employment, which is defined as working an insufficient number of continuous quarters. Migrant workers, the poor, and ethnic and racial minorities have the highest rates of marginal employment and thus are excluded disproportionately from such coverage. Such restrictions on marginal employment, therefore, penalize the very groups of workers who already are denied equitable access to good jobs.[15]

Marginal employment, which is due, in part, to the absence of good jobs for all who wish to work and the lack of wages for critical family caregiving roles, nonetheless, is interpreted by some policymakers as a personal deficit and problem in motivation. Figure 1 depicts how problems that are created by the society are recast as individual deficits and how this reformulation negates the need to change the system and intensifies such victim-blaming initiatives as restrictions on eligibility for unemployment insurance or punitive workfare strategies for welfare recipients.

Implications of Decreased Rates of Unemployment

It generally is believed that when the unemployment rate drops, the economy and the labor market are improving. Statistically speaking, such declines may even be seen as healthy social indicators of improved human functioning and a cause for optimism. However, employment and unemployment figures are not adequate measures of hardship, job security, or the utilization of skills. With the increasing deindustrialization of the U.S. economy and the attrition of better-paying manufacturing jobs, reemployment may equal underemployment for many people. When underemployment is the antidote to unemployment, neither the health and well-being of the economy nor of the work force can be assured. Underemployment is a form of demotion and devaluation that affects not only its victims but society as well through lost productivity, underutilization of talents, and reduced revenues. Previous gains made by women and racial and ethnic minorities in manufacturing jobs have been eroded, for the most part, by the steady loss of jobs and subsequent occupational reversals in their lives. Snyder and Nowak, for example, reported that female blue-collar workers who, after years of enduring the stress and challenges of succeeding in historically male industries, have lost their jobs.

Market does not create enough
jobs, let alone good jobs.

Frequent job losers are seen as
having a weak attachment to the labor
force and are castigated for being a drain
on the unemployment insurance fund.
They also are suspected of quitting their
jobs so they can claim unemployment
benefits.

Unemployment compensation becomes
more restrictive for those with multiple
spells of unemployment.

Those receiving restrictive benefits
are increasingly forced to take any
job if it pays more than unemployment
insurance, rather than being allowed to
hold out for a job that is commensurate
with their previous jobs and livelihoods.

Market does not recognize or
place a monetary value on family
caregiving roles.

Absence of subsidies for these
caregiving roles leaves many women
a man's wage away from welfare and
poverty.

Seen by society as a drain on
the public purse and as unmotivated
in their pursuit of jobs, they may be
victims of punitive workfare strategies
and sanctioned for noncompliance with
employability plans.

Subject to frequent spells on welfare since
neither entry-level jobs nor employed men
at home are sure routes to self-sufficiency;
women may experience such stress from
going on and off welfare and from
working as unpaid caregivers and low-paid
entry-level employees that they develop
occupational and health problems that
make them eligible for Supplemental
Security Income. Thus, they escape bad
jobs as a result of their impairment.

**Figure 1. Punitive Responses of Policymakers and of the
Public Assistance and Unemployment Insurance
Systems to Frequent Job Losers**

Additionally, these workers are being forced to lower their life-styles and to work two jobs at minimum wages just to make mortgage payments on their homes.[16]

It is understandable that many people assume that an improving economy will allocate equitably jobs to those who need them at the level at which they worked before. Studies, however, show that over the past two decades, postrecession economies have not restored good jobs to workers and, because of the increased restructuring of labor markets throughout the world, may be intensifying the inequitable access to good jobs.[17] Moreover, the terror of increasing economic hardships and losses may force workers to take low-level jobs to stabilize themselves and their families.

Recessions may produce aggregated forms of labor market restructuring, but, even in the absence of a recession, some jobless people are forced to take any job to become reemployed. The dynamics of unemployment, including self-blame, increased self-doubts, and economic insecurity and hardship, not only may lower jobless workers' expectations of returning to their former levels of income and jobs but may weaken their ability to hold out for good jobs.

Many jobless people complain that rising employment rates reflect the movement of already employed people into newly created jobs, rather than reflect the reemployment of those people who have lost the jobs. Hence, some jobless people may never return to the labor market; each recession results in the further permanent attrition of jobless persons from the labor market.[18]

To demonstrate the hidden human consequences of declining unemployment rates, McDermott showed that despite a period of economic growth and a declining unemployment rate, the participation of various groups in the labor force decreased (because they dropped out of the labor market) and part-time rather than full-time employment increased, as did the number of discouraged workers and welfare recipients.[19] In effect, economic well-being was not well gauged by the use of unemployment rates during this same period of "recovery." Per capita income dropped dramatically for a substantial proportion of the state's citizens and wages were lower because of the increase in jobs in the service industry and the demise of manufacturing jobs; only those with financial assets from investments, such as stocks or rental property, showed a rise in per capita income. Thus, a decrease in the unemployment rate is not only a poor measure of economic and employment well-being; it is an inadequate index of the distributional effects of income from wages versus wages and other financial assets and resources.[20]

Multigenerational Effects of Unemployment

Little is known about the multigenerational effects of occupational problems. Official rates of joblessness among groups such as women and racial minorities camouflage the incidence of their exclusion from the work force and the effects of their exclusion on their offspring. Although such unemployment rates as 8 to 10 percent among women, 10 to 20 percent among racial minorities, 20 to 40 percent among youths, and 10 to 20 percent among workers aged 55 and over help to sensitize some of the public to the disproportionate inequities some groups face in finding jobs, they fail to denote the political and sociocultural consequences of exclusion.[21]

Some nonlabor market roles may involve careers in what is called the *informal labor market,* which includes noncash exchanges and a "subterranean" or underground economy, such as trafficking in drugs. Other roles may span the realm of family caregiving. Despite the "gains" that women have experienced in the labor market, the fact that no substitute labor force has emerged to perform caregiving responsibilities in the family may help to ensure the predominance of nonlabor market roles in many women's lives. Like caregiving responsibilities for women, retirement has been normalized by society as an often desirable alternative to participation in the labor force. Increasing evidence about the human costs of retiring from paid work, especially the involuntary retirement of men, illuminates the artificial nature of exclusionary regulations even though they are less subtle than the regulatory forces that affect women, persons with disabilities, and racial and ethnic minorities.[22]

Mason wrote about the "long arm" of labor market work that begins to shape our lives in the early years and affects our socialization and life pursuits until we retire from paid jobs in our aging years.[23] Perceptions of the right to jobs in the labor market are derived in part from a societally imposed hierarchical pecking order that places white married men at the head of the list. Moreover, because women, racial minorities, persons with disabilities, youths, and the aged are seen as victims of structural unemployment and thus are subject to specialized job-creation and training opportunities, their blunted access to jobs is taken for granted. Caught between an economy that has never produced enough jobs and the expectation that they will require extra help in acquiring jobs or in fighting discrimination, the public may come to think that structural unemployment is normal and intractable. To make matters worse, programs that focus on training and on inculcating the norms and behaviors of the world of work, rather than on changing an economy that marginalizes many such workers either within or outside the workplace, deflect attention from the systemic bases of these workers' problems.

Although it is caused by the absence of full employment and discriminatory job rationing, structural unemployment may shape differential life expectations and occupational development among its victims. Little is known about how occupational scripts and developmental processes become implanted and nurtured in childhood and adolescence. Nonetheless, the unemployment of a parent or both parents may convey a message to children about the uncertainty of work opportunities while it directly undercuts their development through physical, social, and emotional deprivation.

The correlations among poor school performance, dropout rates, and unemployment further attest to the hardships endured by those with educational problems. Although the schools may help groom children for future occupations, the original precipitants of poor school performance may be the occupational scripts that rule out steady and meaningful work, which parents may inculcate in their children at an early age. The result of these occupational scripts may be a heightened risk of drug addiction, teenage parenthood, and crime instead of steady paid work.

The absence of jobs may intensify teenage pregnancy while preempting the formation of family units through marriage. Research by the Children's Defense Fund found that the number of young men with fulltime work declined from 82 percent in 1974 to 76 percent in 1985 and that the access of young men to well-paying manufacturing jobs declined 25 percent.[24] When paid work roles are nonexistent or uncertain, teenage pregnancy may be the only meaningful alternative, even if the young people are unable to create a stable economic and marital base for their children.

Figure 2 shows how a stable versus an insecure economic and employment environment may influence children's expectations of their future performance in school and occupations and their behavioral development. This is a hypothetical charting of children's occupational development; it may conform to some of the memories of high school dropouts.[25]

The multigenerational effects of exclusionary labor market policies must be subjected to some of the same types of research as are other social indicators. Just as medical research may discover the effects of a medicine on offspring and develop interventions to counter negative consequences, so, too, must social work research on the multigenerational effects of unemployment and underemployment. The absence of data on these effects reinforces the belief in rugged individualism as a solution to exclusion

3-5 years

Attends Head Start. Believes all people can make it if they use the talents they possess. Mother is underemployed; father is jobless.

6-8 years

Father is jobless. Family moves frequently in search of stable employment. Mother and father divorce. Family moves three times. Mother skids onto welfare. Child is not learning to read, which triggers emotional frustration and verbal abuse by both parents.

9-11 years

Grades are poor and behavioral problems develop because of the family's economic problems. Is seen by teachers as a problem student. Mother does not have the emotional resources or confidence to participate in school conferences over the child's performance. Tells the child to behave in school, so learning can occur.

12-14 years

Career talk begins, but youth cannot visualize the connection between school and career. Is exposed to drug use and sexual experimentation. Grades are poor. Is in lower reading group and has increasing difficulty functioning in school. Cannot afford to join in sports. Has falling self-esteem. Psychologically, the youth is dropping out of school. Neither parent can afford counseling to aid the youth.

15-17 years

Arrested for petty theft. Drops out of school. Drug use intensifies. Cannot get job after school or in the summer. Adolescent pregnancy occurs.

Figure 2. Variations in Childhood Occupational Development

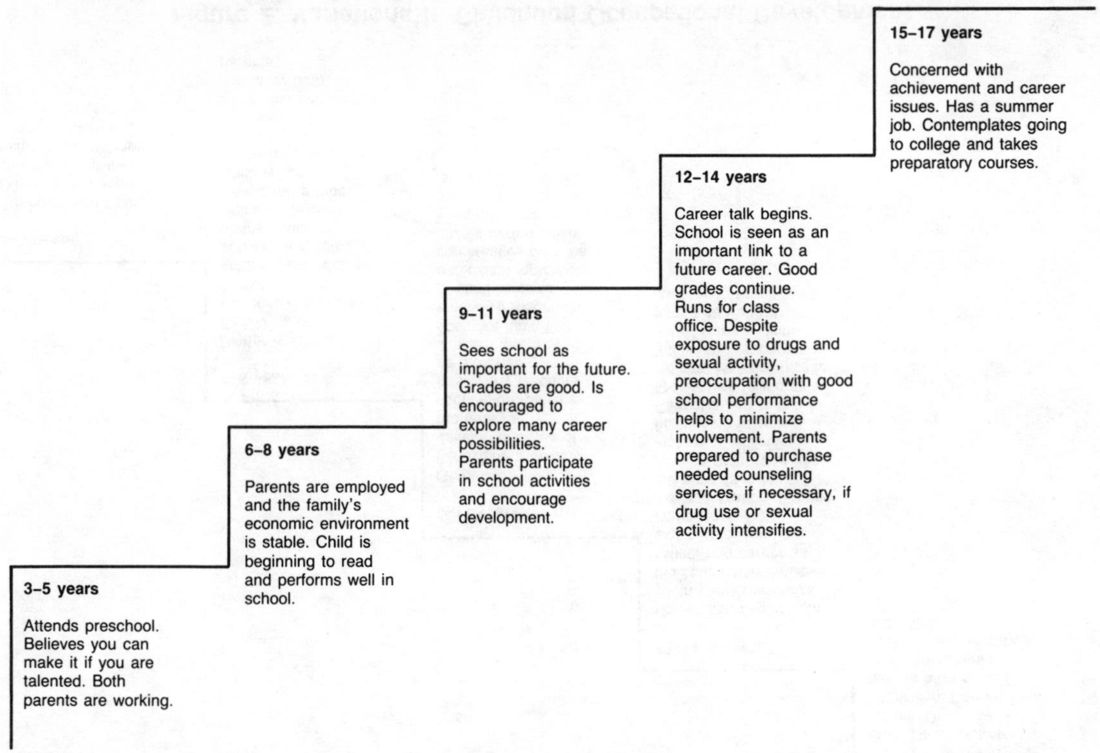

3–5 years

Attends preschool. Believes you can make it if you are talented. Both parents are working.

6–8 years

Parents are employed and the family's economic environment is stable. Child is beginning to read and performs well in school.

9–11 years

Sees school as important for the future. Grades are good. Is encouraged to explore many career possibilities. Parents participate in school activities and encourage development.

12–14 years

Career talk begins. School is seen as an important link to a future career. Good grades continue. Runs for class office. Despite exposure to drugs and sexual activity, preoccupation with good school performance helps to minimize involvement. Parents prepared to purchase needed counseling services, if necessary, if drug use or sexual activity intensifies.

15–17 years

Concerned with achievement and career issues. Has a summer job. Contemplates going to college and takes preparatory courses.

Figure 2 (Continued)

from the labor market and a victim-blaming approach to those who experience occupational problems or failure in late adolescence. Youths who have not been socialized for jobs and careers may increase their criminal activity or use of drugs when they get low-paying jobs that provide little satisfaction.[26] Certainly, once one has adapted to a jobless life-style, short-term jobs may provide resources that exacerbate an earlier occupational script. The provision of a single job through public works or private-sector initiatives may not be sufficient to counter the many years and, in some cases, generations of expulsion from the labor market of a class, race, or community of workers and their offspring.

Social Work Interpretations of Labor Market Statistics

Periodically, a national commission is appointed to review the utility and validity of unemployment statistics. Recommendations for better measures of the functioning of the economy and of the needs and problems of workers are included in the 30 or more background papers prepared for the 1978 Commission on Unemployment Statistics. These recommendations may help guide some of the future advocacy efforts of the profession.

One recommendation was to replace unemployment rates with labor-utilization data, thereby making more definitive the losses to the nation of those who are barred from participation. These data could be presented in terms of hours, weeks, and years of lost productivity, revenues, and contributions to society. Historically, such "lost-labor" analyses have been used to dramatize the plight not just of the jobless but of a nation that is left with idle talent and costly transfer payments. Social workers might also be able to convert such data into equivalent measures of lost opportunities for women, racial and ethnic minorities, persons with disabilities, and others who are less likely to be counted in labor force statistics. Conversely, women's unpaid labor in the home could be documented and used to measure risk. Any woman whose unpaid labor is subsidized by a man's wage is vulnerable because when the man loses his job or his support of the caregiving roles is undercut by divorce, separation, or death, she and those who depend on her are at a high risk of sinking into poverty.

Social workers have major roles to play in the assessment of the impact of a worker's joblessness on his or her family and community. Statistics generated from special studies of the unemployed might include an analysis of the risk of unhealthy functioning among workers, their families, and communities. In many families, the husband's unemployment may cause the wife to give up her multigenerational caregiving responsibilities and to acquire a temporary job to stave off poverty. The decreased functioning; the loss of a home, a car, and other possessions, as well as savings; and the adjustments in life-styles that must be made because of unemployment have not been well documented. Furthermore, little is known about the likelihood that long-term unemployment may reduce a worker's capacity to earn and even impede reemployment. In addition, little is known about what types of jobs workers acquire at the end of their search and the implications of the type of job they get for their improved well-being and that of their families. As analysts of unemployment data have argued, the assessment of mobility is not factored into the social indicators used to gauge the health of the economy, the labor market, or workers.

Assessments of Risk

Because the incidence of unemployment is so great, affecting 20 to 30 percent of the official labor force each year, researchers in social welfare should address the risks to which such workers are subjected. The assessment of thresholds of risks is important even when some workers may have short spells of joblessness or may have left their jobs voluntarily. Ideally, joblessness should not impair or leave workers, their families, or their communities any worse off than they were before unemployment. In the absence of full employment, social welfare initiatives must be accelerated to prevent the incapacitation that now occurs. The analysis of risks may suggest more timely and comprehensive interventions. For example, in the case of Mary, it might be noted that up until now, her functioning has been relatively adaptive. Despite her increased headaches and sleeplessness, she has not developed some of the more severe behavioral symptoms that are associated with long-term joblessness. However, the impending loss of her house because of her inability to make mortgage payments may set in motion an array of dysfunctional reactions.

The analysis of risks can be tied to critical junctures when private pain is thrust into the public eye. Such critical junctures include the timing and news of a job loss; the way the termination of the job is handled; the denial of benefits (unemployment insurance, workers' compensation, public assistance, and trade adjustment assistance); the termination of benefits; defaults on loans; utility shutoffs; the repossession of a car and foreclosure of or eviction from a home; bankruptcy; the failure of a small business; and an arrest. Job-search rejections may be the most compounding risks that such an assessment must address. However, such rejections are often less amenable to scrutiny than are some of the other actions taken against unemployed workers. Although such critical incidents may not be the most difficult problems faced by jobless persons, nevertheless, they may help statistical data gatherers generate profiles on the well-being of jobless workers. For example, the knowledge that each month 10 percent of the labor force may be jobless and that 10 percent of the jobless may experience a repossession; 30 percent, a denial of benefits; and 20 percent, the termination of benefits may compel public responses that are more consistent with the needs of jobless workers, their families, and communities and promote prevention and earlier interventions.

The assessment of the risks to communities, states, and regions also is critical, not just to trigger special aid but to promote extended unemployment benefits as well. Measures of community distress are becoming political footballs; overnight, a distressed community may be dropped from the distressed list, not because the community is no longer distressed but because it may be registering different outcomes that are as bad as joblessness that are no longer picked up in the jobless rates. Thus, although some counties may be declining continually because of the loss of a major industry, the rate of unemployment may decrease, implying that employment is rising. Actually, such a rate decrease may be the result of the increase in the number of discouraged workers who are going on welfare or of the number of part-time workers who no longer are counted in the unemployment rate. Thus, the unemployment rate alone may not be a sufficient index of the dynamics of risk and decline in economically impaired communities. More composite indexes may include the following:

Income: per capita wages, social security, Supplemental Security Income, Aid to Families with Dependent Children (AFDC), food stamps, general assistance, Medicaid, Medicare, unemployment insurance, investment income from financial, rental property, and related assets.

Economic climate: revenues from property taxes, tax levies, and sales taxes; business failures and turnovers; bankruptcies; foreclosures on homes; new housing starts; retail sales; and utility shutoffs.

Utilization of social services: child protective services, community treatment and detoxification services for alcoholics and drug abusers, community mental health services, and adult protective services.

Emergency social services: crisis services, food banks, clothing banks, and emergency shelters for the homeless and for abused women.

Employment and unemployment rates: part-time rates and involuntary and voluntary rates.

Population parameters: in migration, out migration, age demographics, and the presence of school-age children.

Vital statistics: deaths from homicides, suicides, and stress-related diseases (cardiovascular diseases); infant mortality; and rate of teen pregnancy.

Health: mortality and morbidity rates of stress-related diseases.

Crime: adult and juvenile crimes of violence and against property and arrest and conviction rates.

Institutional inventory: institutional stability, shifts in funding and popula-tions (hospitals, public and private schools).

Because the lag time after a job loss may span months or years, it may be that data on trends need to be tracked for as long as 18 years.

Such dynamics are symptomatic of a changed economy. Thus, declining unemployment rates in the face of the increasing use of welfare programs are critical warnings that new indexes of the well-being of workers and families must be used. Research suggests that food stamps, AFDC-R (for single parents), AFDC-E (for unemployed parents), and general assistance rates may offset the unreliability of the unemployment rate in reflecting growing economic distress and measures of social functioning.[27]

Occupational Trends and the Availability of Jobs

Along with the analysis of risks, another minimal requirement for job seekers is data on the availability of jobs in various fields. That it is up to Mary to find the hidden job market in computer programming, as well as job vacancies, reflects policies that place unnecessary and aggravating burdens on potentially high-risk individuals. If Mary were able to deter-mine through a public directory of job vacancies not only where the jobs are but the frequency of openings in her line of work, she might gear herself up for a different kind of search or change her career focus. In Mary's town, many people are looking for jobs in computer programming. Each year, the local community college graduates a large group of persons with such skills, who then descend on Mary's small semirural community trying to find computer programming jobs. Data on job-vacancy rates might have helped Mary gear up for a 12-month search or develop contingency plans if she learned that only three openings occurred in the past six months. Uninformed about job-vacancy rates and unsure about her competition, she treated the two rejections she received as signs that she was perhaps unemployable in her line of work or that the hiring patterns in the com-munity were discriminatory. Had she known the probability of rejection, she might have prepared herself better emotionally, financially, and oc-cupationally for alternative types of reemployment. Clearly, if the state employment service were able to list all the jobs that are available, rather than just 12 percent of the job openings, Mary might have been better prepared to organize a systematic job search.

Similarly, workers should be able to track the viability of their occupations. Analysis of trends should be routinely provided to workers; such analyses should document those occupations that increased or decreased 5 percent each year over a 5- to 10-year period. Such data are essential for early warnings of the uncertain nature of an occupation.

Implications for Social Workers

The social work profession has much to contribute to debates about the nature, prevalence, scope, and consequences of unemployment for workers, their families, and communities. Without the comprehensive data proposed in this chapter, unemployment statistics and related indexes of distress will remain inadequate for the purposes of planning social welfare services and changing policies. Moreover, until the problem is defined more broadly to capture the dimensions of women's roles as caregivers, work roles in the informal and subterranean economy, and the hidden impact of unemployment on communities, no analysis of the problem can be complete. The profession has a primary role to play in serving the jobless because of its unique capacity to move beyond symptom-specific responses to promote multimodal interventions that involve clinical, programmatic, and policy innovations. Without an adequate data base and accurate measures of needs, change will be constrained.

Because unemployment measures shape the public's images of the problem and its victims, improved indicators of human needs might prompt more public support for comprehensive services. Not only do current measures lessen the public's concern, they may even impede advocacy for new rights and services that groups such as social workers might mobilize on behalf of jobless workers, their families, and communities.

Notes and References

1. *Handbook of Labor Statistics* (Washington, D.C.: U.S. Department of Labor, December 1983).

2. *Employment and Training Report of the President* (Washington, D.C., 1980, 1981, 1982).

3. National Committee for Full Employment, *Jobs Impact Bulletin*, 7 (July 1987).

4. D. G. Glasgow, testimony before the U.S. Senate Subcommittee on Social Security and Family Policy, Senate Finance Committee, Washington, D.C., February 2, 1987.

5. B. Gross, "Toward Global Action," *The Annals,* 492 (July 1987), pp. 182–193.

6. *Handbook of Labor Statistics,* p. 63.

7. Labor Force Statistics Derived from the *Current Population Survey: A Databook* (vol. 2; Washington, D.C.: U.S. Department of Labor, Bureau of Labor Statistics, September 1982), p. 445.

8. *Handbook of Labor Statistics,* p. 75.

9. These rates are derived, in part, from the Phillips curve doctrine, discussed in chapter 9, which postulates an inverse relationship between unemployment and inflation. "Full employment" rates thus are pegged officially at tolerable levels of employment and inflation.

10. *See* "Married and Jobless," *Wall Street Journal,* January 19, 1985, p. 1.

11. *For a review of these debates, see* R. S. Goldfarb, *Measuring Types of Unemployment: Implications for Unemployment Statistics.* Background Paper No. 8 for the National Commission on Employment and Unemployment Statistics (Washington, D.C.: U.S. Government Printing Office, June 1978).

12. *See* G. G. Cain, *Labor Force Concepts and Definitions in View of Their Purposes.* Background Paper No. 13 for the National Commission on Employment and Unemployment Statistics (Washington, D.C.: U.S. Government Printing Office, March 1978), p. 30.

13. *Handbook of Labor Statistics.*

14. Goldfarb, *Measuring Types of Unemployment,* p. 7.

15. A. Colon, "For Jobless, Times Getting Tougher," *Everett Herald* (Everett, Washington), August 27, 1985.

16. *See* K. A. Snyder and T. Nowak, "Job Loss and Demoralization: Do Women Fare Better than Men?" *International Journal of Mental Health,* 16 (1987), pp. 92–106.

17. *See* Bowles, D. M. Gordon, and T. E. Weisskopf, *Beyond the Wasteland* (Garden City, N.Y.: Doubleday Anchor Books, 1983). *See also,* R. B. Reich, *The Next American Frontier* (New York: New York Times Books, 1983).

18. G. A. Akerloff and B. G. Main, "Unemployment Spells and Unemployment Experience," *American Economic Review* (December 1980).

19. *Report to Governor Booth Gardner and the Legislature* (Olympia, Wash.: Joint Select Committee on Unemployment Insurance and Compensation, December 1986).

20. R. Nafziger, "The New Washington Economy: Implications for Public Policy." Report to the Washington State Legislature, House of Representatives, November 7, 1985.

21. *Handbook of Labor Statistics.*

22. F. F. Furstenberg, Jr., and C. A. Thrall, "Counting the Jobless: The Impact of Job Rationing on the Measurement of Unemployment," *The Annals,* 480 (March 1975), pp. 45–59.

23. R. Mason, *Participatory and Workplace Democracy* (Carbondale, Ill.: Southern Illinois University Press, 1982).

24. A. Sun and C. M. Johnson, "Declining Earnings of Young Men: Their Relation to Poverty, Teen Pregnancy and Family Formation" (Washington, D.C.: Adolescent Clearinghouse, Children's Defense Fund, 1987).

25. The author thanks Thelma Payne for her comments on and further development of this chart.

26. E. Greenberger and L. Steinberg, *When Teenagers Work: The Psychological and Social Costs of Adolescent Employment* (New York: Basic Books, 1986).

27. *See Report to Governor Booth Gardner and the Legislature;* and *see* K. Briar et al., *Dynamics of Economic Distress in Mason, Clallam and Stevens Counties: Report to the Governor* (Olympia, Wash.: Office of the Governor, 1987).

7

Workplace Services for the Underemployed and Unemployed

In addition to the aid they provide through social service agencies, another avenue through which social workers can help the unemployed and underemployed is the development of programs in workplaces and labor unions, because these are the primary sites through which the needs of workers and their families are met and thus through which preventive and early intervention services may be introduced.[1] The reemergence of workplace social services, such as employee assistance programs (EAPs), as well as expanded benefit, training, and organizational development programs, sets the stage for the development of innovative policies and services on behalf of workers who are threatened by layoffs, closures (and the consequent loss of a livelihood), and cutbacks in wages and benefits.

Recently launched social services in the workplace often seem to be directed toward ameliorating the symptoms of the problems of individual workers and working conditions. However, it is hoped that the long-run focus of social work practice in this area will be the health and welfare of the work force and the effects of work roles and work organizations on individuals and their families.[2] The increasingly turbulent working environments of many workers that affect their livelihoods and identities compel social work practice to go beyond troubled employees to stabilize and prevent some of the damage to workers that is occurring from these organizational changes. Because the goal of the workplace is to achieve efficient and profitable outcomes, the workplace may thwart human needs and dynamics and deform the human organization itself.

This chapter addresses the job-retention mission of occupational social workers, as well as ways to aid victims of layoffs through EAPs and outplacement services. Collaborative practices with labor unions also will be discussed, because they serve as focal points for providing innovative services to both union and nonunion employees. Finally, practice principles that should guide services for underemployed workers are delineated.

Mission of Occupational Social Work

The profession's historic responsibility for mitigating and attempting to prevent the human casualties of the mobility of capital and the maximization of profits in businesses compels new types of practice in this era of unprecedented changes in local workplaces and regional, national, postindustrial, and developing economies. Capital is not bound by moral, social welfare, or legislated codes of human transactions. The challenges to social welfare have become global because more and more corporations are transcending national boundaries and laws and operating freely throughout the world. Thus, these corporations are exporting to developing nations some of the same practices that have been fought in U.S. communities.

The roles of capital, business practices, and business outcomes are viewed from different perspectives in our society. A predominant focus of social workers may be the human and community casualties that warrant restorative and preventive practices. However, non–social workers may view the development and inequitable distribution of products and services, income levels, and jobs and the general lowering of the national per capita standard of living as inevitable while marveling at the changes wrought by technological advancement. Some even may prefer to look at the overall strengths, rather than the harms, of the modern workplace, especially because it has the potential for promoting more effective human functioning both in and outside the workplace.

As social services become a more fixed attribute of the modern workplace, it is appropriate to review the original goals of the EAP movement and to harness them as the rationale for broader interventions. One such original goal was the retention of employees through systematically provided services to address personal or workplace problems. Clearly, the goal of providing services for alcoholism, mental health, family stress, and related problems was to restore the functioning of workers and to prevent them from losing their jobs.[3] Given the thousands of workers whose jobs have been retained by their use of the treatment services of EAPs, it may be said that social workers in both management and union-based employee assistance services have been in the business of what might be termed "layoff prevention." Seen from this light, it is appropriate that EAPs reaffirm and further extend and develop their employee-retention capacities. This is a particularly pressing mission, given the millions of laid-off and permanently dislocated workers throughout the country.

Well-conceptualized plans for intensifying employee-retention strategies must be predicated on formal recognition by both labor and management that the EAP mission indeed centers on employee-retention services. Once EAP strengthens its preeminent concern for and value of preventing layoffs and terminations, it may begin to reframe for the workplace the importance of jobs, livelihoods, and sensitive treatment in the allocation of jobs and in layoff policies. EAP social workers may want to promulgate statistics on how many jobs were saved because of EAP interventions or because the supervisor, employee, or employee's relative initiated timely help seeking. Thus EAP's preventive capacity—an understated attribute—can be expanded, in effect, to help the workplace implement and intensify its "corporate social responsibility" through expanded retention services. To this end, in-house advisory committees and agency boards for externally provided services may want to tailor brochures, promotional materials, and communications to employees to foster the more expanded image, role, and responsibility of EAP.

The retention and prevention services that EAP can offer must be predicated on the concurrence of management and labor of the desirability of promoting alternatives to layoffs. Otherwise, EAP is caught between promoting retention devices through EAP services, on the one hand, and not preventing or seeking alternatives to layoffs, on the other hand.

The occupational social worker can draw on the profession's history of promoting equity in the distribution of society's goods and resources.[4] In some situations, alternatives to layoffs involve similar types of distribution because jobs, job descriptions, timing of shifts, work hours, wages, and benefits are entities that can be meted out more evenly or disproportionately.

Layoff Services

Employers in most industrialized European nations cushion their layoffs with one or two years' advanced notice, retraining, and job placement services to minimize the destabilizing effects on workers, their families, and communities. Researchers are beginning to document some of the mitigating effects of these practices. Beckett, for example, found that the typically negative by-products of layoffs, such as depression, health problems, and family stress, did not occur when workers were given an early warning and preretirement and reemployment-related services.[5] Such research helps to magnify the centrality of problem-solving services that in the absence of job-retention rights, ultimately must be available as a minimal response to employees, their families, and communities.

Some EAPs have addressed unemployment in a systematic way. For example, at Detroit Diesel Allison in Indiana, layoff support groups were formed by the EAP social work director in conjunction with fieldwork students from the University of Indiana School of Social Work.[6] As recalls occurred, reentry groups were formed to help the workers ventilate their anger and to treat what the EAP social worker defined as posttraumatic stress syndrome. Returning workers had lost homes, family members, and their health during their prolonged joblessness. The attention paid to their tendency to collapse once they were rehired and to the related traumas they endured was one of the many innovative services provided.

Some EAPs are unable to acquire the resources, supports, and access to policymakers in the work organization that they need to aid terminated employees. Yet, this problem has not slowed their problem solving on behalf of the jobless. One director of an externally based EAP, who considered it her responsibility to serve both employed and unemployed workers, mobilized support groups for the jobless under the auspices of a church in the community.[7]

Some EAP social workers are able to contribute to, if not design, plans for alternatives to layoffs by examining hiring practices, job vacancies, and overtime. Furthermore, early retirement incentives, although controversial, at least represent additional attempts by employers to reduce the need for layoffs.

Few employers have experimented with workload sharing to the extent that all employees equally bear the effects of cutbacks and none is subject to catastrophic hardships. For example, by reducing the work hours of all employees, hardships are collectivized. Despite the impediments of already existing prior contracts that involve layoff procedures based on the degree of seniority, new formulations could be introduced to make the effects of retrenchment more equitable.

Some EAPs have worked extensively with employees who have avoided termination during a layoff. One EAP director facilitates programs for these "survivors" that address their sense of vulnerability, insecurity, and guilt and the stress of heightened workloads.[8]

Like layoffs, major reorganizations in a workplace, especially in times of takeovers and mergers, displace workers from their previous occupational roles and statuses. EAP intervention can help to cushion the effects of powerlessness and the consequences of dysfunctional personal reactions to decisions. EAPs are critical to cushioning the destabilizing effects of corporate mergers, acquisitions, and hostile takeover. The experiences of Bob in this regard are an example:

> Bob, a well-paid executive of a large aluminum processing operation, has just learned that, despite growing profitability, a disinvestment strategy is afoot. As a victim of a hostile takeover by a conglomerate several years back, Bob was determined to keep his operation viable through creative management to improve the employees' morale and productivity. However, the conglomerate, although using the takeover as a source of tax relief, now has decided to milk the profits from Bob's plant for speculative investments in the hope of bringing 40 percent in tax write-offs and greater overall profits to the conglomerate and its stockholders. The tax disinvestment will involve a two-year closure process. Bob is to fire half his management staff and lay off two-thirds of his work force in the coming year. What might have been an opportunity for an outright employee buyout of the company becomes a slow process of demise, preempting an organized effort to look at alternatives for the plant and for the workers.
>
> Six months after the first wave of layoffs, Bob suffered a cerebral hemorrhage and consequent brain damage, forcing him into early retirement. Had he not retired because of his stroke, he eventually would have been laid off, too. His two sons have been forced to drop out of college, and his wife seeks work as a receptionist. They sold their home and one of their two cars to get by.

Unfriendly takeovers are on the increase because they produce what Reich called "paper profits."[9] The vulnerability of companies to hostile takeovers has increased to the point that, in 1981, almost 50 percent of the chief financial officers of the largest U.S. firms believed that a takeover of their firm was possible. What such takeovers and mergers reflect is the growing instability of the workplace for managers and employees alike. Bob's story reflects a level of servitude, a lack of control, and human consequences that may not be any different from those of his workers.

It is critical for social workers to remember that managers may be no more immune to the stresses of joblessness than are their work forces. Moreover, in looking at the destabilizing consequences in the lives of work organizations, managers, and employees, social workers can avoid some of the adversarial interactions that focus on symptoms while failing to address the need for stabilization for all as an entitlement.

Corporations hire outplacement services, which usually involve the self-directed job development of employees, to address the problems of displaced middle-level and upper-level managers. The recognition of the hardships they face in finding jobs, accompanied by a sense of accountability for their welfare, has resulted in specialized treatment for these high-ranking personnel.

Corporations have outplacement firms partly because of the frequent reorganizations and layoffs that have occurred in the past decade. It is estimated that in 1982, 30,000 workers were aided by outplacement services.[10] One outplacement firm estimated that it provides 30 to 65 hours of counseling per jobless employee, while the employee may spend up to 300 hours in self-assessment and job-campaign activities.[11] Even though many outplacement services focus on middle- and upper-level managers, the strategies pursued for self-assessment and reemployment are similar to those suggested in chapter 3, especially the use of "reclaimed dreams" to ferret out occupational goals and interests and to stimulate an intensive self-directed job campaign.

Outplacement services benefit both the corporation and the laid-off employee. Cost effective for the corporation, they reduce the utilization of unemployment benefits and minimize the number of lawsuits filed during the termination process.[12] Many laid-off workers are able to continue using their offices and titles, which increases their access to other jobs. In addition, the provision of severance pay further cushions the economic chaos of the loss of a job. Ideally, all laid-off employees should transfer from their current jobs to others without a break in employment. Outplacement firms aim for a 90-day transition from the old job to a new job.

In a sense, outplacement services help to signify a more positive model of social welfare for jobless employees than is practiced in many corporate layoffs. Although outplacement services address a small fraction of the laid-off work force, such initiatives should be expanded to become part of all employee benefit systems.

Capacity Building in Labor Unions

Just as some corporations provide outplacement services for their managerial employees as a bridge between old and new jobs, unions also have programs that are effective bridges for workers. Even if they are not members of a labor union, laid-off workers may find a union-sponsored or union-affiliated program to be a sound forum for collectivizing their pain, anger, and self-help efforts to become reemployed. Not only has the labor movement fought for job security and full-employment initiatives since its inception, it has functioned as an advocate for unemployment compensation, workers' compensation, and the extension of such benefits as health insurance.

In communities in which the labor movement may not be strong or as systematically focused on the needs of its jobless members, social workers still can engage in incremental capacity building to enhance the responsiveness of a union. Like the help needed by the relatives and friends of jobless individuals to refrain from personalizing the anger that may be directed at them, so, too, do union leaders require skills to reframe whatever negative demands their jobless members place on them. For many, the union is like a family, and its members believe they have the same rights to skills and knowledge to promote effective problem solving as do other primary groups. For example, business agents may complain that the jobless members are too frustrated, cannot be helped, or eventually will drift into nonunion jobs and thus might not be worth the investment of promoting their reemployment, especially when the union is accountable to its dues-paying members.

The time of layoffs and displacement may be the most critical juncture for social workers to enable union leaders to extend themselves, through services, rather than to expel symbolically or "lay off" their disenfranchised members. Many workers may choose not to participate in a union in future jobs if they are left with the taste of an unsupportive union at the time of a layoff or plant closure.

Some labor leaders may believe that the ability to survive a layoff or dislocation may be similar to the ability to "tough" out a strike. Thus, the idea of specialized services for long-term unemployment may seem either unnecessary or beyond the resources or capacity of the local union. Moreover, because an array of services to address the human costs of unemployment was not provided in the past, union leaders may not believe that they have the resources to develop them unless they work collaboratively with social workers and social service agencies.

Despite the uncertainty of local unions about the place of their jobless members, the national leadership of the AFL–CIO encourages an array of services for jobless members. Research has documented the effectiveness of directories of helping services as organizing tools for survival workshops and support groups.[13] Such directories, which include descriptions of health and social services, training, and educational and reemployment resources, also may help to normalize the jobless workers' symptoms by describing the types of feelings and problems that warrant help seeking. In assessing the effectiveness of such a directory as a capacity-building tool for a union's support of its jobless members, a pre–post test was conducted.[14] The pre-post test showed that business agents of key unions affiliated with the AFL–CIO labor council became more willing, interested, and able to reach out to and better serve jobless members through the provision of such a directory when it became an educational and organizing, as well as self-help, tool.

Most large United Way agencies have an AFL–CIO community services arm. A labor union representative actually may be on the staff of a United Way agency, or United Way funds may support a freestanding social service agency called a labor agency. Labor agencies, which now operate in a number of cities across the country, provide an array of housing, food, and alcoholism treatment services to the community. Because help seekers do not have to be union members, these services are presented as being critical for all workers and their families and for retirees.

Within either the United Way agencies or the labor agencies, creative labor counseling courses are held that help union members and nonmembers develop some initial skills in reaching out to troubled workers and neighbors.[15] Speakers for the courses include representatives from many of the key social service agencies in the community. Skills in outreach and referral also are provided. Such counseling courses also are ideal sources of capacity building for local union leaders to help them better serve their jobless members. Several sessions, if not the whole series, can address the dynamics and need for services of jobless and underemployed members. Such forums are a systematic route for social workers to infuse knowledge about occupational stress into self-help networks of workers and to reaffirm the social service orientation of the labor movement and its leaders.

The Community Services Division of United Way or the labor agency may be the most appropriate auspice for conducting specialized self-help job-search classes, survival workshops, and outreach services to the jobless and to victims of lockouts and union busting. It may be less stigmatizing to workers to use their local union as a conduit to social services than to go to an outside specialized agency. Thus, when the social service auspice is labor based or labor linked, workers believe they are claiming services they have paid for through their union membership and that these services are going to be compatible with their social class and values.[16] It is critical that providers of social services be connected to the labor union culture so they are seen as "one of the family"; otherwise, some of the best-cherished and well-funded services will fail. The low rate of use of services by jobless union members in a demonstration project in the East has been attributed to the incongruence between the style and values of the service provider and of the jobless union members.[17]

Labor leaders and providers of community services also have been able to conduct job clubs that are provided through the state employment service for their laid-off members who were victims of a plant closure.[18] By using the helping network and cloak of legitimacy for help seeking that the union provides for its members, service providers can coordinate creative supports, ranging from job placement services to self-initiated job searches. The long heritage of struggle to advance the needs of workers through political action and binding agreements places the labor movement in a position to spearhead reforms on behalf of the jobless and underemployed. Furthermore, political action, rather than services, may be the predominant response to the needs of jobless members. Thus, the addition of the service approach to the unions' well-developed ability to engage in political action will encourage the development of a multimodal continuum of policies and services.

The pressing needs of the jobless may dwarf the symptoms and hardships that are faced by the underemployed. However, labor unions may prove to be a major rallying point for publicizing the increasing seriousness of underemployment as a social problem. Although unions have focused on the lower wages that are associated with underemployment, the human costs of wasted talent and energy may need to be addressed by social workers.

Serving the Underemployed

Some of the symptoms addressed by EAPs, such as poor work performance, substance abuse, and emotional and family problems, may result from boredom and dissatisfaction with a job and the corrosive effects of the sense of entrapment that is inherent in underemployment. Often the underemployed worker's feelings of powerlessness may manifest themselves in symptoms like the ones experienced by the unemployed. However, some workers may fear that their disclosure to a social worker of their dissatisfaction with underemployment may threaten the jobs that entrap them. The employees' time-limited relationship with another overburdened EAP social worker also may minimize the extent to which working conditions can be addressed. Employees who are referred by their EAP social worker to social service agencies in the community that have a less-direct connection to the employer may be able to discuss more openly their work constraints and the self-anger these constraints perpetuate.

It is not threats to confidentiality alone that may prevent an employee's disclosure of frustrations with a job. Like jobless workers, underemployed workers may feel they have no choice, believing that if they were "any good," other workplace opportunities would have emerged. Furthermore, those who believe they are only as competent as the job they are in will be reluctant to explore the possibility of changing.

Thus, such self-recriminating thoughts and attributions may even impede the learning of new skills and the expansion of responsibilities. Some workers may feel convinced that change is not possible or requires adjustments that are too fraught with new problems (like a period of unemployment, increased economic woes, and interpersonal adjustments in the family). For some, especially those whose expectations for a better job or working conditions are consistent with their training and previous work roles, the feelings of being entrapped may surface easily. But for those whose hopes are buried by years of little recognition for their broader repertoires and who have felt like supplicants in a hierarchical work organization, disclosure may be much more difficult. Moreover, when the worker is referred because of problems with his or her work performance, job retention needs to be addressed first and the worker stabilized in the job, if desired, before underemployment is tackled. Lerner suggested, on the basis of his work with underemployed workers, that insight into the source of their pain may help workers externalize some of the blame and relieve symptoms.[19] In their problem-solving role, social workers can empower employees to take baby steps in initiating change or reclaiming at least a portion of their earlier occupational dream. Some of the steps in effecting change for an underemployed worker are similar to those used with a jobless worker. They are as follows: the reframing and normalization of symptoms, the abatement of symptoms and the stabilization and retention of a job, and the addressing of underemployment and the structure and content of the work.

Reframing and Normalizing Symptoms

Employees often voluntarily seek help from an EAP, an agency, or a private practitioner when the symptoms of underemployment overwhelm them, their co-workers, supervisors, or family members. When a supervisor refers a worker to EAP, the worker's presenting problems may be low productivity, absenteeism, the excessive utilization of health benefits, sickness, and accident-prone behavior.[20] Unearthing the possible working conditions that caused or set in motion the personal, family, or work dysfunction may be central to enabling the worker to make changes.

Moreover, rather than "fixing" their symptoms, some workers may prefer to leave their jobs, especially when the disappointment of the jobs is analyzed and the tools to help them find work elsewhere are offered.

Despite the fact that it may be warranted clinically, focusing on a negative behavior when a worker is already feeling down and marginalized may be like double punishment. Thus, until the worker has taken steps to consider job alternatives, he or she may not be ready to work on symptoms. For this reason, it is important that job-acquisition strategies (discussed in chapter 3) parallel the clinical process of assessing and abating symptoms and related activities to stabilize functioning.

Stabilizing the Situation

Traditional interventions that focus on the "presenting problem" will seek to stabilize the situation, especially if the worker's job will be terminated soon or other crises are escalating in or outside the workplace. For example, when conflict with co-workers and family members reaches an untenable level, the social worker may want to postpone discussing the workplace shapers of the problem until the immediate crisis is resolved. Helping the worker to keep his or her job by undergoing treatment for such problems as alcoholism may be a critical precursor to a long-run analysis of the extent to which underemployment or other workplace stressors have contributed to the presenting problem. However, plans for treating these workplace precipitants should be made early, especially when the step-by-step contract is developed. For example, in the following case, the social worker was cautious about promising to intervene in the system until the worker's situation was stabilized:

Sara was referred to the EAP social worker by her supervisor because of her excessive absenteeism. Her absenteeism from the multimedia production and sales office was tied, she claimed, to the demotion she experienced in the sales unit, which left her and two other workers with more desk work and less responsibility for sales. She admitted, in her first counseling session with the EAP social worker, that she was absent throughout segments of the day because she was "medicating" herself with marijuana. Her partner's unemployment had placed her squarely in the role of breadwinner for herself, her partner, and four children. When her confusion and anger increased over being demoted, along with the self-doubts that she already had about her competence, she slacked off, "sneaked" home to get high, and then was afraid to return to work. She also resented the desk work and felt that she had worked many hard years to move out of a clerical role.

Genevieve, her EAP counselor, normalized Sara's anger and self-doubts about the reorganization that occurred in her work unit. In addition, Genevieve discussed the need to address the underutilization of Sara's talents and skills either through empowerment strategies to support Sara or through direct intervention with the supervisor. Some of Sara's reframing included the acknowledgment that the production requirements placed unprecedented pressure on her just when her coping skills were undermined by the self-doubts and depression brought about by the reorganization.

Sara believed that the need to hold onto the job, no matter how poorly it reflected on her, was so important that she decided that her first tasks were to eliminate her frequent absences, to encourage her partner to join her in some counseling sessions to address the stress she was feeling as a provider and caregiver, and to work on the abatement of her substance abuse (at least during working hours). Although Genevieve would have liked to address Sara's problems of being underutilized in the work unit, Sara had asked that she have two weeks to prove that she could stabilize her work habits.

With the confidence Sara derives from her improved work performance, Genevieve hopes that Sara will be ready to look at long-term plans for changing jobs or developing in her current job. Meanwhile, Genevieve has arranged for Sara to have counseling at a private agency to address her stresses at home and her substance abuse problems.

Addressing Underemployment

Like Genevieve, other practitioners should operate with the tentative hypothesis that many workers may be underemployed both at home and in the workplace. Their assessment and intervention at least will be shaped by attempts to test these assumptions. It may be unsettling for a worker to probe the desirability of a job and working conditions when he or she is consumed with anxiety about losing the job. The timing and sequencing of interventions may be as significant as the stabilization of symptoms, and retention of the job may be a precondition for some to work on longer-term occupational goals.

Some social workers may seek to expand their EAP responsibilities to include the enrichment or enlargement of jobs. Much work is being pioneered in this area through the promotion of staff training and the development of work roles. Such enrichment, especially when grounded in employee-developed formulations of more desirable work opportunities, may prove to be fertile avenues for altering the conditions of underemployment.[21]

Like other initiatives, the enrichment of jobs can unleash new abilities of workers or can be oppressive, for example, demanding that more tasks be accomplished without increased resources, status, and benefits. Because some underemployed workers are resigned to the nature of the jobs they hold or are cynical because of their thwarted hopes, they may not respond quickly or positively to strategies for change. Therefore, pilot projects, rather than whole-scale changes, may provide the opportunity for more trial-and-error tests of a variety of approaches; such initiatives also should give them a chance to control what is being changed, which will reduce the likelihood of failure and sabotage.

Unless workers are viewed as experts on their problems, the most valuable solutions to and definitions of problems will be overlooked. Thus, the presence of social workers in work organizations should signal that workers have the opportunity to engage in participatory problem-solving and management processes.

In Sara and Genevieve's situation, Sara was reluctant to challenge her supervisor about her "demotion" and the rationale for the reorganization until she was sure that her job was more secure. When another worker from the same office was driven to seek help through EAP for the same stressors, Genevieve was able to develop, with the help of these two workers, the rationale for a training session on the effects of stress and change as well as the need for developmental opportunities for all employees.

In addition to the sources of underemployment, economic factors must be addressed as well. Some workers may feel trapped because they cannot acquire the same wages and benefits elsewhere. Good economic payoffs for jobs that are dehumanizing and do not tap skills are indeed legion in some industries and occupations. Workers should not be driven to lesser paying jobs just to derive intrinsic satisfaction from their work and working conditions. By addressing a production issue or documenting the effects of underemployment, social workers can develop a database that may stimulate or reinforce reforms in the workplace that are championed by workers, their unions, or management.

As with unemployment, it would be naive politically to assume that a social worker in EAP or an agency-based private practitioner could do more than pioneer some exemplary models of innovative approaches to reducing underemployment. More realistically, EAP, like the community social service agency and the private practitioner, functions as a database, a clearinghouse, and a capacity builder, providing some of the mandates for reform. Until data on underemployment are collected and generated and then used to influence powerful allies in the marketplace, as well as in the courts and legislative bodies, little beyond individual or small-group strategies can be undertaken to address the issue.

Roles for Social Service Agencies

Some facets of underemployment can be addressed more effectively by service providers who are external to the work environment, particularly when the need for a career change is threatening to the employer. As with unemployment, the community-based social service agency, whether it participates formally in contracts with workplaces or simply receives voluntary referrals of workers, can highlight the significance of underemployment as it affects the workplace, the family, and the community. By documenting the consequences of wasted talents and the loss to the community, these agencies can reframe the issue of untapped skills as a community-wide problem. In fact, documentation of underutilized skills and talents may help foster alternative types of community-based economic development to ensure that such skills are used. Workers who are marginalized by their frequent utilization as temporary or contingent labor may be one of the first groups who are empowered to demand access to the resources of economic development and to initiate alternative ventures for localities.

The social service agency can be a spearhead in the formulation of evidence for community-based change. Thus, if one-third of a community's work force is underutilizing its talents and skills, for example, if persons with college degrees are working on an assembly line, both workplace initiatives and community-based initiatives are warranted. Jobs should be tools for self-development. The gravest injustices persist when development is deformed by practices that divide jobs into functional minutia.

Numerous avenues exist for practitioners to address human needs in the "work community." Practitioners may offer one-time-only classes and related support services, including self-help materials, on issues such as local educational and career resources, loans for school and business, small-business startups, work sharing, and home-based entreprenurial activities.

One reason why so many workers may be trapped and discontent with their jobs is that there are few readily accessible resources to help them with occupational development. Social service agencies not only play a key role in offering such services to the community, but they ensure efficient use of the resources that exist. As it is, much loan money may go unspent that could support retraining and small business ventures.

Changes in the Workplace and Adaptability

The underutilization of talents and the stress of jobs are exacerbated by the incipient changes that are transforming many workplaces. One-third of the work force may be touched by unemployment each year and another third may be afflicted by bad jobs.[22] However, changes in plant locations, hiring patterns, reorganizations, mergers, buyouts, bankruptcies, and the disinvestment of capital suggest that lives of individuals and communities are undergoing unprecedented changes. Boom-bust business cycles, long recognized as a feature of modern economies, add to the predictable fluctuations in workplaces and to their effects on workers, families, and communities. The major restructuring of U.S. work institutions, which their European and Japanese counterparts undertook after World War II, also is accelerating changes in the workplace.[23] Moreover, as the global marketplace becomes the basis for business transactions, the movement of plants and money to labor forces around the world will intensify. Such mobility of capital is not due to the lowered productivity of U.S. workers, but to the fact that developing nations are more "profitable" business climates because wages for workers in these countries are lower, as are the costs of resources. Unrestricted, unregulated labor policies, along with strategic positioning for competing in world markets, have forced the closure of even profitable plants in the United States.

It is ironic that antidiscrimination laws have been passed to curb the maltreatment of employees and communities but that few, if any, policies have been adopted to regulate the movement of jobs. This lack of regulations has necessitated not only more welfare state innovations but the extension of problem-solving efforts both to cushion the effects and to initiate alternative policies to promote the well-being of workers and communities.

Regardless of their economic ideologies, business management experts and scholars are arriving at similar conclusions. The way we organize to do business with people and communities may vary in relative effectiveness and may prove to have differential outcomes in terms of ultimate profitability. Increasingly, strategies for leadership, for organizing for effective employee-based innovations, and for making business both civically appropriate and profitable are reflecting the growing knowledge about the ultimate costs of ignoring the needs of people and their communities.[24]

Important changes can be brought about by showing, for example, that it may be less costly to retrain workers than to spend time and resources to replace them with more highly skilled workers.[25]

Machine Model of Organizations

One major source of stress on and underemployment of employees stems from the machinelike approach to people taken by many work organizations.

The roots of this machinelike approach can be traced to schools of thought espoused by persons such as Jeremy Bentham, who believed that organizations could be run like finely tuned clocks and that unruly members could be brought in line by imposing regimentation and order that the members might soon internalize.[26] This line of thinking influenced not only the way in which the poor were treated in the early 1800s in England, but the way in which institutions such as prison systems to this day have come to rationalize the anonymity, alienation, depersonalization, and regimentation of individuals. The theories of Taylor, who advocated scientific management to increase the efficiency of workers through time-motion studies, undergird some of the regimentation and hierarchy, reductionism, and overspecialization in tasks that are prevalent today.[27] Assembly lines do not give workers the opportunity to expand their repertoires of tasks, but they make it easier to replace employees either with new employees or with automated machines.

Many organizations distribute power judiciously so that little power is shared with line workers. Yet, the dedication of or sabotage by workers clearly may be tied to the control they have over and how involved they feel with their jobs. Under the banner of maximizing profits, this organizational model has denied to the workplace many of the attributes of family life in which individual needs are preeminent and the development of the self is nurtured. Dichotomous worlds and the values of work and family make it possible for the family, despite its patriarchal organization, to be perceived as the haven for more desirable human relationships and practices. Expectations that the workplace could legitimately operate according to a machine model have normalized the dichotomous values, systems, and "bicultural" norms that operate between the spheres of the workplace and the family. Thus, family members may be expected to live according to one set of values and interactive practices in the home but be required to adopt diametrically different values and practices in the workplace. A machine model minimizes human needs as well as the organization's responsibility to enhance well-being. Even in public service agencies, in which profits are not the goal, the need for efficiency through a bureaucratic structure may supersede the need to develop the capabilities of workers.

The machine model might be of less concern if the well-being of workers was not so abridged. For this reason, many workplaces have persisted in mechanistic exchanges of labor for wages. That is not to say that at higher levels in the hierarchy individuals are not groomed for the display of talents in new and challenging roles and responsibilities. But for an estimated one-third or more of the work force, blunting conditions prevail.[28]

Because this book focuses on underemployment and unemployment, it does not delve into the hardships of professional or managerial employees who may not have sufficient resources to carry out their jobs. The corporate raids and takeovers that are unsettling many workplaces are taking an increasing toll on corporate managers.[29] The strokes, heart attacks, and related conditions of persons in high-ranking positions are also important issues for social work because the profession's concern for the well-being of workers is universal, not selective.

The same machine–profits–efficiency model that permits labor to be reduced to a production unit rather than a subsystem of the human organism also expels all or part of its work force without moral or legal constraints. The ability to discharge a work force without forewarning and to disregard the impact of this action on communities, families, and individuals epitomizes the grimmer side of the machine model.

Given the profession's knowledge of and experience in working with small groups, families, and communities, it is time that it addresses some of the structural deficits in the workplace that affect and reinforce the stress placed on workers. The profession can transfer its techniques for working with families to the workplace to make it more equitable for and supportive of individual and group development. Principles and values that guide the development of the talents and contributions of family members, derived from several centuries of normative practices, may prove more effective, healthy, efficient, and profitable than many traditional practices in the workplace. Social work can help to reduce the perseveration in values and practices that dichotomize work and family life and thwart human development. The profession's rich heritage in serving individuals in their families or support networks makes its expertise vital for correcting some of the dysfunctional workplace systems that blunt the development and the utilization of the talents of so many workers.

Instituting democracy in the workplace by redistributing good and bad tasks and roles and the power to make decisions about working conditions and jobs, is a critical challenge for the future development of organizations. Showing that what is good for workers, their families, and communities is also good for productivity, profits, and efficiency is essential if debilitating structures and practices and nonproductive outcomes are to be reformed.[30] Social work has the technology for demonstrating the cost-effectiveness of and testing preferred ways of organizing workers, the work flow, various tasks, and work organizations as a whole. It would be naive to think that work organizations can be transformed quickly, given the many centuries in which the current machine model has been implemented. However, the restructuring of local economies because of changes throughout the world may hasten the introduction not just of new business ventures to replace dying or relocated businesses but of improved ways of organizing the workplace for more humane and productive work systems.

Notes and References

1. H. J. Weiner, S. H. Akabas, and J. Somer, *Mental Health Care in the World of Work* (New York: Association Press, 1973). *See also* B. C. Reynolds, *Social Work and Social Living* (reprinted; Washington, D.C.: National Association of Social Workers, Inc., 1975); and S. H. Akabas and P. A. Kurzman, "The Industrial Social Work Specialist: What's So Special?" in Akabas and Kurzman, eds., *Work, Workers and Work Organizations* (Englewood Cliffs, N.J.: Prentice-Hall, 1982).

2. K. H. Briar, "Occupational Social Work Services for Unemployed, Underemployed and Employed Workers." To be published in *Social Work Papers*.

3. *See* J. T. Wrich, *The Employee Assistance Program* (Center City, Minn.: Hazelden Foundation Books, 1974).

4. *See* N. Gilbert, *Capitalism and the Welfare State* (New Haven, Conn.: Yale University Press, 1985).

5. J. O. Beckett, "Plant Closings: How Older Workers Are Affected," *Social Work,* 33 (January–February 1988), pp. 29–33.

6. Personal communication from J. Kneseck, former director of the Employee Assistance Program for Detroit Diesel Allison in Indiana and currently codirector of the United Auto Workers–General Motors Resource Center, Region III.

7. Personal communication from the director of avenues in Indianapolis, 1983.

8. Personal communication from J. Francek, former director of the Health Services Advisory Committee, Exxon Corporation, and current chair of Watershed Corporate Health Services, Inc., Westport, Conn.

9. R. B. Reich, *The Next American Frontier* (New York: New York Times Books, 1983).

10. L. M. Brammer and F. E. Humberger, *Outplacement and Inplacement Counseling* (Englewood Cliffs, N.J.: Prentice-Hall, 1984).

11. Ibid.

12. Ibid.

13. K. Briar, "Evaluation of the Pierce County AFL–CIO Employment Support Project." Unpublished report for the Community Services Division of United Way, Tacoma, Wash., 1981.

14. Ibid.

15. *See* "Curriculum for the Union Counseling Class, Pierce County AFL–CIO Labor Council" (Tacoma, Wash.: Community Services Division, United Way, 1982). *See also* K. H. Briar, C. S. Jones, and R. C. Vandergrift, "Undergraduate Social Welfare Curriculum and Field Work Innovations with AFL–CIO Labor Council Community Services." Paper presented at the Annual Program Meeting, Council on Social Work Education, Los Angeles, 1980.

16. Personal communication from the participants in the Job Search Workshop, AFL–CIO King County Labor Agency, Seattle, Wash., 1983.

17. Observation made by L. Schore of the Center for Working Life, Oakland, Calif., 1986.

18. Activities of the Seattle Worker Center, Seattle, Wash., attest to such initiatives.

19. M. Lerner, *Surplus Powerlessness* (Oakland, Calif.: Institute for Labor & Mental Health, 1986).

20. *See* E. Chinoy, *Automobile Workers and the American Dream* (Garden City, N.Y.: Doubleday & Co., 1955); and A. Kornhauser, *Mental Health of the Industrial Worker* (New York: John Wiley & Sons, 1965).

21. Guest lectures by Edmund Sheridan at the University of Washington School of Social Work, 1984, 1985, and 1986.

22. D. M. Gordon, *The Working Poor: Toward a State Agenda* (Washington, D.C.: Council of State Planning Agencies, 1979).

23. Reich, *The Next American Frontier. See also* B. Bluestone and B. Harrison, *The Deindustrialization of America* (New York: Basic Books, 1982).

24. *See, for example,* R. M. Kanter and J. N. Warner, *The Change Masters* (New York: Simon & Schuster, 1983); and R. Peters and R. H. Waterman, *In Search of Excellence* (New York: Harper & Row, 1982). *See also Initiating Social Work Services in Labor and Industry* (Silver Spring, Md.: National Association of Social Workers, Inc., 1984).

25. M. Ozawa, "Work and Social Policy," in S. H. Akabas and P. A. Kurzman, eds., *Work, Workers and Work Organizations* (Englewood Cliffs, N.J.: Prentice-Hall, 1982). *See also* R. S. Eckley, "Company Action to Stabilize Employment," *Harvard Business Review,* 44 (1966), pp. 51–61.

26. M. P. Mack, *Jeremy Bentham* (London: Wm. Heinemann, 1962), p. 284. In contrast, *see* J. D. Adams, ed., *Transforming Work* (Alexandria, Va.: Miles River Press, 1984).

27. *See* F. W. Taylor, *The Principles of Scientific Management* (New York: Harper Bros., 1911).

28. Gordon, *The Working Poor.*

29. D. L. Commons, *Tender Offer: The Sneak Attack in Corporate Takeovers* (New York: Penguin Books, 1986).

30. S. H. Akabas, P. A. Kurzman, and N. S. Kolben, eds., *Labor and Industrial Settings: Proceedings of a National Conference* (New York: Council on Social Work Education, Columbia University School of Social Work, and Hunter College School of Social Work, 1978).

8

Work and Welfare:
Untangling the
Dilemmas

Several years ago, Karen and Joe graduated from high school together and took jobs at a local department store where they earned similar wages. Both Karen and Joe married other people, and each couple now has one child. Karen's husband, Milton, lost his job, which led to a series of marital stresses that prompted their divorce. His joblessness and ineligibility for unemployment benefits added to his difficulties in paying child support.

Karen's wages make it impossible for her to afford day care; Joe's wage does not have to cover day care costs; his wife Veronica has remained at home to provide complete child care for their baby. Karen's emotional and physical exhaustion over the divorce, trying to make ends meet, and caregiving worries over her 17-month-old daughter eventually resulted in both she and her daughter getting pneumonia, which necessitated that she quit her job. Karen's next few years will be spent on welfare, while Joe will receive two promotions and wage increases.

There are many reasons why people need public assistance. Clearly, the destabilizing effect of unemployment on the family may be a major contributor. However, the absence of jobs, especially decent paying jobs, is only one factor. Caregiving costs and responsibilities strike at the heart of the human need for welfare. A man with a family may be a layoff away from unemployment compensation and welfare (at least in those states that provide welfare for two-parent families). Not only may a woman with a family be just a layoff or even a divorce away from welfare, but caregiving responsibilities themselves may plummet her onto the welfare rolls.

Much has been written about the role of the welfare system in regulating a surplus of labor and in cushioning the casualties of the economic system.[1] This chapter looks at the welfare system, not just as a repository for the market's failures but as one of the sole, although inadequate, resource systems that support caregiving functions. Additionally, this chapter shows that welfare reform depends not just on improved jobs, educational resources, and entitlements to child care and medical care, but a rethinking of work itself and the placement of a monetary value on caregiving roles in the home.

Devaluation of Caregiving

As was shown in earlier chapters, one's relationship to the labor market determines one's identity, status, sense of contributions to society, and ability to support the functioning of oneself and one's dependents. In the United States, market relationships play an all-pervasive role in determining one's life chances.[2]

The rise of capitalism increased the segregation of men's and women's roles, while a racist and class bias emerged in the allocation and hierarchy of statuses and rights within these roles.[3] Moreover, women's home-based caregiving inadvertently may have even depressed the wages of men, who could be paid less because women were providing free labor at home to dependent family members. The impoverishment and marginalization of women in the labor market has been caused not just by occupational segregation and the receipt of wages that are lower than men's but by the fact that when many women work out of the home, they must hire others to care for their dependent family members. Hence, women with dependents are placed in the position of being both employers and employees.

Thus, women who are the sole providers and caregivers for their families face a dilemma that has not been addressed fully by the welfare state. When, as Karen's situation suggests, wages are insufficient to employ others to perform these dependent care functions, then women must be subsidized by welfare or face the breakup of their families. Elderly persons may be placed in nursing homes and children and disabled persons in foster homes or institutions. When members of an extended family (usually women) are provided free care, such institutionalization could be avoided. Today, the nuclear family cannot do so easily because of isolation from familial networks owing to geographic mobility and the growing number of women who are working outside the home.

The nostalgia for such free labor by family members ignores the costs to the caregivers. For instance, the number of displaced homemakers increased threefold between 1976 and 1987.[4] Furthermore, despite the growing regard among social workers for natural supports for families, Belle's research suggests that support networks for poor women may enmesh them in burdensome reciprocity and thereby reduce their utility and effectiveness.[5] Consequently, even when free labor is available from a relative, the social costs may outweigh the benefits.

Caregiving is a devalued function in society because it is done primarily by women outside the labor market and often involves the support of and care for the powerless and, therefore, the most vulnerable members of our society. Until recently, welfare policies did not just attempt to cushion those who were marginalized by the labor market; they partially ensured that caregiving was a supported activity even at subsistence levels. The mothers' and widows' pension movement, which swept the nation before 1935, sought to enhance the caregiving capacity of mothers by relieving or diverting them from their labor-market roles so that their children could remain in their care, rather than be institutionalized or exploited as sources of cheap labor. The use of income transfers to divert women and children from labor-market roles was paralleled, in part, through the introduction of family and children's allowances in Europe. Family allowances ranged in intent from increasing the birthrate (after World War II) to regulating or providing women with choices regarding their participation in the labor market.[6]

Like other welfare state schemes such as Aid to Families with Dependent Children (AFDC), such benefits may be questioned as inherently sexist and regulatory in terms of human rights and behavior; nevertheless, the fact that men have not been seen as caregivers underscores their limited access to welfare benefits. Only 28 states currently provide welfare to two-parent families; few men are single heads of households and on welfare.

Although preindustrial societies may have had more gender equity in the sharing of caregiving and provider roles, such role equity has been diminished by the development of the industrial economy. Perhaps with the decline of the industrial economy, a resurgence in shared caregiving responsibilities will occur.

Current debates about welfare imply that women, children, and the public are better off when women labor in the workplace rather than at home. Research on the benefits of employment for women has shown how jobs may be tools for improved self-esteem, power, and mental health.[7] What these studies have failed to depict is the extent to which such improvements are attributable either to the benefits of jobs or to women's escape and respite from isolating, undervalued caregiving roles. Moreover, what has not been studied are the effects of employment on low-income women whose jobs may be in the secondary or tertiary labor market; such research might help qualify the data base that now tends to show that any job is better than being on AFDC. For example, preliminary research by the author and her colleagues has begun to uncover the social and psychological consequences of work outside the home for low-income women whose jobs in the secondary labor market are not necessarily antidotes for or improvements over their jobless, impoverished, and round-the-clock caregiving situations. Jobs with no benefits or opportunities for advancement, that cause heightened physical or mental stress, or that make women feel powerless and stuck may place some women at a high risk for persistent feelings of suicide, depression, and anxiety.[8] Both the nature of their jobs and some of the discriminatory and dysfunctional dynamics of the workplace may impair their mental and physical functioning. We know that gender differences may profoundly affect not just moral development but the depths of emotional involvement with others.[9] It is these caring, emotionally involved behaviors that may make others see women as highly desirable for low-paid caregiving and service-related jobs outside the home and as prime candidates for unpaid caregiving labor in the family. It is these roles into which some women are conscripted, especially when welfare reform is tied to low-wage work.

The Myth of Self-Sufficiency

Over the centuries, the goals of public policy have been to make the poor and jobless self-sufficient. What makes these values so attractive in the United States is their kinship with beliefs that rugged individualism is important and that anyone can make it from a "log cabin to the White House" if he or she just tries hard enough.

The belief that hard work will ensure self-sufficiency persists despite centuries of evidence to the contrary. Women work extraordinarily hard at family caregiving, performing two-thirds of the world's work; yet it is estimated that they receive only 5 to 10 percent of the world's income.[10]

As welfare reform proposals increase, the theme of self-sufficiency will ring loud and clear. Social workers can make a major contribution to the debates about self-sufficiency and independence by demonstrating how jobs are a sometime thing, not a guarantee. Moreover, jobs with plummeting wages brought about by the expansion of the service economy and forced wage concessions may intensify the reliance of workers on food stamps, Medicaid, and even welfare allotments just to get by while they work full time. (According to 9 to 5, The National Association of Working Women, two-thirds of part-time workers are female, and women constitute 62 percent of the temporary workers.[11]) Thus, social workers must demonstrate how low wages and temporary part-time jobs militate against self-sufficiency. In fact, these are times when social workers may want to promote debates about "aid in wages." As these become germane, they may be reminiscent of the Speenhamland Act in England or the Post-World War II European movement for children's and family allowances.

Carried to the extreme, self-sufficiency brings up images of homeless individuals and families begging in the streets and scrounging food from dumpsters while using a park bench as an address. We witness daily the plight of battered women and children who strike out on their own to be independent of an abuser only to find themselves without shelter, transportation, and food. The terrorizing aspects of independence are well rooted in the horrific stories of the past centuries of waves of peasants thrown from their lands and forced to seek wage-based work in cities or of freed slaves, who, despite their new status, were blocked from or unable to find paid employment.[12] More and more studies are finding that the more social supports a family has, the more successful it may be.[13] Hence, the notion of an isolated family that functions independently does not correspond with the empirical realities of the resources of strong capable families. Rather, the socially isolated are often those whose "independence" and "self-reliance" may impair their well-being and effective functioning.

Wage solidarity (involving the reduction in wide-ranging disparities in wages) and a sense of collective interdependence that permeates much of Western Europe is preempted in the United States by the prevalence of social Darwinism. Ideally, the concept of interdependence should replace the earlier ethos of independence. Similarly, European trends should shape our own, with the belief that one person's injury hurts all; this belief would reinforce the growing sense of social solidarity and collective welfare. In a sense, society pays for its discounting of some persons in long-term, welfare-state-type outlays, perhaps for generations to come, because the effects on the family of marginalization sometimes are passed on through the offspring.

Self-help groups of empowered recipients, such as those who are benefiting from the nationwide movement Helping Ourselves Means Education (HOME), have helped to publicize the successes of women who leave welfare, and to destigmatize recipients. These mentoring, role-model, and mutual aid relationships are valuable only if the resources are available for self-directed problem solving. HOME has shown, for example, that concrete resources like scholarship aid, child care, and work study must be made available to ensure that these networks of recipients who are learning from each other have a viable base from which to develop collectively new skills, visions, and successes.[14]

Toward Occupational Development

Welfare programs have fared less well than did the Comprehensive Employment and Training Act (CETA) in placing people in long-term jobs. The CETA and Work Incentive (WIN) programs have produced slightly better outcomes than have recent workfare programs.[15] Nevertheless, the relatively low absorption of jobless workers into durable employment reflects the inherent barriers to self-sufficiency when "symptoms" (poverty, welfare dependence, and joblessness) are treated in the absence of the wholesale redistribution of paid work activities that would enable all who seek it to be employed at a decent wage and durable livelihood.

The lack of child care, medical benefits, and transportation is a critical barrier to job and career development for many women who are on welfare.[16] Moreover, these resources need to be extended over a period of months and years until participants have reached a level of income and benefits that makes it possible for them to make a smooth transition from welfare to wages, rather than face a drop in income that forces them to skid back onto the welfare rolls. Postjob-placement casework may help the worker move from an entry-level job to another job at the next step in his or her occupational goal plan. As it is, many shuffle between low-paying jobs, partial schooling, and welfare. Because many jobless and impoverished workers have been conscripted to think in short-term ways about what they require in a job, they inadvertently may be forcing themselves unnecessarily to remain both underemployed and vulnerable to a relapse in unemployment compensation or welfare.

What is proposed is an alternative to the assembly-line model of practice. This model predominates when the caseworker—usually an adult-service, self-support, or employment-related counselor—promotes the voluntary use of employment services and addresses barriers to employability, such as problems with child care, mental health problems, or substance abuse, and then passes the recipient to an employment service worker, who may work for the state employment service. Despite attempts to consolidate functions, different philosophies of practice may create interdepartmental friction; such friction can be minimized, however, if a holistic model of service is pursued. Moreover, as chapter 3 suggests, services may be more effective if job placement and the client's personal problems are addressed simultaneously. After all, why should a public assistance client work hard on substance abuse, parenting, or mental health problems if there is no sure job payoff for seeking help? In some cases, being told that one has a problem or "pathology" that needs to be treated before one can look for a job may increase the likelihood of failure, rather than maximize the benefits of help with personal problem solving and the job search. Whether the jobless worker is abusive or an alcoholic, inattention to occupational dreams and the steps toward fulfilling those dreams may leave the worker with untapped positive emotional energy and a lack of focus on self-care. Meanwhile, such a linear model may increase the client's defensiveness and, because of competitive relations that may ensue between bureaucracies and those they serve, may cause the client to sabotage the most needed treatment. For this reason, a service model is proposed that is an adaptation of the model suggested in chapters 3 and 4.

Ideally, the caseworker would either engage in job development or would use the help of the employment service worker as part of a more comprehensive case plan. Rather than turning the jobless, impoverished worker over to the employment service and yielding responsibility for coordinating his or her family and work needs, the caseworker must include the employment service worker in the team of service providers and natural helpers who are aiding the client. Once the service plan has been developed by the jobless worker and his or her family, in collaboration with the caseworker, a case-managed team meeting can be convened. It is important that the family, especially its adult and adolescent members, be present. They may even be the conveners, which would give them a sense of power over the process and over those who are to act in a coordinated manner on their behalf.

Family members may begin by stating their concerns and need for occupational aid (when getting a job or going to school may be a means toward a long-term occupational goal).[17] They then may describe the barriers to achieving their goal. Barriers may include health or mental problems, substance abuse, and the lack of child care, housing, or transportation. The caseworker may help each family member to articulate his or her goal (if this was agreed on earlier) and then explain how members of the service team can address those goals. In turn, each service provider reacts to the goals of service and describes how he or she plans to get started, the schedule, and the adjustments that must be made. The service providers also clarify what they will and will not be able to do. The family's reactions are sought at every opportunity, for if the family members think they cannot control the plans and process, they may sabotage it or it otherwise will fail. After the service plan is tested and modified in this meeting, the caseworker suggests a timetable for staying in touch with the family to verify the progress that is being made or to seek an alternative plan. Service providers use the caseworker as a sounding board for determining whether the service plan or the timetable needs to be altered.

In this approach, failure can be reframed as less of a problem of the client and more of a deficit of the service plan. Moreover, when appropriate, the caseworker may be able to hold in abeyance a hypothesis about the client's behavioral barriers to the acquisition of a job, which either may be improved or disrupted when the job search occurs. Service plans are first steps, not the answers, to a client's needs. They allow the service team to test which of the symptoms and services need to be addressed first, they give the family help while the assessment is being done, and they permit the family to assume control over the process and the terms of the help they have asked for. Nonetheless, many service plans must be reworked when it is discovered that the parent did not like a particular service provider or the natural helper was less effective than a formal service provider might be. All of these adjustments should involve collaboration between the family and caseworker on what works best for the family.

Ideally, this "case-managed" model makes it possible for the participant and family to seek assistance with work and family issues long after an entry-level job has been obtained. Because the female worker often is underemployed because of the nature of the labor market and her gender, this period is perhaps the most critical in that it requires an exceptional outpouring of skills and tools to keep the newly underemployed worker from feeling stuck. Thus, the most intensive services and resources must be deployed when job placement has occurred to promote occupational mobility and the coverage of benefits. Otherwise, emotionally and financially, the only recourse may be to go back on welfare if the employer's wages and benefits do not cover child care and medical costs and if there seem to be no stepping stones beyond a low-paying, dead-end job. Cost-effective accounting might show that preventing a family from going back on the welfare rolls through the provision of medical benefits and in-kind supports, such as educational vouchers, food stamps, and child care, may be far more desirable than the emotional, social, and fiscal costs of going on and off welfare.

Although incentives to get and keep a job may well depend on the provision of benefits that at least are comparable to those for welfare families (especially medical assistance), many studies of incentives and of the exit from welfare reveal that incentives alone do not account for whether a person gets off the welfare rolls. In fact, the stigmas of welfare may propel many thousands of women to take low-paying jobs that do not provide benefits, which may put them and their families in greater overall jeopardy. Yet, some women and their families may remain on welfare when the incentives to move into paid jobs may seem to be more fiscally beneficial. What accounts for variable responses to welfare incentives remains a critical subject of inquiry; it also may help generate new perspectives on human behavior. Thus, to assume that fiscal incentives motivate all or most people, especially women, may be to overlook the critical dimensions of women's behavior and motivation that are known to feminists and scholars of gender differences, but not to policymakers. More feminist and multiethnic analysis is needed of welfare reform proposals to ferret out whether assumptions made about the dependence on welfare and motivation to work are based on suppositions about the patterns of behavior of white men but that ignore alternative plausible assumptions and policy options.

Barriers to and Prospects for Reform

The welfare system was created to cushion the hardships caused by the economic system and to regulate the surplus of labor and women's behavior.[18] Thus, it would be expected that an economic system that has been as unhelpful to millions as has ours would compel policymakers to make dramatic improvements in the welfare system and welfare state programs. However, some of the barriers to developing such stabilizers and cushions are derived from several attitudes. The first is the belief that anyone can find a job or make a living if he or she is inventive and hard working. This traditional view has impeded policymakers from substantially overhauling either the economy or the welfare system because the victims of the economy are blamed for their failures. The second is the persistent myth that people who are unemployed and poor are "lazy and immoral," which makes inaccurate inferences about the results of poverty and confuses them with the causes of poverty. In fact, observers historically may have misconstrued what they thought to be laziness, a lack of motivation, and lethargy for what probably was depression or malnutrition. Substance abuse, sometimes the major means of coping with the pain of expulsion from or marginalization by the labor market, was interpreted as immorality. Thus, rather than seeing how the homicidal and genocidal tendencies of the economic system generate such results, observers throughout the centuries have blamed poor people for their reactions to their condition and considered these reactions to be the cause, rather than the consequence, of their marginalization. The third attitude is the shame and consequent lack of power that has accompanied the condition of the poor and has created barriers to their self-advocacy in recent decades. Instead of taking their case to the courts, the legislatures, and the press, poor people have been consumed by self-recrimination and a preoccupation with getting out of their condition. The fourth attitude is the belief that full employment or more comprehensive welfare state benefits will be too costly. However, the reverse is true.[19]

On a more positive note, research by Ellwood has shown that a small group of recipients (especially young mothers) use a disproportionate amount of welfare resources.[20] Other studies have found that half the welfare recipients move off welfare in less than two years.[21] Thus, it is proposed that resources to enhance employability should be targeted to those who will remain longer on welfare. Occupational development strategies should be intensified for this small group of recipients. Even during the pregnancy of a new welfare recipient, the vision of a long-term occupational goal can be sustaining as tiny steps are planned and supported systematically, such as vocational tests or obtaining resources for education.

Social workers need to strengthen their advocacy for educational resources for recipients. Of the thousands of women and men who are on welfare, many lack the education (including literacy) and job skills to accelerate their careers beyond entry-level jobs. Zimlich's analysis showed that recipients who acquire a college education are in a far better position not only to be taxpayers but to be better providers for their families.[22] Given the disproportionately lower wages earned by women than men with the same educational qualifications, it is imperative that access to education be accelerated as a welfare-reform strategy. Unfortunately, most proposals for welfare reform seek the least expensive routes to getting people off the welfare rolls, rather than consider the long-run costs of frequent relapses onto welfare because of low-paying unstable jobs.

If recidivism is as high as 50 percent over the short term, then the pressure to get recipients into any job may need to be tempered with long-term economic development and other job-creation strategies. Welfare reform strategies should combine research on recidivism with the obvious requirements of child care, transportation supports, and medical care.

The Role of Welfare in Protecting Children, Families, and the Community

There are several destabilizers of families. If underemployment and unemployment do not rupture marital functioning, then eligibility for welfare may do so in states that do not provide AFDC for two-parent families. Ironically, however, AFDC may be the only durable stabilizer of whatever is left of the family and marriage. Moreover, AFDC plays a role in protecting children and families. Women and children may escape physically abusive situations because they can set up households that are independent of their abusers. Moreover, correlational research conducted by the author and her colleagues has found an inverse relationship between the utilization of welfare and child abuse, which may open the door to future probes of the possible stabilizing functions of welfare.[23]

At a time when the economy is going through such a radical restructuring, it is critical that welfare and unemployment insurance benefits be seen as leveraging resources or investments in new community-based jobs and entrepreneurial undertakings.[24] It is expanded welfare and unemployment benefits that may help protect declining communities from becoming ghost towns because benefits can be reframed as potential investments in entrepreneurial and caregiving activities. Recipients may know best what communities need. Moreover, as wages and benefits are being downgraded as a temporary workforce expands, welfare benefits, such as medical aid, help to offset deficits in wages and benefits. Enormous opportunities exist at this critical juncture in the restructuring of the economy to press for government-provided health care, housing, day care, dependent care, and related benefits, because employers are either unable or unwilling to assume full responsibility for these basic insurances.

Department of Labor policies historically have produced programs involving "creaming" rather than the intensive problem solving that is essential for mainstreaming disadvantaged populations.[25] The reimbursement of programs, based, for example, on placement outcomes, helps to ensure that the least needy, rather than the most needy, gets served. It is understandable that many welfare systems have considered their job-ready recipients as the preferred candidates for job placement services, rather than welfare participants who are least likely to be employable. Social workers can make a major contribution not only in targeting resources but in setting new priorities for access to such services to ensure that those people who historically have been "last in line" at least get moved up to the front of the line. The thousands of recipients who are "banked" because they are not ready to get a job or those workers who are eligible under the Job Training Partnership Act but are the last to be enrolled in training programs constitute the persons who are most in need of attention. The setting of new priorities also should embrace economic development resources and educational institutions, to make venture capital, tuition waivers, waivers of admissions fees, and financial aid available to welfare recipients before all others.

From Workfare to Community Economic Development

A number of states have offered an array of initiatives to accelerate the movement of recipients off the welfare rolls. Most well known, perhaps, is the Massachusetts program Employment and Training Choices, popularly called ET, which mandates that recipients choose among retraining, education, and job-placement options. Child care and medical benefits are ensured for an extended period. Because of pressure from advocacy groups, recipients reportedly must be placed in jobs that pay at least $5 an hour. Although the successes of the program are publicized in anecdotal form, they have not been evaluated. The American Friends Service Committee studied ET participants and found that despite their jobs, they were still earning an income that did not put them above the poverty line.[26] Nevertheless, studies conducted by the Manpower Development and Research Corporation of the earnings of recipients in workfare programs in other states have found that earnings increased 8 to 38 percent.[27] In San Diego, savings owing to the employment of recipients resulted in an 8-percent reduction in welfare payments over an 18-month period.[28] However, two test sites—Baltimore and West Virginia—did not show such savings. Nevertheless, the overall increase in employment in these test programs ranged only from 3 to 9 percent.[29]

Workfare programs in states with poor economies are beginning to link up with local economic development initiatives. In Baltimore, for example, the economic development program Investment in Job Opportunities was instituted to increase the job opportunities of the Maryland welfare recipients enrolled in its workfare program called Employment Initiatives. Similarly, because of its shaken economy, Maine found that registrants in the WIN program could not support their families with the jobs they found. Thus, durable job placement may depend on locally based economic development initiatives. In Maine, Coastal Enterprises, Inc.— a private nonprofit community development corporation—helps fund company expansions on the condition that at least one-third of the jobs must be reserved for the economically disadvantaged and jobless workers with disabilities.[30] Moreover, displaced homemaker groups are being helped to become more entrepreneurial and are linked more systematically to economic development resources.

In Washington State, a proposed welfare initiative, Family Independence Plan, seeks to promote economic development through the creation of child care jobs for recipients. Such jobs, if well subsidized with long-term career paths, will constitute a burgeoning new "industry" that is central to the overall health of the state's economy, especially for women workers, both on and off welfare.

Caregivers' Wage and Pension Movement

As the foregoing suggests, welfare is not just a cushion for the vagaries of the market but a resource for caregivers. Welfare reform cannot be relevant unless it addresses caregivers' double burden of full-time, out-of-home jobs on top of caregiving and housekeeping. Welfare reform will fail if it depends solely on the market to absorb adult welfare recipients. Although many recipients may prefer market labor to work in the home, they may be impeded from leaving the rolls until they earn enough both to support their families and to employ a substitute caregiver. The nature of entry-level wages, particularly for women, never will be sufficient for some to cover the costs of hiring a substitute caregiver and of supporting the family's household needs.

Moreover, because most women are on loan to the labor market until a family caregiving crisis occurs, all women without another source of income (the wages of a spouse, the sale of property, or social security) are economically vulnerable to poverty. Such vulnerability may occur after children are grown but a parent, sibling, or spouse requires their care. When no welfare or social security is available, caregivers of persons other than chidren may be at great risk of impoverishment if they are forced to give up their paid work.

Social workers need to reclaim their longstanding heritage of spearheading reforms on behalf of caregivers. As they promoted the mother's and widow's pension movement at the turn of the century, they now must foster a caregivers' wage and pension movement. Because caregiving and household management continue to be excluded from market work, this movement also would demand that caregiving functions be seen as part of the gross national product (GNP) as they now are in Sweden. If these functions were viewed this way in the United States, such work would add $65 billion to the U.S. GNP.[31]

Such a movement might do more to alleviate some of the long-term societal confusion over the source of and solution to poverty that stems from women's responsibilities for the care of dependents. It would not stop women from attaining their rightful place in the labor market, but, at the least, it would help minimize some of the lost opportunities and wages for those who do perform such care, while increasing the opportunity for men to become full-time nurturers and caregivers. Those who sought full-time market work then could use their caregiver pension or wage to hire a substitute.

Support for a caregivers' wages and pension movement may be forthcoming from the United Nations, which, in 1980, appealed to all governments to count all forms of women's unpaid work in the home and in other fields, and from feminists who, although divided over the risk to the further occupational segregation of women in caregiving roles, nevertheless, may be a base of support for effective debates. Thus, leadership support may come from the National Organization for Women (NOW), the Women's movement, and the Wages for Housework Campaign, based in Los Angeles, which emerged from the 1987 International Women's Conference in Nairobi. This campaign promotes a petititon—"Women Count—Count Women's Work"—that states that women's unwaged work may produce as much as 50 percent of the GNP of some nations. Yet, the campaign argues, raising a child is not considered work while serving in the military and killing one is. Likewise, the campaign notes that while women produce all the workers of the world, reproduction is not considered work and women are not considered workers in such roles.[32]

Until wages for caregivers become a policy issue, gender roles will remain segregated, men will remain relatively excluded from caregiving roles and responsibilities, and their obsolescence in the family may increase as women perform both caregiving and provider functions. Sweden has taken one of the leads in promoting more symmetry in the roles of men and women. Although relatively fewer men than women make use of the parental leave policies in Sweden, these policies, nonetheless, make an important public statement about the desirability of gender equity.[33] Without attention to the issue of caregivers' wages and pensions, neither welfare reform nor full employment movements can succeed fully.

To launch a caregivers' wage and pension movement, numerous groups need to be allied, namely, women's advocacy groups like the Older Women's League, Displaced Homemakers, support organizations of caregivers for dependents with physical and mental disabilities, NOW, the newly developed Superwomen Anonymous, and members of the

Wages for Housework Campaign. Other sources of coalition building are families who provide health care to members, foster parents, and adoptive parents. The standards for the wages, benefits, and pensions of caregivers might have to be pegged at a lower income level than the actual monetary value of the work (estimated to be anywhere from $13,000 to $40,000 a year) to enhance the political viability of the proposal and to establish a basis from which improved benefits can develop. (Bonnar estimated that the value of caregiving is about $260 billion, which rivals the defense budget.[34])

Because mothers' pensions were one of social workers' key initiatives during the Progressive Era, it is time that the mother's pension movement be reviewed by social workers, so that gender- and work-role equity can be enhanced. Some of these ideas are mere visions, but signs that they are already informing European practices may be harbingers of innovative policies to come. For example, although child care is not a wage-based work role in the family, caregiving benefits are awarded to families who are raising disabled children and caring for aged members who would otherwise be institutionalized on a costly basis in England, Sweden, and even in parts of the United States.[35]

Ideally, men and boys must have access to caregiving roles and benefits, so that caregiving is not seen as a women's issue and thus the values it reflects are not relegated only to females. Caregiving careers should be freely chosen by both genders. Wages and pensions should be sufficient to enable men and women to choose to perform the family services for those who love and depend on them. Wages and benefits also could be used to purchase respite care, thereby treating respite as part of the entitlement package. Boys and girls could be prepared for caregiving roles in schools, followed by a stint in a national youth service that would focus on community caregiving roles (for shut-ins and latch-key children).

No matter how costly, such wages and benefits can never approximate the millions of dollars spent on institutional or professional care outside of the home. The recognition that many persons may be better off in family caregiving arrangements than in large depersonalized institutions has led welfare states to deinstitutionalize some of their high-risk, long-term dependent populations.[36] Moreover, the presumed economic savings brought about by shifting the care of these populations from institutions to unpaid family members has hastened these trends. Therefore, the caregiver's wage and pension movement can be seen as the next phase of deinstitutionalization, diversion, job creation, and gender equity in the reallocation of work roles.

Notes and References

1. *See* N. Furniss and T. Tilton, *The Case for the Welfare State* (Bloomington: Indiana University Press, 1977); *Report from Working Group 9 on the Unemployed: Policies and Services* (Helsinki, Finland: Finnish National Committee, International Council on Social Welfare, 1986); and H.L. Wilensky and C.N. Lebeaux, *Industrialized Society and Social Welfare* (New York: Free Press, 1966).

2. D. N. Ashton, *Unemployment Under Capitalism* (Westport, Conn.: Greenwood Press, 1986).

3. P. A. Roos, *Gender and Work: A Comparative Analysis of Industrial Societies* (Albany: State University of New York Press, 1985); J. Jones, *Labor of Love, Labor of Sorrow* (New York: Basic Books, 1985); B. R. Bergmann, *The Economic Emergence of Women* (New York: Basic Books, 1986); S. Rothman, *Woman's Proper Place: A History of Changing Ideals and Practices, 1870 to the Present* (New York: Basic Books, 1978); B. Ehrenreich, *The Hearts of Men* (Garden City, N.Y.: Doubleday Anchor Books, 1983); and C. N. Degler, *At Odds: Women and the Family in America, from the Revolution to the Present* (New York: Oxford University Press, 1980).

4. "Focus on Displaced Homemakers," *Jobs Impact Bulletin* (National Committee for Full Employment), 7 (September 1987).

5. D. Belle, ed., *Living in Stress: Women and Depression* (Beverly Hills, Calif.: Sage Publications, 1982).

6. *See* E. Burns, ed., *Children's Allowances and the Economic Welfare of Children* (New York: Citizen's Committee for Children of New York, 1968).

7. P. Warr and G. Parry, "Paid Employment and Women's Psychological Well-being." *Psychological Bulletin,* 91 (1982), pp. 498–516.

8. K. H. Briar, K. Knighton, and A. Van Ry, "Human Costs of Unemployment and Poverty for Women." Paper presented at the Annual Program Meeting, Council on Social Work Education, St. Louis, Mo., 1987.

9. C. Gilligan. *In a Different Voice* (Cambridge, Mass.: Harvard University Press, 1982); and A. W. Schaef, *Women's Reality* (New York: Winston Press, 1981).

10. *See* D. Bonnar, "Women, Work and Poverty: Exit from an Ancient Trap by the Definition of Work," in D. G. Gil and E. A. Gil, eds., *The Future of Work* (Cambridge, Mass.: Schenkman Publishing Co., 1987), pp. 67–84; and H. Scott, *Working Your Way to the Bottom* (Boston: Pandora Press, 1984).

11. *Working at the Margins: Part-time and Temporary Workers in the United States* (Cleveland, Ohio: 9 to 5, National Association of Working Women, September 1986).

12. Jones, *Labor of Love, Labor of Sorrow;* S. Mencher, *Poor Law to Poverty Program* (Pittsburgh: University of Pittsburgh Press, 1967); T. J. Sampson, *Welfare: A Handbook for Friend and Foe* (Philadelphia: United Church Press, 1972); and W. E. B. DuBois, *Black Reconstruction in America, 1860–1880* (reprinted edition; New York, Atheneum Press, 1969).

13. J. K. Whittaker, *Social Support Networks: Informal Helping in the Human Services* (Hawthorne, N.Y.: Aldine Publishing Co., 1983).

14. Personal communication from Carol Sasaki, founder of HOME, Seattle, Wash., 1986–1987.

15. J. M. Gueron et al., *Summary and Findings of the National Supported Work Demonstration* (Cambridge, Mass.: Ballinger Publishing Co., 1980). *See also* J. M. Gueron, *Reforming Welfare with Work* (New York: Manpower Demonstration Research Corp., December 1986).

16. *See, for example,* M. Rein, *Dilemmas of Welfare Policy: Why Work Strategies Haven't Worked* (New York: Praeger Publishers, 1982); N. S. Dickinson, "Women and Welfare Work Strategies." Paper presented at the Workshop on Women and Unemployment, held before the Annual Program Meeting, Council on Social Work Education, Detroit, Mich., February 17, 1985; and N. S. Dickinson, "Contributions to the Employment of AFDC Recipients: An Experimental Comparison of Work Experience and Job Search Assistance Strategies." Unpublished doctoral dissertation, University of Washington, Seattle, 1986. *For a review of poverty trends and policies, see* S. Danziger and R. D. Plotnick, "Poverty and Policy: Lessons of the Last Two Decades," *Social Service Review,* 60 (March 1986), pp. 34–51.

17. *For innovations in aiding poor young families, see* H. McAdoo and T. M. Parham, *Services to Young Families* (Washington, D.C.: American Public Welfare Association, July 1985). *For an innovative reform proposal, see Investing in Poor Families and Their Children: A Matter of Commitment* (Washington, D.C.: American Public Welfare Association, 1987).

18. F. F. Piven and R. A. Cloward. *Regulating the Poor: The Functions of Public Welfare* (New York: Pantheon Books, 1971); and M. Abramowitz, "Social Policy and the Female Pauper: The Family Ethic and the U.S. Welfare State," in N. Van Den Bergh and L. B. Cooper, eds., *Feminist Visions for Social Work* (Silver Spring, Md.: National Association of Social Workers, Inc., 1986), pp. 211–228.

19. *For a more thorough analysis of current welfare reform issues, see* G. S. Goldberg, "The Illusion of Welfare Reform and Some New Initiatives." Unpublished paper, Center for Social Policy, Adelphi University School of Social Work, 1987.

20. D. T. Ellwood, *Targeting "Would-Be" Long-Term Recipients of AFDC* (Princeton, N.J.: Mathematica Policy Group, 1986).

21. J. M. Gueron, "Reforming Welfare with Work," *The Entrepreneurial Economy*, 5 (February 1987), pp. 5–9.

22. N. Zimlich, "Comparative Benefits of College for AFDC Mothers." Unpublished policy paper, Region 10, Seattle, Wash., U.S. Department of Health and Human Services.

23. K. Briar, et al., *Dynamics of Economic Distress in Mason, Clallam, and Stevens Counties: Report of Research Prepared for Governor Booth Gardner* (Olympia, Wash.: Office of the Governor, 1987).

24. *See* L. Wilcox, "Jobs for Welfare Recipients: The Maine Experience," *The Entrepreneurial Economy*, 5 (February 1987), pp. 12–14; L. Wilcox, "The Self-Sufficiency Collaboration: Developing a Comprehensive Self-Sufficiency Strategy for Low-Income Women," *The Entrepreneurial Economy*, 5 (December–January 1986), pp. 14–17; S. Barkin, "Self-Employment for Low-Income People: A Real Option," *The Entrepreneurial Economy*, 5 (March 1987), pp. 2–4; and B. Bohley, "Former Welfare Mom Helps Others Succeed in Business," Neighbornews, *The Columbus Dispatch*, April 29, 1987, p. 1.

25. M. Johnson, *Counterpoint: The Changing Public Service* (Salt Lake City, Utah: Olympus Publishing Co., 1973).

26. I. L. Amott and J. Kluver, *ET: A Model for the Nation? An Evaluation of the Massachusetts Employment and Training Choices Program* (Philadelphia: American Friends Service Committee, 1986). *See also* S. Terry, " 'Workfare' Problem: People with Jobs Still Live in Poverty," *Christian Science Monitor*, October 21, 1986, p. 3.

27. Gueron, "Reforming Welfare with Work."

28. Ibid.

29. Ibid.

30. Wilcox, "Jobs for Welfare Recipients."

31. *See* Bonnar, "Women, Work and Poverty."

32. As stated in the petition, "Women Count—Count Women's Work," 1987, promoted by the Wages for Housework Campaign, Los Angeles.

33. *See* R. Sidel, *Women and Children Last* (New York: Viking-Penguin, 1986).

34. Bonnar, "Women, Work and Poverty."

35. *See* R. M. Moroney, *Shared Responsibility, Families, and Social Policy* (Hawthorne, N.Y.: Aldine Publishing Co., 1986), p. 163. *See also* R. Perlman, *Family Home Care* (New York: Haworth Press, 1983).

36. K. Briar and R. Ryan, "The Anti-Institution Movement and Women Caregivers," *Affilia, Journal of Women and Social Work,* 1 (Spring 1986), pp. 20–31.

9

Equitable and Full Employment: The Mission of Social Work

Sally, age 42, has a long history of being treated for mental illness. She functions relatively well when on medication, but the most effective stabilizer for her has been the jobs she has held.

The recent closure of the curtain factory where she worked plunged her into a deep depression and has left her disoriented and often needing supervision with her medication. In recent months, she has deteriorated so drastically that her family is encouraging her to be hospitalized.

 If Sally were employed in a full employment economy, she might not experience such relapses that seem to be triggered by fluctuations in work opportunities and in the economy.[1] In fact, news of a closure might come two years in advance so that plans for each worker could be developed more systematically long before the closure. Each worker then might be transferred as smoothly as possible into a new line of work, a process that involves the provision of a series of entitlements, including occupational counseling and income transfers, if necessary.

In a full employment economy, Sally might be seen as a good candidate for retraining, because she eventually would like to move into data processing. She would not experience any break between her old job and the training program in data processing and would have worked closely with a social worker to identify a career shift that fits her current needs. She also would be assured of a continued income; if she moved into a new job rather than a training program, the job might involve either a subsidized wage in the workplace of her choice or job placement. However, she is at a juncture in her vocational life; she feels stuck in industrial sewing jobs and wants to move into a less physically stressful line of work.

In a full employment economy, such considerations would be critical because, in the end, it might be better for Sally and for society as a whole (morally, socially, and fiscally) to support and invest in her future contributions than to force her out of the labor market, either because of her mental illness or her physical strains. Her training subsidy would put her at 90 percent of her former wages with a promise of an increase in the subsidy after she finished the first segment of her training program. Because Sally would not experience a break in her work life other than the two-week vacation that she took before she started her training program, she would be far less susceptible to a relapse and return to the hospital. The social worker would stay in close contact with her during the transition phase of her training program. The specialized social work care that Sally would receive is characteristic of a full employment society, because funds for intensive social work services would be made possible not only by increased tax revenues but by a market that valued and invested in the long-term contributions and well-being of workers like Sally.

Although in many cases, social work skills can be mobilized to aid jobless people such as Sally to regain their functioning, to survive unemployment, and even to become reconnected to the labor market, greater professional attention must be paid to the societal conditions that cause or reinforce much human dysfunction, namely, the inequitable distribution of work, jobs, and incomes. The techniques and suggestions discussed in the earlier chapters are not a substitute for working toward full and equitable employment. In fact, once social work practice incorporates the known techniques of job acquisition and some of the tools of community-based economic development; the limitations of such interventions will give the profession an even firmer rationale for demanding changes in this country's employment policies.

The profession's commitment to achieving greater equity in the distribution of goods and resources makes the goal of full and more equitable employment central to social work practice and advocacy. Some might find this mission more pressing, given depressed conditions throughout the United States and the economic restructuring of the local, national, and global economies. However, the inequities and harms of the market have been with us for several centuries and always have afflicted ethnic minorities, women, sexual minorities, persons with disabilities, the young and the old, and working-class persons. Thus, solely as an antidiscrimination tool, the merits of full employment transcend the immediate reaction to current economic crises and address the multicentury legacy of the labor market's oppression of some groups and classes of individuals. This chapter presents rationales and strategies that support full employment initiatives. It also addresses the many roles and contributions of social workers who seek to promote employment entitlements and suggests ways to integrate these roles into practice.

Human Rights Issue

The progress achieved in civil rights in the 1960s and 1970s cannot be furthered without the more equitable access of all people to jobs.[2] Otherwise, the human rights agenda that seeks to end the various forms of discrimination will fall short of remedying one of the greatest impediments to human functioning and to human rights. Full employment will counter some of the job rationing that pits one group against another by gender, race, ethnicity, age, class, disability and sexual affiliation. The more equitable allocation of jobs helps to create the power base for improving working conditions, wages, benefits, and work roles. When there is a surplus of labor and unemployment rates are high, the wages of both union and nonunion workers may decrease. Power is weakened, if not destroyed, when workers are considered to be easily disposable and replaceable. Moreover, the resistance of workers to changes in the workplace, such as automation and new methods of organizing work, might be reduced if workers, assured of their jobs, were given the power to determine the pace and benefits to themselves of the introduction of new practices and automated equipment into the workplace.[3]

The absence of full employment intensifies underemployment and the bumping-and-skidding phenomenon discussed in chapters 1 and 2. Although employers may think that they benefit from hiring overqualified workers or hiring workers part time rather than full time, economic and noneconomic costs still are incurred. These costs may shift, in part, to the worker and his or her family, the work group, the community, and the welfare state.

Low-paying, part-time jobs in the service sector compel workers and their families to become dependent on public resources, such as Aid to Families with Dependent Children, Medicaid, and food stamps. If ineligibility or pride forces them to forego these benefits, a catastrophic event may heighten the need for state intervention. Thus, when workers are powerless, the human costs of unemployment may scar them severely, and the fiscal costs may outrun the short-term profits derived from corporate exploitation of their condition. Consequently, the absence of full employment not only necessitates supplemental or substitute state aid but encourages cutbacks in the very welfare state programs needed to counter the effects of the inadequate economy. Decreased funds for programs and restrictive eligibility, therefore, increase the number of people who may be thrust below the "safety net." Homelessness, a symptom of such marginalization, is attributed primarily to joblessness.[4] Moreover, a substantial number of homeless people work full time but cannot afford housing.

As Durkheim found in his classic studies, work is a protective shield, especially for persons who are susceptible to mental illness, violent behavior, substance abuse, or addictions.[5] Comparative analyses of the rate of such pathologies in other countries underscore how preventable these symptoms may be in the United States. For example, Warner's cross-national research on schizophrenia showed that the absence of an occupational role may be a predictable contributor to schizophrenia and its relapse.[6] Thus, as Schore argued, the best mental health protection and prevention workers can receive is economic justice.[7]

Full Employment and the Welfare State

Welfare states in Western Europe emerged after World War II to ensure a steady, healthy supply of labor. "Cradle-to-grave" programs were founded on the assumption that most people would be employed and would pay for them through insurance schemes. As Warner discussed, the focus of social services in Western Europe may be rehabilitation; because so many lives were lost during World War II, even impaired workers were needed in the economy.[8] The United States is at a crossroads not only because the economy is in crisis but because the welfare state is not functioning as a countercyclical tool to combat economic hardships. In fact, as the economy unravels, so, too, do many welfare state programs and voluntary and private schemes, such as bread lines and food banks.[9] At best, advocates fight just to maintain the status quo or to create budget-neutral innovations.

The demise of fundamental innovations in social welfare policies is attributable to the economic decline that began in the 1970s and that has continued through the 1980s. Where this decline will lead us, as chapter 10 suggests, depends partly on the actions that are taken now.

The U.S. welfare state cannot develop more fully without full employment; the U.S. population needs to be needed for welfare state programs to develop. As long as the market determines, in great part, one's "utility" in a society, social investments in people will be minimal and will continue to be based on whether they support the market, not people. The market, then, dictates the terms of the debate and the basis for organizing services and supports for human needs. Thus, mandates for full employment, so eloquently urged by the National Committee for Full Employment, affiliated groups of religious leaders, the National Conference of Catholic Bishops, the Black Congressional Caucus, the National Urban League, and such social scientists as Gross and Gil, also will help to improve benefits and social services offered by the welfare state.[10] It may be increasingly difficult for social workers to eke out of the current state and national coffers the basic entitlements and services that are so obviously required by those we serve. Thus, pressure for full employment may have the double advantage of creating new entitlements and services while promoting a new political-economy ecology in which people are needed. If localities take action to redefine work, to experiment with the redistribution of work, and to eliminate gender roles and promote locally based goals for full employment, the groundwork will be laid for a national movement for full employment.

Job Redistribution, Creation, and Conversion

The absence of full employment involves more than the aggregated individual, family, and community costs of joblessness. In their persuasive work, *Beyond the Wasteland,* Bowles, Gordon, and Weisskopf cited the consequences of an economy that excludes so many from participation.[11] They argued that the results of such a wasteful economic practice haunt the national treasury, the Gross National Product (GNP), and even the deficit. Moreover, the huge budget deficit might be reduced, if not eliminated, if a full employment policy were enacted. Lost productivity, foregone tax revenues, and the blunted economic, social, and emotional resources of unemployed workers and their families are just some of the costs of not pursuing full employment.

Full employment involves the redistribution, creation, and conversion of jobs. Redistribution requires shorter workweeks and workyears, so that more equity occurs. Furthermore, when a monetary value is placed on work in the home and such work is considered a redistributional resource, society, communities, and families have many more jobs from which to choose. Redistribution cannot stop with market and nonmarket roles but must attempt to infuse qualitative improvements into jobs.

Workplaces have the capacity to redistribute the intrinsic and extrinsic attributes of work. *Intrinsic* means a sense of control over jobs—the ability to solve problems regarding the whole work process and larger workplace issues. *Extrinsic* means wages, wage levels, benefits, promotion policies, and profits. Moreover, undesirable work does not need to be relegated to one sector of the labor force but can itself be distributed more equitably. Workers need a more equitable allocation of the rewarding and growth-enhancing attributes of good jobs. For example, when the workplace is assessed for all the tasks and functions that are performed, it is clear that many of the esteem-building roles are allocated to those who have power, more income, and more benefits. These roles could be built into everyone's job or at least better shared. In social service agencies, for instance, shaping policies, working with the press, giving speeches, and organizing community committees often are not seen as clinical tasks and thus clinicians may not have the opportunity to grow in these areas and to share some of the multiple opportunities for community capacity building that may be relegated to those in the "higher ranks."

Movements for democracy in the workplace are critical especially to such a reexamination of the decision-making power that workers should share over work roles and the allocation of new roles. Thus, thinking of each workplace as a forum for maximizing the participation of workers in many, if not all, decisions affecting their work lives opens up avenues for the more equitable reallocation of work roles, tasks, and benefits.[12]

In relation to job creation, full employment must close the multicentury gap between jobs and the persons who seek them. Beveridge's definition of full employment is helpful; Beveridge argued that there should be more jobs than workers who are available to fill them.[13] Thus, the creation of numerous jobs in the public and private sectors is a central way of achieving full employment, while job-generation activities can benefit from placing a monetary value on nonmarket work roles.

Job-generation activities also must depend on community-based definitions of needed work. The process of planning for full employment at the local level should empower workers and their families to build more effective communities while offering them a democratic process for determining the future work careers in their localities.[14] Representatives of the National Urban League have promoted diligently the rebuilding of infrastructures in communities through public works projects, representing one of the many job-generating options that can be pursued.[15] Intensified community-based economic development should be another major source of jobs.

The least helpful of the job-generation activities may be those that rely on a traditional aggregate trickle-down aproach. Attempts by the Federal Reserve Board to "prime the pump" by increasing access to money and thereby stimulating the demand for goods and services may not necessarily ensure the expansion of jobs or even the recalls of laid-off workers because it is the restructured economy, rather than a cyclical downturn, that now compels action. Moreover, the courting of big business by policymakers often is ill advised, because the majority of new jobs are developing in small businesses, which reaffirms the need for small business loans and more technical support to reduce the failures of small businesses.

Job conversion is also a critical component of a full-employment agenda. Employment that is dependent on militaristic or environmentally hazardous enterprises cannot be considered desirable. Thus, the long-term challenge of jobs that involve human or environmental annihilation will put critical new demands on the economy and intensify the need to generate jobs that are based on community definitions of need and improvements in the quality of life. The conversion mandate is important because a huge amount of government spending during the Reagan Administration involved jobs in the military. Kazis and Grossman showed that full employment is critical to ridding the environment of its hazards to life and that the environmental movement has helped to generate, rather than supplant, jobs.[16]

It is possible that structural changes brought about by full employment would not yield their long-term benefits for 30 to 100 years. It may take several generations to erase the intergenerational effects of being socialized by society into the "excluded track." Moreover, it might require at least 100 years to understand fully the effects of a healthy, stable economy that provides work for as long as one wishes to be employed.

Women and Equity

Traditional estimates of the number of jobs needed to reach full employment may be based on sexist assumptions. In Japan, for example, unemployment rates have been as low as 2 to 3 percent in recent years, which has led some to conclude that Japan is nearing full employment. However, such rates are misleading, because they primarily reflect a labor force in which men are the main source of labor. Traditionally, married women are not supposed to work outside the home. Moreover, 20 percent of the marriages in Japan are still arranged, which further regulates women's roles within and outside the labor market.[17]

In the United States, studies have shown that full employment might draw out many persons who are not in the labor market. Expanding the elasticity of the labor market is critical to planning for a fuller use of the talents of the citizenry. Furstenberg and Thrall, for example, found that in the 1960s, 3 to 5 million women were ready to work if they were assured that other groups such as blacks were gainfully employed first.[18] This queuing up for jobs, described by Borrero, reflects an attribute of a system of job rationing that would be reduced in a full employment economy.[19]

To correct a potentially sexist bias, it is essential that policymakers view caregiving and household management as central work roles that are valuable socially and monetarily, that should be allocated to both men and women, and that are seen as essential to the nation's productivity. Because full and equitable employment implies that the sexes should be treated equally, the disproportionate access of women to income and to labor-equalizing roles should place the condition of women at the forefront of debates about full employment and hasten the caregivers' wages and pension entitlements discussed in chapter 8. The fact that women receive no wages for family caregiving and that those who are employed must labor at home as well as in the labor market reflects inequalities because work at home is an unpaid and thus an exploited by-product of a market economy while employment outside the home on top of family labor is an excessive burden. Moreover, men's relatively low rate of performance of caregiving and household management jobs necessitates that they have equal access to and equal support and equal responsibility for these work roles.

Equitable employment initiatives must not segregate men and women's labor or that of various age groups. One example of labor market segregation is the fact that women's jobs primarily span 14 categories of work that have not changed since the turn of the century. Yet this segregation must be seen more broadly, because women have been relegated to home-based work roles as their societally sanctioned duty and calling.[20]

Labor equity in a full employment economy involves the same principles as comparable worth: workers with similar responsibilities, levels of skills, and training should receive the same rates of pay. Equity also suggests uniform labor practices for all workers so that labor practices no longer are a function of which employer one works for or the type of work one does. Thus, a six- or eight-hour workday, whether at home or in the labor market, should involve respite, paid vacations, and support from co-workers.

Without a full and equitable employment movement that promotes caregivers' wages and pensions, it is certain that societal regulation of work roles in the home and labor market will intensify in the years to come. If the unemployment rate increases, efforts to drive women out of the labor market back into the home may increase. Such banishment of women from the labor market is not only sexist but is ill advised economically, because two-thirds of the women who work outside the home are the sole providers for their families or they have husbands whose incomes are below $10,000 a year.[21]

Job-Creation Schemes

There are several routes to full employment. One is a massive jobs program in which the government is the employer of first resort. Although this strategy has been castigated in the past for its makeshift jobs, research may help to counter much of the negative publicity about public service jobs.[22] Nevertheless, if public service jobs are not valued by society and do not offer opportunities for long-term growth, they will be set up to fail as the country's strategy to alleviate joblessness. Such public job-creation schemes actually could catalyze locally based entrepreneurial and service initiatives in communities to ensure that growing human needs (caregiving crises) are addressed and that new industries and enterprises are developed. They could be based on an "enterprise wage" that each person acquires as he or she joins job clubs and collectives that seek to promote community development. It would be possible to reconvert or relabel much of the welfare subsidies into enterprise allowances that would include subsidies for dependents. In a sense, to build up distressed communities, what is needed most may be a portable wage that enables workers to direct their skills and interests to community-defined needs.

Obviously, the traditional approach to the creation of jobs that is being pursued in the United States is derived from the trickle-down expansion of the economy, which is discussed later in this chapter in the case histories of Rosa and Miguel. Yet, this is an inflationary route to take that benefits the market but usually does not help those people who are excluded from it. Thus, it may be one of the less desirable forms of intervention, even though it is the one intervention that is pursued most frequently. In some circles, European leaders are coping with their restructuring economies by debating the merits of a leisure society that would use current income guarantees to enable those who do not have paid jobs to coexist with the rest who do but to relabel their activities as work.[23] Such schemes seem less applicable to the United States because of its work ethic and the fact that this country does not even provide a basic income entitlement.

Economic Theories and Policies that Affect the Unemployed

Over the past several centuries, competing perspectives have led to different analyses of unemployment. These perspectives form some of the dichotomous approaches to market and nonmarket labor today.[24]

Dichotomous Approaches

Traditional economic thinking defined economic crises and unemployment as fluctuations in an equilibrium state of expansion and growth. It was believed that the unfettered market economy, run on laissez faire or "free-market" principles, eventually would be stabilized. Those without jobs were assumed to be unemployed voluntarily; it was thought that if jobless workers would only lower their wage demands, they would be reabsorbed by the economy. In contrast, Marxist concepts held that the accumulation of wealth requires the maintenance of an industrial "reserve army" that keeps wages down and forces workers to labor harder.

Riccardo. Riccardo's alternative to such competing notions was that society must bear a fixed cost for labor whether or not workers are employed. After all, society could not reproduce itself if its citizen work force was damaged by the economy. Riccardo thus helped elevate the needs of workers and their families beyond the confines of the market; to him, these needs were to be considered independent human issues and rights, which is consistent with social welfare principles. The economist, Kapp, suggests that Riccardo's principles help set the stage for Maslow's hierarchy of human needs, which begins to provide a unifying basis for promoting workers' rights and needs, regardless of the performance of the market.[25] As a theorist of personality and motivation, Maslow argued that human needs and aspirations are organized hierarchically; work is central to this hierarchy and when thwarted, it may result in or exacerbate human suffering and social pathology.

If one thinks in lateral rather than hierarchical terms, one can theorize that work is the central basis on which members of a society are affirmed and contribute as needed nonmarginalized members. When it is defined more broadly to reflect the tasks needed to ensure a stable cohesion, progression, and reproduction of the human race, especially within a protective cultural, social, and physical environment, work can be seen as the basis of the economic, social, and psychological functioning of the species.

Despite this author's attempt to establish a base for theory building, more theoretical development is needed. That no one theory has been developed is due, in part, to the specialization and segmentation of perspectives in the social sciences. Social work, as an applied arm of social science theory, has the opportunity to be both the integrator of a unified, holistic theory of needs and rights and the promoter of a database that tests economic and social welfare concepts and the effectiveness of various policies and practice interventions.

Separation of Economic and Social Concerns

Dichotomous aproaches to the jobless may flow not just from the absence of a unified theory of needs, but from the separation of economic and social concerns and beliefs about who is culpable for the problem. Conservative views about the causes of unemployment include the beliefs that unemployment benefits increase the rate of joblessness because benefits may be a better deal than wages and that unemployment figures are padded by persons who do not want to work but who are required to register for work to receive some form of public assistance. Such beliefs have been countered by evidence to the contrary.[26] For several decades, policies to aid the jobless have relied primarily on indirect benefits from aggregate attempts to stimulate the economy, rather than on direct and swift attempts to provide jobs, income, and services to the unemployed. Rationales for interventions with the economy instead of with the jobless stem from economic principles and preferences for policies that aim to build the capacity of the market, not the welfare state, to aid jobless persons.

The emergence of capitalism helped reinforce the centrality of the market economy as the allocator of goods and services that are essential for material well-being. Nevertheless, during the twentieth century, pressures on governments to cushion the human costs of business cycles and fluctuations in markets led to the adoption of Keynesian economic principles.

Keynesian principles. Essentially, Keynesian principles validate the way in which government spending can be a stimulus to economic activity. Countercyclical interventions that are undertaken by the government through intensive spending to pull the economy out of a recession depend on the easing of credit and the trickle-down effects of the circulation of more money. These initiatives theoretically stimulate the demand for more goods and services and thus increase the supply of jobs.

Keynesian policies, antidotes to some of the human costs of capitalism, have come under increasing attack in recent years because monetarism has been on the upswing. The staunch defender of monetarism—Friedman—argued that money should be kept tight through contractions in the money and credit supply, which will slow growth and keep wages and prices down.[27] Monetarism seeks to curb workers' wages and power by augmenting the accumulation of capital. A rival philosophy is that of the supply-siders, which had its heyday in the early 1980s.

Supply-siders argue that tax cuts are stimuli to growth and hence will ensure more investments and thus more jobs. Moreover, supply-siders contend that reducing the federal regulation of business practices also will be a stimulus to growth. The failure of supply-side ideologies was due, in part, to the absence of empirical evidence that deregulation and tax cutting would be sufficient stimuli for jobs and growth. Thus, supply-side strategies failed, especially when used by the Reagan administration in conjunction with monetarism and Keynesian practices. Moreover, all these strategies did not address the prominent restructuring of the economy that was occurring, which further negated the impact of some Keynesian practices of the past.

Phillips curve doctrine. Like Keynesian policies, the Phillips curve doctrine has been increasingly discredited by some economists, yet it has guided modern-day thinking about the inevitability and even necessity of unemployment. On the basis of correlational analyses of patterns of unemployment and inflation, this economic theory postulates that an optimal tradeoff between unemployment and inflation is achieved when there is a balancing effect of some inflation and some unemployment. This optimal tradeoff between unemployment and inflation has been used to calculate "desirable" or "natural" rates of unemployment not only as guides to employment policy, but as indexes of when "full employment" has been attained.[28]

Stagflation—a condition in which rates of unemployment and inflation rise without the counterbalancing effects postulated by the Phillips curve—dominated the U.S. economy, especially in the 1970s. The presence of stagflation strengthens the realization among some economic and social policy analysts that inflation and unemployment are not necessarily causally linked. Nevertheless, rising inflation in the 1970s compelled the Reagan Administration to reduce the growth rate of money dramatically and to control access to credit that raised interest rates, dampened spending, and plunged the economy into a deep recession in the early 1980s. Meanwhile, the recession camouflaged, in part, the restructuring of the economy.

Effects of Economic Policies

The following case of Rosa and Miguel is a microcosmic and simplified example of the human side of some of the dynamics that are inherent in using policies to curb inflation and raise unemployment. The social welfare implications of such patterns and human outcomes suggest critical new roles for social workers. Questions can be raised about whether workers should have to be so burdened by attempts to regulate the economy and to curb inflation. Why, it may be asked, are employers allowed to cut costs by laying off workers, while workers must, as a consequence, forego life possessions and healthy futures?

Rosa and Miguel work for a computer assembly plant. The rising demand for computers has pressured their employer to increase production and to work them overtime. Because of the rising demand for computers and an inadequate supply of new workers, Rosa and Miguel have leverage to raise their wages. Their employer already may have raised prices in anticipation of a wage hike or set prices in a way that ensures increased profit margins that are far beyond the real increment in their wages. He also may need to expand the plant to keep up with the increased demand, so he will take out a loan for construction and equipment, which may be available at still-manageable interest rates.

At the same time that some are enjoying the benefits of "an expanding economy" at work and at home, others may be feeling a pinch. Miguel's parents who are on a fixed income may be especially hurt by inflation and may need him to supplement their Social Security benefits, which, although indexed to keep up with inflation, still are insufficient. Rosa's sister is on welfare and finds that rising prices are strapping her as well as making it more difficult for her to finish school and to survive on her public assistance allotment.

As concerns about inflation intensify, the Federal Reserve Board acts to reduce the degree of credit and money in circulation by hiking interest rates and making it harder for the large money handlers, investors, bankers, and speculators to get money. Rosa had planned to buy a house, but the sudden hike in interest rates deterred her and stopped others, who might have enjoyed the benefits of easier access to money, from buying computers. Despite their increased earnings, Rosa and Miguel are not getting a proportionate increase in goods and services for the money they earn and are buying less and spending their money more cautiously.

The slowdown in the economy, caused by the lack of money in circulation and reduced spending, affects the demand for computers. This decreased demand catches the employer at a time when he is stuck with fixed construction costs from expansion and a profit margin he needs to maintain, in part because of the dividends his stockholders hope to continue to receive. Thus, despite the declining demand, the employer is unable to reduce prices and thinks he has no choice but to cut labor costs, because they are the only "flexible" source of cuts he can look to. So he calls in his work force (which is nonunion) and tells them that one-third will be laid off at the end of the week because of the declining demand for computers. Those who are to be laid off will receive their notice with their Friday paycheck in the form of a little pink slip. He reassures them that when the economy picks up, he will rehire them.

On Friday, Rosa and Miguel, with an average of 10 years of service in the plant, receive their layoff notices. Miguel feels like he has been kicked in the stomach. Rosa expected it, so she feels relieved now that the word has come. One worker attempted to commit suicide; another bashed in three cars in the parking lot.

Rosa and Miguel fare poorly on their unemployment compensation. Miguel's drinking has become a family problem. They have had to pull their son out of college, the first in his family ever to attend, and Rosa is depressed. Their frustration is further fueled by the fact that their employer is working some of the remaining employees overtime rather than hiring others back.

By the end of a year, with mounting worries about a recession and political pressures to get the 10 percent of the jobless back to work, the Federal Reserve Board loosens up the money supply, and the trickle-down effects make it possible for demand to intensify. However, because of the uneven way in which the demand for goods and services has increased, inflationary pressures are felt early at the computer plant. One of the suppliers has had a bottleneck problem and an insufficient number of workers. Thus, the supplier passes the consequences of increased wages and prices onto Rosa and Miguel's employer. Compounding these rising costs is the fact that their employer has installed updated equipment, automating some of the assembly processes. Uncertainties about the improving economy, coupled with automation and the rising costs of parts, make it difficult for the employer to reabsorb all the laid-off workers. Hence, although Miguel returns to his job, Rosa just works odd hours and is forced to seek work elsewhere.

Policymakers might have viewed Rosa and Miguel's unemployment as cyclical. However, given the restructuring of world markets, especially in manufacturing, it is possible that the recession hid from view the actual shifting of the assembly of computers from the United States to another nation, such as Taiwan, where labor and parts are less expensive. Thus, Rosa may find that what would have been deemed cyclical unemployment by labor market economists becomes, in the end, long-term structural or chronic joblessness.[29]

Rosa's structural joblessness is compounded by job rationing and discrimination owing to her gender and ethnic minority status. Moreover, that she is a woman and that her skills as a machinist are no longer in demand may place her in the ranks of the long-term structurally unemployed. Therefore, despite her hopes for eventual recall, she may be a victim of skill and occupational obsolescence. Who will level with her? Who even knows that she will not be recalled? Who will help her identify her retraining needs? Because few problem-solving pathways exist except occasional publicly created jobs and retraining funds, it is unclear that her reemployment and perhaps her need to find a new livelihood will be addressed systematically. Although models of holistic approaches are being tested in Canada, they are not widely replicated in the United States.[30]

The stress of unemployment and strife in awaiting recall warrant improved social welfare responses. Despite the trickle-down effects of more money in circulation to stimulate the demand for computers, Rosa and Miguel's joblessness left them worse off. Miguel returned to work with a severe drinking problem and marital stress and had to forego plans to send their son back to college. Rosa's depression worsened to the point where she had to seek mental health counseling. In a full employment economy, the deliberate creation of recessions not only would be immoral but unnecessary. Moreover, the uncertainties over the security of one's job, income, and life-style, as well as the long-term scars of unemployment, would or should not occur.

Sherraden developed a paradigm for targeting interventions for the jobless to the kinds and types of unemployment they face.[31] He argued that frictional unemployment may warrant such initiatives as job placement, the provision of information about the labor market, and additional job-acquisition supports. Structural unemployment, he suggested, requires numerous interventions, including job training and tax credits for hiring the unskilled. Cyclical unemployment may necessitate, among numerous options, short-term public service employment, monetary and fiscal stimulants, and a reduction in the workweek, while chronic unemployment may require such initiatives as long-term public service employment, long-term wage subsidies, job sharing, and early retirement incentives. If these differential strategies were made available to the jobless as entitlements, the current crises that engulf many workers and their families would be minimized. In fact, Rosa might not slip from the status of a cyclically jobless worker to that of a structurally or chronically unemployed person.

Historical Perspectives on Unemployment and Full Employment

Unemployment as it is known in the United States is directly traceable to the wage-based economies that emerged in the fourteenth and fifteenth centuries. Mercantilism, capitalism's predecessor, while freeing workers and their families from their servitude on feudal estates and advancing opportunities for multiple kinds of employment, denied many people access to wage-based work. Moreover, wage-based economies imposed new regulations and limits on one's tasks and mobility as a worker.

As early as 1349, English laws denied workers opportunities to search for better working conditions. Poor-law regulations, which followed from 1601 onward, not only blocked the cooperative entrepreneurial endeavors of industrious residents of workhouses but, in many cases, punished the jobless by subjecting them to conditions similar to those faced by imprisoned criminals.[32] The historic identification of social work with the workhouse poor may have intensified some of the repulsion the profession felt toward some forms of employment, especially given the compulsory basis on which it has been proffered to the victims of labor market marginalization. Moreover, the colonization and building of the United States depended on the generation of a labor supply, which was created, in part, by the kidnapping and enslavement of Africans and by the expulsion of some of Western Europe's surplus labor and workhouse poor.[33]

As was discussed in chapter 8, men and women worked side by side on an equal basis at home and in the trades before the Industrial Revolution. For many years, home chores were performed by men. The emergent economic system, based on the specialization of skills and the view of workers as commodities, increasingly dominated the organization of family life and gender roles so that men were socialized for labor market work and women were socialized for caregiving in the family. In addition, dichotomous values evolved for each domain so that both sexes came to have different roles and rights.

The home was to be a haven for the flourishing of family and women's values. However, the emergence of the so-called self-regulating market reduced workers to commodities and their labor to fragmented specialized tasks and assumed that how they performed their jobs depended on punishments and payoffs.[34] Although the home was elevated as the cult of domesticity, it nonetheless was built on the employment of immigrant women as well as the enslavement of black women. Thus, despite beliefs about the home as the preferred base for inculcating values, the degeneration of the home into an often-exploitive workplace, both for the mother and then for those she employed, suggests that, in many respects, market processes and values overtook some of the family life as well.[35]

Equitable Employment

The struggle to legislate full employment in this country reached several high points in this century that are instructive for future organizing efforts. The first landmark occurred during the Great Depression of the 1930s, when social workers and others actively pressed President Franklin D. Roosevelt and Harry Hopkins, his domestic affairs adviser and a social worker, to guarantee jobs for all. Hopkins was the primary architect of the New Deal economic and employment programs. Hopkins actively promoted the notion of jobs for all as a human right. However, had social service leaders not decried the ill effects of the economy, the depression would not have been recognized as quickly and the need for government interventions would not have been revealed so graphically.[36] Even though guarantees of jobs were reaffirmed in speeches and in written promulgations, the full employment movement was stifled politically when inflation rose and when an increasing number of people finally returned to work.[37]

Explicit job rationing was practiced during the Great Depression. For example, in numerous communities, it apparently was illegal for married women to hold a job. Therefore, some married women concealed their marital status, even when pregnant, to bring home wages that were sufficient to meet their families' needs.

World War II. As of 1938, 20 million workers, or less than two-thirds of the work force, were covered by unemployment insurance. As of 1985, 92.5 million, or 96 percent of the work force was covered.[38] Yet, currently only one-quarter of the jobless are drawing benefits.

World War II not only produced an unprecedented low rate of unemployment in the United States but demonstrated that groups of individuals, including women, racial minorities, and disabled persons, who were once thought to be unemployable, were indeed able workers. Millions of new workers who traditionally had been marginalized by the labor market were thrust into jobs. Because the demand for labor was so great during World War II, workers were able to bargain for higher wages and benefits and better working conditions.[39]

Minority workers were subjected to controls on their power to advocate for better pay and positions and so, too, in a sense, were women. Told that it was unpatriotic not to work outside the home because their labor was needed, women were induced further to work by the government's provision of child care. Although the child care that was provided fell dramatically short of meeting the needs of employed mothers, the promulgation of such policies nonetheless demonstrated the ability of policymakers during World War II to recognize and alleviate some of the caregiving responsibilities of women.

The post-World War II years brought fears that the country would relapse into a depression. Countries like Denmark, England, France, Germany, and Sweden chose to enact full-employment policies that linked the right to paid jobs to citizenship. Unlike England and other Western European nations, the United States pursued a more equivocal initiative that guaranteed that the federal government would promote economic prosperity, on the one hand, but that fell short of establishing the goals of and tools for full employment, on the other hand. Thus, the Employment Act of 1946 (once slated to be called the Full Employment Act), promised maximum purchasing power (or freedom from inflation), maximum employment opportunities, and productivity. An earlier draft of the act guaranteed the outlay of federal funds to ensure the right of everyone to employment. Representative Augustus Hawkins recently suggested that this provision would have saved $20 trillion in the GNP and 125 million woman/man years of joblessness.[40]

The 1960s. Political inattention to the mounting needs and problems of the jobless during the 1950s created some of the momentum that led directly to the election of President John F. Kennedy in 1960. In retrospect, it has been argued that the vote margins produced by jobless workers ensured the Kennedy victory and helped to renew the public's concern for the poor.[41]

The Equal Opportunity Act of 1964 implied that the poor should "seize opportunities" rather than be guaranteed certain outcomes (such as jobs). Like they did during World War II, unemployment rates declined dramatically during the late 1960s because of the Vietnam War. Nevertheless, unemployment rates of black workers continued to be disproportionately high. In fact, discriminatory hiring patterns in the labor market were one of the many sources of pressure to place jobs for all on the human rights agenda. It was argued, for example, that civil rights would not be fully achieved if black workers were at last allowed to sit at the same lunch counter as white workers but did not have the money to buy a cup of coffee.

Social work services to the jobless expanded again during the Johnson administration's War on Poverty (through the Manpower Development and Training Act and the Neighborhood Youth Corps). Job-creation activities of the 1970s were marked by the Nixon administration's Comprehensive Employment and Training Act (CETA). CETA provided up to 1 million jobs annually and, at its peak, brought the unemployment rate down by about 1 percent each year.

More recent public service employment programs, such as the 1983 Emergency Jobs Appropriations Act, have not necessarily been fully implemented. A 1987 report by the General Accounting Office found that the 1983 appropriation resulted in the creation of only 35,000 jobs, compared to the 200,000 to 500,000 anticipated by advocates.[42]

Also among such initiatives was the Job Corps, which sought to increase the employment and earnings of disadvantaged youths. Findings from several studies showed reduced dependence, teenage pregnancy, and criminal activities. Despite these findings, the Reagan Administration scuttled a public proclamation of the findings that economic returns were 1½ times greater than the costs of the program. Additionally, that administration sought to abolish the program after 20 years of its demonstrated successes. Although the Office of Management and Budget argued that the functions of the Job Corps could be absorbed more effectively by the Jobs Training Partnership Act (JTPA), evidence to the contrary has been mounting. For example, eight out of every 10 Job Corps enrollees were high school dropouts, whereas only 10 percent of JTPA enrollees are dropouts.[43] This difference is attributed to the fact that JTPA placements necessitate that the program serve only the most job ready, rather than the more difficult to place.

The 1970s. Despite beliefs about the inverse relationship of inflation to unemployment rates, both inflation and unemployment seemed to rise simultaneously in the 1970s. Stagflation destroyed many people's belief in the inevitability of the tradeoff between unemployment rates and rising inflation. Moreover, civil rights activism, fed by fluctuating unemployment that was caused, in part, by major slumps in key industries during the 1970s, helped to generate a movement for full employment. Growing concerns about joblessness among women, ethnic minorities, sexual minorities, youths, the aged, the disabled, and Vietnam veterans intensified the efforts of individual social workers to build employment-relevant social services. Several initiatives gave a focus to these activities. For example, Representative Augustus Hawkins introduced the Full Employment and Job Guarantee Act (H.R. 50), which fostered the emergence of full employment councils and committees in a number of states and communities.

H.R. 50. So dedicated was Representative Hawkins and his fellow members of the Black Congressional Caucus to the principle of the enforceable guarantee of jobs that earlier drafts of H.R. 50 referred to local employment offices as "job guarantee offices." Although state and local full employment councils debated issues such as how to enforce the guarantee clause, some lawyers envisioned new forms of litigation to ensure that the law would be implemented. Economist and House Budget Director Alice Rivlin testified that the costs of a two-year operation might run $16 to $44 billion, but, when offset by tax revenues, the real costs would be reduced to $17 to $18 billion.[44]

To foster such legislation, full employment councils and committees were organized as broadly based coalitions of the unemployed, civil rights and labor leaders, rank-and-file union members, policymakers, and church leaders and members, as well as social workers and allied health and human service workers. At the local level, these councils and committees sponsored educational forums and drives that attempted to heighten the public's awareness of the possibility and desirability of jobs for all, that evidence for the inflation–unemployment tradeoff was suspect, and that states and localities could do their part to promote full employment by adopting full employment principles as guides for economic initiatives and citizens' rights. During one year, mayors and governors were asked to acknowledge and proclaim a full employment week that would include educational events, petitions, and drives to garner support for H.R. 50. A recapping of some of these initiatives along with suggestions for launching locally based, full employment campaigns is included in Table 1.[45]

Table 1. Action Ideas for Locally Based Full Employment Coalitions.

■ Organize or join a coalition involving the unemployed and poor, homeless, sexual minorities, young and aged, labor, churches, multiethnic groups, women's groups, social service groups, representatives of cooperatives, environmental and peace groups, and small businesses.

■ Document the locally based consequences of the economic marginalization of workers and their families: the increasing rates of child abuse, death from heart disease, utilization of welfare, homelessness, foreclosures, repossessions, reduced tax revenues, the failure of tax levies, high school dropouts, and teenage pregnancies.

■ Document the hidden benefits of caregiver labor that mitigates the costs of the institutionalization of dependents or long-term hospitalization for health care problems.

■ Document all the work on the community infrastructure that needs to be accomplished.

■ Compare the costs of some of the consequences of unemployment and personal marginalization with the human and tax benefits of full employment, as well as the benefits to small businesses.

■ Document the estimated value of caregiving labor, especially as it applies to the welfare state, and savings to insurance carriers. Some benefits may seem clearer if one imagines a strike of caregivers as was pursued by women in Iceland in fall 1986.

■ Document the profits, tax exemptions, and costs to the government of toxic waste cleanup of large local corporations.

Table 1 (Continued)

■ Estimate the loss of revenue that occurs when corporations leave an area, including the income spent elsewhere and profits invested elsewhere.

■ Present a full-employment resolution to local policymakers that focuses on the need for national and locally based full employment.

■ Review economic development loans and initiatives: Are they supporting job-generating small businesses or absent employers?

■ Use your coalition to screen the impact on employment of corporate as well as regional, state, and local policies on the generation of jobs.

■ Establish subcommittees on mature industries, reindustrialization, and locally based economic initiatives that should spawn their own legislation and freestanding commissions.

■ Organize petitions for jobs or income now.

■ Organize an early warning system on a voluntary or legislated basis to prevent closures and the flight of capital and to promote buyout of troubled industries. Meet regularly with state and congressional representatives on full employment goals and requisite policy initiatives. Develop a network of coalitions or councils on a local or regional basis.

■ Lobby for full employment, jobs, and income policies.

■ Work with the mass media to educate the public on the costs of economic decline and the benefits of full and equitable employment to workers, families, and communities.

■ Call press conferences and seek media coverage of the human and community costs of lockouts, union busting, plant closures, mergers, and takeovers.

■ Document the gap in jobs for your locality on the basis of estimates of the jobs that are needed, the range of skills that are unused, and the number of persons who need jobs.

■ Seek work-sharing options that combine reduced work hours with unemployment compensation in plants that are laying off but not closing by ensuring that work-sharing laws are passed and intensively implemented, whenever possible.

■ Initiate educational forums that lead to legislative agendas to promote helpful economic, employment, and social service policies.

Many of these activities came to an end with the passage of the Full Employment and Balanced Growth Act of 1978, known as the Humphrey–Hawkins bill. Nonetheless, such local initiatives demonstrated how critical communities are in promoting moral mandates that everyone is entitled to a job. These beliefs were hallmarks of an emerging economic literacy in persons who once had been relegated to the sidelines during technical economic discussions. They helped reaffirm the centrality of social welfare goals as overriding responsibilities of the economy and gave local citizens some sense that economic change was indeed within their domain and possible control.

Not all were satisfied with the version of the Humphrey–Hawkins bill that was enacted. Despite the diligence of Hawkins and of many groups in repudiating what was once believed to be an inevitable yet questionable tradeoff between unemployment and inflation, congressional acquiescence to the business lobby resulted in the incorporation of some of the tradeoff language in the final bill. Although H.R. 50 is primarily a planning document, it requires Congress to report annually on the progress that has been made in its implementation. In addition, its goals of reducing inflation to 3 percent and unemployment to 4 percent by 1983 (which obviously were not achieved) serve as benchmarks against which the next wave of legislation will be compared.[46] Despite the number of proposed initiatives and local attempts to aid the jobless, a federal full employment framework is a precondition for effective local strategies.[47]

Current Initiatives

Worker adjustment assistance is being proposed in Congress to provide a rapid coordinated response to layoffs and closures, a 90-day advance warning system (for employers who are planning to layoff 50 to 100 workers), and up to 120 days of notice for employers of a work force of 500 or more.[48] Moreover, although pieces of legislation have been passed to alleviate some of the hardships of some of the jobless, they never reach all who are in need, and benefit levels are not adequate. Even worse, the absence of a framework for promoting full and equitable employment,[49] make the few initiatives, such as JTPA or trade adjustment assistance, important but seemingly insignificant, compared with the great need for a comprehensive array of full employment and income supports. For example, the Trade Adjustment Assistance Act provides critical benefits that are similar to unemployment compensation (about $150 per week) to workers who have been displaced by foreign trade. Although only 100,000 workers participate, it is a little-advertised income assistance program. Within this act, provisions are made for training, relocation assistance, and aid to failing firms.[50]

The disjuncture between what is passable politically in Congress and the lives that are placed at risk because of inaction creates both the crisis and the mandate for social work intervention. As Gross has suggested, grass roots organizing for effective full employment in the local and national economy is the most democratic approach to this essential policy responsibility.[51]

History suggests that no singular legislative initiative will do the job of ensuring enforceable guarantees of jobs and equitable employment for all. It may take multiple consecutive bills before Congress and many state legislatures fulfill the policy directives needed to guarantee jobs. In addition to a service continuum that would promote training and job guarantees, bills also are needed to ensure early notification of layoffs and plant closures, retraining vouchers, and the creation of resources for an intensive community-based economic development movement.

The Quality of Life Action Act (H.R. 1398), a later version of the Jobs and Income Act, introduced by Representatives Charles A. Hayes and John Conyers in 1986 may be one of the cornerstones of new efforts to achieve full employment. Although the premises of this bill are similar to those of the Humphrey–Hawkins Act, the Hayes–Conyers bill focuses on community definitions of work and assumes that grass roots organizations will be co-decision makers and implementors. The legislation also requires jobs to serve socially useful ends, rather than militaristic goals. Finally, it may provide a forum for debates on how to institute wages for the care of dependents.

The power of full employment as a tool of promoting self- and family development, higher wages, and improved working conditions has not been tested in the United States. Nonetheless, a weakened or broken down labor force, which lives with the ravages or the threat of unemployment, runs counter to the social welfare principle of the right to self-development. Therefore, full and equitable employment must be one cornerstone of a plan for meeting and advancing human needs and rights. Clearly, there is plenty of work and plenty of income to be distributed more equitably. The principles of full employment should preempt debates about the inevitability of joblessness, poverty, and extreme income differentials by reframing the issue as one of a more equitable distribution of work, income, and benefits.

Barriers to Full and Equitable Employment

Given the many benefits that full employment would bring to our economically and socially troubled nation, what barriers have prevented the redirection of the economy and the welfare state? There are many explanations for the resistance to full employment. The central one is the concern that full employment will cause inflation, which is assumed to be a by-product of labor shortages and power shifts. One way to address such a fear is to pinpoint and control only those pockets of inflation that may occur in some segments of the labor market but not in others. For example, one industry might experience price hikes and wage increases, while in other industries, there still may be a glut of labor and little pressure for wage increases. Despite the unevenness of inflation in the economy, its rise in one sector may lead to overgeneralizations about the "inflationary economy."

Because price hikes occur irrespective of wages, the assumption that inflation in prices is driven solely or even primarily by labor is false. In the past decade, one-third of the inflation has been attributed to increases in the price of oil.[52] Inflation also may be attributed to greed. Greed is a human characteristic that those who are schooled in human dynamics, especially social workers, may be well equipped to address.

The institution of voluntary wage and price controls that occurred during the Nixon administration as a way of combating rising inflation became a game of anticipatory moves. Thus, inflation may have been exacerbated by the anticipation of the imposition of inflationary controls. In Sweden, it is just this understanding of human dynamics that has led labor, business, and the government to negotiate wages and price hikes. This three-way problem-solving and planning effort ensures that wages and prices are seen not as natural by-products of economic forces but as negotiated human decisions that take into account the needs of the various stakeholders.[53]

The Swedish model assumes that most workers are represented by unions and that the government has a hand in planning wage and price increases. In the United States, however, supply-siders complain that business already is hampered by too much governmental intervention that inhibits the creation of jobs and prosperity. Yet, the flight of capital and the rash of mergers and takeovers suggest that the destruction of jobs is on the rise. The message is clear: unless democratic controls are placed on the behavior of corporations and the movement of capital, much of the industrial and social fabric of the United States will dissolve in a short time. In contrast, planning for full employment may involve community and government-based initiatives that empower disenfranchised communities and workers to retain mature industries, to reactivate plants that were abandoned, and to build more accountable enterprises for localities that are in demise.

Despite these well-known barriers to full employment, especially the fear of inflation and regulatory controls, social workers have joined leading economists who supported H.R. 50 and current efforts to achieve full employment. They claim that because this nation has never tested full employment, it is premature to assume that the effects of full employment would be inflationary.

Objections to full employment come not just from the Right or from the business community. Some skeptics are activists who are concerned about the human conditions of the workplace and of work itself.[54] Such criticisms are cogent reminders that a campaign for full employment cannot ignore underemployment and that full and equitable employment involves not just the reallocation of jobs and income but the qualitative attributes that involve wide but unnecessary disparities in the allocation of desirable and relatively undesirable tasks in the workplace. Moreover, work that does not tap innate abilities does violence to the intention of full employment policies.[55]

Another central barrier to the discussion of full employment in the United States is mystification about the workings of the economy. The symbols, equations, and analyses used by economists, which may seem unfathomable to the public, inhibit workers and their families from becoming involved in weighing and choosing among various economic policy options. However, economic and employment rights must be seen as moral issues, not technical issues that only can be fathomed by economic experts.

Recent work in the Massachusetts Chapter of the National Association of Social Workers (NASW) to pass legislation calling for constitutional amendments that guarantee employment is but one of the many initiatives that social workers have launched to advance full employment.[56] In 1987, the NASW Delegate Assembly was presented with a policy statement on "Full and Equitable Employment," developed by the NASW Commission on Employment and Economic Support. The policy statement was passed. New Initiatives for Full Employment, in which some social work educators and practitioners have participated, further attests to the critical campaigns in which social workers are engaged in building a movement for constitutional guarantees.[57] As another example of social work leadership, the Adelphi University School of Social Work, Garden City, New York, through its Center for Social Policy and Social Services, has focused not only on full employment but has been the home base for the Long Island Coalition for Full Employment.[58]

The recent reaffirmation of the meaning of work and the morality of full employment as a fundamental human right by the National Conference of Catholic Bishops, as well as numerous other religious bodies, is a significant reminder to social workers and all who are served by them that anyone can enter the debate about equitable jobs and income.[59] Similar analyses have been undertaken by Baptist, Congregational, Episcopal, Jewish, Lutheran, Presbyterian, Universalist Unitarian, and United Methodist bodies, along with the National Council of Churches.

According to Rabbi David Saperstein, Washington representative of the Union of American Hebrew Congregations, there is a consensus that the moral implications of unemployment and underemployment must be addressed. In a report to the National Committee for Full Employment, Saperstein noted that the Reagan Administration has created fewer public jobs than any of the previous four administrations.[60]

Demystification of the Economy

Economic analyses conducted by economists are not the equivalent of tracking the human costs and benefits of the macroeconomy on human lives and communities. Few disciplines undertake impact analyses that pertain to the human consequences of the economy. As with the Great Depression of the 1930s, social workers may be the first to witness and diagnose the effects. Thus, the profession should take seriously its responsibility to track the human side of macro-economic activity, which may reaffirm the role that social workers can play in debates about reforms in the welfare state and cutbacks in programs.[61] It also may help reformulate agendas so that the rising utilization of social programs is not seen by some as a sign that programs create dependence or do not work but, rather, is viewed as a by-product of increased human dysfunction in the impermanent and hurtful economy, both in its boom and bust phases. It is easy to get mired in debates among economists over monetarism, sources and causes of inflation, or even the future prospects of capitalism. What social workers bring to the policy arena are data on the human side of the economy and the interconnection between social and economic domains and problems. Moreover, social workers must demand interventions that help people—not just the market economy.

The restructured global economy inevitably will create greater conflicts over economic theories of the past, while encouraging new explanations of some of its problems. The need for new analyses and new courses of action place social work practice in the United States in the center of a worldwide campaign for human, economic, and occupational rights.

Notes and References

1. *For perspectives on a full employment policy, see* H. Ginsberg, *Full Employment and Public Policy: The United States and Sweden* (Lexington, Mass.: Lexington Books, 1983). *For a report on new dimensions to the problems that jobless*

people face in Sweden, see H. Berglind, "Unemployment: A Challenge for Social Work." Paper presented at the International Conference for Social Development, Montreal, Quebec, Canada, August 1984.

2. *See* K. Thode, ed., *Freedom from Want: Towards More Equality,* proceedings of a conference sponsored by the Seattle Urban League (Seattle, Wash.: Seattle Urban League, 1976).

3. *See* R. Howard, "Brave New Workplace," *Working Papers,* 7 (November–December 1980).

4. Testimony of David Mosley, director of the Department of Community Development, Seattle, before the Joint Select Committee on Unemployment Insurance, Washington State Legislature, 1986. *See also* K. Hopper and J. Hamberg, *The Making of America's Homeless: From Skid Row to the New Poor, 1945–1984* (New York: Community Service Society of New York, December 1984).

5. E. Durkheim, *Suicide* (Glencoe, Ill.: Free Press, 1951).

6. R. Warner, *Recovery from Schizophrenia* (Boston: Routledge & Kegan Paul, 1985).

7. Presentation by L. Schore at the conference "Toward Full, Fair, and Gratifying Employment for Quality Life and a Liveable Earth," held at the University of California, Santa Cruz, May 29–30, 1987.

8. Warner, *Recovery from Schizophrenia.*

9. G. Riches, *Food Banks and the Welfare Crisis* (Ottawa, Ontario: Canadian Council on Social Development, 1986).

10. The National Committee for Full Employment is a longstanding coalition of 80 religious, civil rights, union, and related organizations and individuals; it publishes the *Jobs Impact Bulletin. See also* B. Gross, *Friendly Facism* (Boston: South End Press, 1980); M. D. Hoff, "Response to the Catholic Bishops' Letter on Economic Justice: Implications for Social Welfare." Unpublished doctoral dissertation, University of Washington, Seattle, 1987; *Pastoral Letter on Catholic Social Teaching and the U.S. Economy* (2d draft; Washington, D.C.: National Conference of Catholic Bishops, October 7, 1985); D. Rasmussen and J. Sterba, *The Catholic Bishops and the Economy: A Debate* (New Brunswick, N.J.: Transaction Books, 1987); D. G. Gil, "Toward Constitutional Guarantees for Employment and Income" (Waltham, Mass.: Florence Heller Graduate School for Advanced Studies in Social Welfare, December 19, 1985); *Urban League Review,* 10 (Summer 1986), entire issue; and *Congressional Record,* 131, Wednesday, March 6, 1985.

11. S. Bowles, D. M. Gordon, and T. E. Weisskopf, *Beyond the Wasteland* (Garden City, N.Y.: Doubleday Anchor Books, 1983).

12. R. M. Mason, *Participatory and Workplace Democracy* (Carbondale: Southern Illinois University Press, 1982).

13. W. Beveridge, *Full Employment in a Free Society* (London: Allen & Unwin, 1944).

14. B. Gross, "Toward a Human Rights Economy: A Task for Social Workers Who Will Not Become Unwilling Agents of Social Control," *Report from Working Group 9 on the Unemployed: Policies and Services* (Helsinki, Finland: International Council on Social Welfare, 1986), pp. 195–196.

15. D. G. Glasgow, "Welfare: Reform or Replacement." Testimony given before the Senate Subcommittee on Social Security and Family Policy, Senate Finance Committee, Washington, D.C., February 2, 1987.

16. R. Kazis and R. L. Grossman, *Fear at Work: Job Blackmail, Labor and the Environment* (New York: Pilgrim Press, 1982).

17. J. Condon, *A Half Step Behind, Japanese Women of the 80's* (New York: Dodd, Mead, & Co., 1985).

18. F. F. Furstenberg and C. A. Thrall, "Counting the Jobless: The Impact of Job Rationing on the Measurement of Unemployment," *The Annals,* 418 (March 1975), pp. 45–59.

19. M. Borrero, presentation for Working Group 9 on the Unemployed: Policies and Services, held at the 13th Regional Symposium on Social Welfare, International Council on Social Welfare, Turku, Finland, June 1985.

20. H. Remick, ed., *Comparable Worth and Wage Discrimination* (Philadelphia: Temple University Press, 1984).

21. L. Westley and J. DeGooyer, *Women's Work: Undervalued, Underpaid* (Washington, D.C.: National Commission on Working Women, 1982). *See also* S. A. Hewlett, *A Lesser Life* (New York: William Morrow & Co., 1986); and B. R. Bergmann, *The Economic Emergence of Women* (New York: Basic Books, 1986).

22. K. Briar et al., "The Impact of Unemployment on Young, Middle-Aged and Older Workers," *Sociology and Social Welfare,* 7 (November 1980), pp. 907–915.

23. G. Fragniere, "Work, Unemployment and Marginalization: A Vicious Circle or a False Problem?" Paper presented at the Regional Symposium of the International Council on Social Welfare, Rome, Italy, 1987.

24. *For a wide-ranging discussion of these theories, see* K. W. Kapp, "Socio-Economic Effects of Low and High Employment," *The Annals,* 418 (March 1975), pp. 60–71.

25. Ibid.

26. *For a discussion of and response to some of these conservative ideologies, see* J. S. Henry, "Hallelujah I'm a Bum: The New Conservative Theories of Unemployment," *Working Papers,* 6 (March–April 1979), pp. 71–79.

27. M. Friedman, *Capitalism and Freedom* (Chicago: University of Chicago Press, 1962).

28. Gross, *Friendly Facism.*

29. M. W. Sherraden, "Chronic Unemployment: A Social Work Perspective," *Social Work,* 30 (October 1985), pp. 403–408.

30. S. McKay, "Helping the Unemployed: A Model for the Development of a Community Response," *Report from Working Group 9 on the Unemployed: Policies and Services* (Helsinki, Finland: International Council on Social Welfare, 1986), pp. 158–176.

31. M. W. Sherraden, "Employment Policy: A Conceptual Framework," *Journal of Social Work Education,* 21 (Spring/Summer 1985), pp. 5–14.

32. S. Mencher, *Poor Law to Poverty Program* (Pittsburgh: University of Pittsburgh Press, 1967).

33. *For an exposé of the human side of colonization, see* H. Zinn, *A People's History of the United States* (New York: Harper & Row, 1980).

34. *See* K. Polanyi, *The Great Transformation* (Boston: Beacon Press, 1944). *See also* H. Braverman, *Labor and Monopoly Capital* (New York: Monthly Review Press, 1974); E. P. Thompson, *The Making of the English Working Class* (London: Victor Gollanez, 1963); and E. Hobsbawn, *Workers: Worlds of Labor* (New York: Pantheon Books, 1984).

35. *See* C. Degler, *At Odds: Women and the Family in America* (New York: Oxford University Press, 1980).

36. J. Fisher, *The Response of Social Work to the Depression* (Cambridge, Mass.: Schenkman Publishing Co., 1980).

37. P. M. Bachrach, "The Right to a Job: Emergence of an Idea," *Social Service Review,* 26 (June 1952), pp. 153–164.

38. D. N. Price, "Unemployment Insurance, Then and Now, 1935–1985," *Social Security Bulletin,* 48 (October 1985), pp. 22–32.

39. S. Moses, "Labor Supply Concepts: The Political Economy of Conceptual Change," *The Annals,* 418 (March 1985), pp. 26–44.

40. A. F. Hawkins, "What Happened to Full Employment?" *Urban League Review,* 10 (Summer 1986), pp. 9–12.

41. J. L. Sundquist, *Politics and Policy* (Washington, D.C.: The Brookings Institution, 1968), p. 432.

42. "$9 Billion Program Fails, Produces Only 35,000 Jobs Says GAO," *Seattle Times,* January 31, 1987, p. A4.

43. "Report Assesses JTPA's First Months," *Job Impact Bulletin* (National Committee for Full Employment), 4 (April 20, 1984), p. 3. *See also* "Job Creation Education Project," *Jobs Impact Bulletin,* 5 (May 10, 1985).

44. Testimony of A. Rivlin, *Hearings Before the Committee on Banking, Housing, and Urban Affairs, U.S. Senate, on the Full Employment and Balanced Growth Act of 1976* (Washington, D.C.: U.S. Government Printing Office, 1976).

45. In the 1970s, the author worked closely with Noel Hagens, Larry Kinney, Paul Pruitt, Kay Thode, and others in developing Washington State's Full Employment Action Council, the local counterpart of the National Full Employment Action Council that exists today. Some of the ideas for developing networks were crafted by them. Since then, the Washington Economic Solidarity Coalition, the Seattle Worker Center, and the Unemployment Law Project have functioned in similar ways I thank especially Tom Croft, Bill Knowles, and Marvin Williams for the opportunity to learn from, and collaborate with, them.

46. Hawkins, "What Happened to Full Employment?"

47. *For examples of local initiatives, see* W. H. McCarthy et al., *Reducing Urban Unemployment* (Washington, D.C.: National League of Cities, 1984). *See also* A. Levison, *The Full Employment Alternative* (New York: Coward, McCann & Geoghegan, 1980). *For a list of some laws on the books, see* Subcommittee on Employment and Productivity of the Committee on Labor and Human Resources, *A Compilation of Job Training and Related Laws* (Washington, D.C.: U.S. Government Printing Office, 1987).

48. *Fact Sheet on Economic Dislocation and the Worker Adjustment Assistance Act* (Washington, D.C.: Industrialized Union Department, AFL-CIO).

49. B. Gross, personal communication, 1987.

50. *See* Office of Technology Assessment, Congressional Board of the One Hundredth Congress, *Trade Adjustment Assistance: New Ideas for an Old Program* (Washington, D.C.: U.S. Government Printing Office, June 1987).

51. *See* B. Gross, "Grass Roots: National Planning in a Global Perspective." Statement presented at the Conference on the Role of the Public Sector in Restoring the Economic and Social Health of the Nation, sponsored by the U.S. House of Representatives, Washington, D.C., February 1983.

52. *See* L. E. Nulty, *Understanding the New Inflation: The Importance of Basic Necessities* (Washington, D.C.: Exploratory Project for Economic Alternatives, 1977).

53. Howard, "Brave New Workplace."

54. *See* B. Gross, "Making an Issue of Full Employment," *The Nation,* January 24, 1987, pp. 72–74; and B. Gross, "Rethinking Full Employment," *The Nation,* January 17, 1987, pp. 45–46.

55. D. G. Gil, "Reversing the Dynamics of Violence by Transforming Work," *Journal of International and Comparative Social Welfare,* 1 (Fall 1984); L. Levi, "Quality of the Working Environment: Protection and Promotion of Occupational Mental Health," in *Working Life in Sweden,* No. 8, pp. 1–15 (New York: Swedish Consulate General, November 1987).

56. D. G. Gil, "Economic Rights: State Takes First Step," *NASW News* (June 1986), p. 9.

57. Organizing Committee, New Initiatives for Full Employment, "A New Movement for Full Employment is Launched," *Social Policy,* 18 (Spring 1987), pp. 21–22.

58. *See Policy Notes,* Center for Social Policy, Adelphi University School of Social Work, Garden City, New York, Fall 1984.

59. *See* Rasmussen and Sterba, *The Catholic Bishops and the Economy;* and *Pastoral Letter on Catholic Social Teaching and the U.S. Economy. See also* G. Baum and D. Cameron, *Ethics and Economics: Canada's Catholic Bishops on the Economic Crisis* (Toronto: James Lorimer & Co., 1984).

60. "Jobs '87: A NCTE Special Report," *Jobs Impact Bulletin* (National Committee for Full Employment), 7 (March 20, 1987), pp. 1–2.

61. *See, for example, testimony by G. Riches to the Commission of Inquiry on Unemployment Insurance,* "Chronic Unemployment and the Failure of Unemployment Insurance in Canada: Moving Beyond the Safety Net," Regina, Saskatchewan, Canada, December 3, 1985.

10

The Global Economy: Toward Economic and Social Stabilization

The United States is at a crossroads. One scenario suggests that deindustrialization and the flight of capital, along with the expansion of the service industry, will dramatically reduce the standard of living and that regions that are in economic decline will see the rise of ghost towns.[1] Another scenario projects a deep and cataclysmic depression in the 1990s; several current economic conditions seem to simulate those of 1929, which ushered in the "crash" and the Great Depression.[2] A third scenario foresees a renaissance in worldwide trade and the potential for trade-based negotiations to replace the use of militarism for sorting out global power. This third scenario suggests the intensified use of negotiation, a form of world federalism, and perhaps a worldwide system of social welfare.[3] A variant of this scenario is one that projects a future in which free trade on a global basis may create world stability.

Another scenario suggests that labor-saving devices and automation will free most workers from wage labor. The concept of a leisure society also has taken hold among some policy analysts in the United Kingdom and Western Europe. On the basis of the belief that full employment has not delivered workers from hurtful hierarchical structures and poor jobs and working conditions, these analysts argue that creative leisure can be considered work, which would reduce the stigma of leisure among the jobless. Not only does this scenario offer no concrete demonstrable model of how unemployment redefined as creative leisure might work, it begs the question of the need for full employment. Rather, its supporters argue, the estimated 1 billion new jobs that would have to be created by the year 2000 to put the world back to work are an unreachable goal.[4]

Others, at least in the United States, claim that the changing demographics of the work force alone will produce fuller employment. As the pool of workers shrinks, with the retirement of the post-World War II baby boomers and the decreased number of young workers as a result of the declining birthrate, the demand for youthful labor, it is said, will intensify and even force retirees back into the labor market.[5] Such projections have been met with considerable skepticism, however.[6]

This chapter outlines some of the challenges that lie ahead and the consequences of the exportation of U.S. business practices to other parts of the world. Linking local action to global consequences, it describes the impact of changes that occur at the local level in the United States on workers, their families, and communities in other parts of the world. It also addresses the need to reformulate some of the paradigms of the practice and knowledge bases of social work in the United States and for social workers to collaborate with others throughout the world. By building alliances with key groups in the United States and their counterparts elsewhere and by sharing a collective mission, social workers may lessen their sense of fragmentation, futility, and stress, while improving the outcomes of practice. Finally, this chapter suggests ways that the profession can become more proactive by introducing its repertoire of win–win skills and problems into the larger systems that impair the functioning of the smaller systems of people and communities.

A National and Global Crisis?

Few social problems are as corrosive to world stability and peace as are unemployment and economic insecurity. The unrest and uncertainty about a future because of joblessness intensifies desperation and win–lose dynamics in the home, community, and nation and throughout the world. Whether violence erupts in the family, in the streets, or in war, the pain and desperation that may fuel it may be masked by elaborate rationalizations and ideological explanations.[7] Nevertheless, the source may be economic deprivation or greed. Central to world stability and peace may be the question of equity in income, jobs, and resources and the democratization of allocative structures to promote the right of all people to occupational well-being.

Covering Up the Crisis

Some analysts believe that the dominant western economies are covering up the extent of the unemployment crisis. One forecast is that by the mid-1990s, 65 to 70 million people in the western industrialized countries and 900 million to 1 billion people in the developing nations will be unemployed.[8] Yet, given the current and projected state of the world's unemployed, there seems to be a dangerous complacency, despite the recent stock market crash, which temporarily has riveted attention on one aspect of the economy. Furthermore, it is not clear what impact the projected shortage of workers, the economic restructuring that is afoot, the increase in occupationally segregated labor markets, and the destabilizing effects of automation and deindustrialization will have on the future of work in the 1990s. For example, in the United States, it is claimed that had banking customer services not been automated, banks would have had to employ every adult woman in the United States.[9] As it is, many bank teller jobs that are relegated to women and are now part time are being replaced by automation.

Social workers can help stop the dynamics of cover-up and denial by exposing the number of jobs that are being exported or lost and the human costs of a restructured economy. In 1986, an unemployment seminar that was sponsored by the International Network on Unemployment and Social Work and involved delegates from 10 nations found that the use of the secondary labor market is a widespread phenomenon in many industrial and developing nations. Low-paid, part-time, and piecework jobs in non-unionized sectors of the labor market, along with relaxed regulations about working conditions and child labor may suggest a return to nineteenth-century labor conditions.

Campaigns to mask the seriousness of the problems of the underemployed and the unemployed may be on the rise. Nevertheless, during the 1970s, General Electric reduced its U.S. work force by 25,000 and added 30,000 foreign jobs and Radio Corporation of America cut its U.S. work force by 14,000 and added 19,000 overseas workers.[10] Bluestone and Harrison found that from 1969 to 1976, 110 jobs were created by new plant openings for every 100 jobs that were lost through plant closures.[11] Meanwhile, the number of exported jobs through foreign investments by U.S. corporations increased from 12 billion to 192 billion between 1950 and 1980, compared with corporate investments in the United States, which grew only at half the pace, from 54 billion to 400 billion. Moreover, a growing percentage of U.S. imports are actually from subsidiaries of U.S. multinational corporations.[12] For example, in 1980, more than 70 percent of U.S.-made goods were in competition with others in the world market.[13]

Such dynamics suggest that unless practitioners probe the source of their clients' layoff or underemployment problems, they will be missing an opportunity to build the public record and open to the public the painful economic realities that require problem solving. The biggest challenge that lies ahead for social workers is not just to expose the level of dysfunction in the lives of those they serve but to uncover the denial or normalization of the harms of the economy. There are some who believe that rapid deindustrialization, accompanied by the expansion of the service economy, is not only inevitable but desirable and that such changes are not happening fast enough. Capital thus may be viewed as both creative and destructive—creative in the building of new products and markets and destructive in the harms, scars, and irreversible damage done to workers, families, communities, and entire nations. Therefore, some would have social workers believe that the destabilizing effects of capital mobility are to be understood as natural and even desirable and that boom towns eventually will spring from ghost towns.[14] Yet, growth or decline at the expense of the human right to economic and social stability is an anathema to social welfare.

Faith in the hidden hand of the market or in the self-regulating market to correct imbalances in employment also may preempt policymakers from focusing on the economic crisis. Some social workers may be met with claims that the economy is generating new jobs and that the unemployment rate has dropped to a lower-than-predicted level and thus may be questioned for their fervor. The masking effect of state or national unemployment rates may need to be exposed. What percentage of jobs keep workers underemployed or are part of the military or depend on nuclear energy or other hazardous materials? What percentage are manufacturing, and what has the attrition rate been for the past five years? How many jobs depend on the microchip, which means that, at any moment, many of them can be exported? It has even been claimed that airline reservations on one carrier in the United States are routed through an airlines receptionist in Singapore.

Effect on Underdeveloped Countries

The movement of industries to developing nations is attributable, in part, to the drive for increased profits to be had by using less expensive sources of labor and resources. Such mobility also is augmented by the absence of developed welfare states that might require corporate responsibility for layoffs, environmental controls, labor policies, labor unions, and the governmental regulation of working conditions.

Multinational corporations enter cultures in which many workers and families support themselves by subsistence farming, fishing, and related resource-based activities. Industrialization may foster the creation of two nations—one in which the old ways of surviving and living persist and one that is dependent on wage-based labor, some of which comes from multinational industries. As was true in the days of feudal England and Europe, unemployment may seem like an anathema to many in these nations. Unemployment is a by-product of undemocratized capitalism. As a result, people in these nations may become more prone to such social problems as substance abuse, conflict, depression, and family dissolution in attempting to deal with the unprecedented stresses caused by the rise of wage-based labor and the further exclusion of those who are outside wage-based jobs. The following example illustrates not only what happens to a family in a developing nation when multinational corporations impose a wage-based economy on an economy that was based on reciprocal exchanges and subsistence work but the repercussions of this multinational structure on an American family:

Tamba's life in a developing nation is fraught with her daily struggle to keep herself and her two children fed. She and her children consume substantially fewer calories than any standard recommended diet. Tamba's husband sends money when he can from his work in a mining town that is over 700 miles away, but his arm injury has kept him from working regularly, and there are no governmental or corporate benefits for industrial injuries or layoffs. Moreover, recent mine closures and layoffs have lowered his chances of contributing a stable family income.

Tamba is no different from any of the other women in her village. Wage-based jobs are not available; but, if they were, they would go first to the men. Tamba has relocated twice to be closer to her husband; each time, she has become farther removed from the natural resources that kept her fed as a child. Now she is forced to get closer to the city, where she can exchange her woven baskets for food commodities.

Thousands of miles away, a single mother and her two children eke out an existence in a two-room house soon to be torn down by the landlord. Sue, the mother, has been unable to find a full-time job since the mine closed in her town. Before that, her husband's wage was sufficient to sustain the family and she was able to stay home with her two young children. Now she works as a waitress twice a week and cleans homes when she can get the work. Her husband's job loss led to major marital conflict; they separated, and he is now searching for work in a nearby city. Sue suspects that he is drinking and has deteriorating health problems. Their tiny but once thriving mining town in the United States has been devastated by the closure of the mine. When the mine closed, more than half the shopkeepers went bankrupt. Other families, unable to sell their homes, have vacated them and now, like Sue's husband, migrate in search of new work elsewhere. New enterprises have not sprung up in this declining town.

The mining company for which Tamba's husband works is partly financed and owned by the company that employed Sue's husband. The bonds that connect Tamba, her husband, and their family to Sue's family and the declining mining community in the United States make their plight mutual although different. A social welfare structure is needed that transcends national boundaries and bridges the gap between the well-being of workers, families, and communities and socially unaccountable capital investments and business practices.

The irresponsible mobility of capital may help unify the human race in a show of solidarity on human rights issues. For example, when workers at a 3M® plant recently went on strike in New Jersey, their black counterparts at a 3M® plant in South Africa also took to the picket lines.[15] Having much more to lose than their mainly white counterparts in the United States, these black South Africans stood firm on the issues that unified them with the New Jersey strikers even when one of their leaders was jailed. Similarly, workers at a NIKE® plant in Oakland, California, recently went on strike to protest the repressive practices in a Korean NIKE® plant that was restricting union organizing.[16] Thus, it is evident that the well-being of people and communities in this country cannot be achieved if economic rights elsewhere are being violated.

Capitalism is the economic system that is spreading throughout most of the world.[17] As this trend accelerates, so, too, will the need for an overarching structure of protections for human welfare. This need is exacerbated by the fact that U.S. companies that export their practices as ''models'' for developing nations are dictating to developing nations the prescriptions for growth. Through loans by the World Bank and the practices of the International Monetary Fund, developing nations are being forced to build their economies along U.S. lines, to participate in free trade, and to reduce protective practices that would limit the penetration of foreign and especially U.S. products.[18] Sanctions and incentives are tied to the continued use of credit and the postponed repayment of loans if debtor nations comply with U.S. business practices as well as free and open trade. Not only is the world's work force at risk of being mechanized and exploited in the same patterns as in the United States, but pressures are increasing daily for indigenous businesses in developing nations to adopt the "profitable" practices of U.S. companies. Although some nations may require joint corporate ownership so that a U.S. company is partially owned by indigenous persons in the host nation (long enough for the transfer of technology to occur), many U.S. corporate practices overseas remain unfettered by environmental, social, or legal constraints or the degree of taxation experienced in the United States.

Toward Stabilization or Depression?

As industrialized nations undergo economic restructuring, the power base of the globe may become more diffused. Few workers, communities, or nations will be self-reliant in their production of goods and services. For example, when many manufactured goods are imported, the United States increasingly will be dependent on nations that it now treats as unequal partners in the production and distribution of goods and services. Accelerated trade among nations may either further fractionalize the globe with outbreaks of war or force negotiated agreements that supersede militaristic attempts to keep peace. Threatened and actual acts of war over the export and transport of oil are recent examples of how violence is bred by a resource in demand.

The Quality of Life Action Act (H.R. 1398), discussed in chapter 9, calls for the imposition of conditions on the federal governments' support of the International Monetary Fund and the International Bank for Reconstruction and Development. Under this act, the use of federal money for such purposes would be tolerated only if the policies of these loan institutions promoted a rise in the standard of living of debtor nations rather than the imposition of economic austerity. It also proposes a series of United Nations-sponsored conferences to promote deliberations on trade, aid, currencies, labor–management relations, and working conditions. These conferences also would deal with alternative methods of reducing involuntary unemployment.

Rosecrance argues that a new interdependence and peace may be forged from pressures among nations to develop an orderly basis for the exchange of resources through negotiated trade policies.[19] He argues that the territorial sources of world conflict are now secondary to pressures for international economic cooperation. The continued preoccupation of the

United States with producing armaments against nuclear war has deflected attention from economic development and trade. Yet the goals of the development and exchange of resources and of trade are derived locally because resources spring from locally based enterprises rather than multinational corporations. Thus, the demand for more local control over trade agreements will intensify. This demand may place governments in the role of what Rosecrance calls "mediative states." These mediative states will emerge to balance pressures from abroad for trade with domestic needs. According to Rosecrance, these mediative states also will be forced to play a "safeguarding" role to cushion some of the continued impermanence caused by the flight of capital.

Rosecrance envisions more U.S., Western European, and Japanese workers on the move around the globe, much like migrant workers from Mexico in the United States and guest workers in Europe. Although Rosecrance does not describe how these safeguards will emerge, it is clear that they must involve a strengthened welfare state and the building of a global infrastructure for promoting human welfare.

As chapter 9 suggested, one driving force for a strengthened welfare state may be the demands of the global marketplace for healthy labor. Pressures for stabilizing the functioning of workers, families and communities also may come from recessions, believed to be a normal part of the business cycle. The standard of living of many people seems to be declining, even though many families have two or more wage earners. Levy and Michel found that from 1973 on, contrary to the previous pattern of growth, the wages of men aged 40 to 50 plummeted by 14 percent and the median income of families dropped as well.[20]

The predictions are, however, that the 1990s will see not just a major recession, but a cataclysmic depression. Drawing on an analysis of business cycles and the belief that depressions in the United States occur every six decades, Batra argued that 35 percent of the wealth concentrated in the hands of the top 1 percent of U.S. families and an insecure banking system may help plunge an ordinary 1990 recession into a depression.[21] The stock market crash forecasted by Galbraith may have just occurred.[22] Kondatief curves suggested a downturn every six decades, making the 1990s bear the brunt of the decline.[23] Even if such predictions prove unfounded, they nonetheless should underscore for social workers the impermanencies in the lives of workers, communities, and businesses. Social work activists should promote more than countercyclical strategies to stabilize lives and economies; instead, they should seek a more permanent structure for economic well-being that transcends the capacity of current economic systems and welfare states. Whether capitalism sows the seeds of its own destruction, as predicted by Marx and others, remains to be seen.[24] Nevertheless, mounting pressures for democratized capitalism or some form of socialism to guide the policies of the next century may grow from the well-documented harms of the current economic chaos.

Global Practice Starts at Home

U.S. economic policies and business practices may be exported more frequently than those of any other nation, and social workers in the United States, in collaboration with allied groups, should play a major role in curbing the effects of these policies and practices and in transforming those that are hurtful. It is often the exportation or replication of U.S. business practices that impairs the well-being of workers, families, and communities in other nations.

Rather than being seen as a composite of separate and dissimilar human populations, the world community can be reframed through a social welfare lens as an interdependent and interconnected network of people.[25] National boundaries must be seen as obstacles to working for the betterment of the world family, especially when some of the world family functions as a labor force for U.S. companies. Concern for the well-being of other people, then, compels an understanding of the similar problems, needs, and conditions of people all over the world and the shared dynamics that transcend cultural attributes to bind nations and peoples together. In a world family, one nation's afflictions may affect us all, whether they involve the threat of nuclear war or disasters like Chernobyl. Whether it is an end to the famine and deaths in Ethiopia or the apartheid in South Africa, the end of pain in one part of the world may reduce its consequences for the rest of the world.

Schwartz and Neikirk argued that the task that lies ahead is to control the damage done by the economies of the world.[26] This task can be accomplished only by the revelations of social workers, unions, churches, the media, politicians, and others of the unmitigated or preventable harms of industrialization, deindustrialization, destabilization, and unfettered capitalism. The disclosure of the conditions in sweatshops in Hong Kong, Korea, Sri Lanka, and countless other nations that produce critical goods for consumption in the more developed nations of the world may help build pressure for boycotts, sanctions, and regulations. Substandard working conditions and the exploitation of workers must be documented, and communities and nations must be examined for the ways in which work roles, good and bad jobs, income, and related resources are to be allocated more equitably. Discrimination is a worldwide phenomenon that is reflected in the distribution and allocation of jobs and the fact that sectoral labor markets relegate various classes, races, ethnic minorities, men and women, and age-related groups to differential working conditions.

The well-known consequences of layoffs and boom–bust economic cycles and the hardships of community and family distress must be documented. Their universal harms may help to mobilize global action.[27] Setting the record straight through such documentation helps raise the consciousness of the public and elected officials and may compel more legislative and legal actions. This is not to say that corporate practices will change, but that the evidence for needed reforms will become the basis for instituting laws, organizing alternative ways of doing business, and holding corporations responsible for the human and community consequences of their actions.[28] For example, before corporations relocate to developing nations, they might be assessed in the community they are leaving as well as the one they are entering with a special worker–family–community tax that becomes a countercyclical fund for the demise of corporations, for layoffs, and for training underemployed workers who wish to use their skills more fully.[29]

Furthermore, a tracking system may begin to spread to the point that a network of labor, social work, and related groups in one nation may be informants to counterparts in another nation about the potential labor problems and harms that may ensue with a particular unregulated corporation. The building of a global database on the damages of industrialization and deindustrialization may be necessary to set new agendas for action by the United Nations. Perhaps Mazzocchio's call for reparations to workers and communities and his appeal for a "superfund" for workers in the United States could guide the mobilization of global efforts to aid injured workers, families, and communities.[30] Such a superfund might be one of the few resource systems other than the World Bank and the International Monetary Fund that transcend national boundaries and sovereignty.

This book began with an analysis of the implications of the human costs of unemployment and economic distress for social work intervention. It examined how increased rates of suicide, homicide, and mental illness are a few of the results of a rise in unemployment rates. Unfortunately, studies by Brenner, among others, on the changed economy as well as the human costs of unemployment may present only half the picture of the ripple effects of U.S. joblessness and the different kind of toll it takes on a developing nation.[31] It eventually should be possible, for example, to tie a 1-percent rise in U.S. unemployment or a 5-percent drop in manufacturing to a corresponding increase in mortality and mental illness in urbanized, wage-based regions in developing nations. Wage equity and stability may be sought not through the downgrading of U.S. workers' wages (as is now occurring) but through improvements in wages in developing nations. Thus, workers who might have made $1,600 a month in the production of footwear in the United States should create pressure for a more equitable wage upgrade for counterparts who are being paid $25 per month in such countries as India, the Philippines, Malaysia, Sri Lanka, and Thailand. The concern for the welfare of workers in such countries necessitates the development of worldwide standards of wages and benefits. Such concerns also should promote a worldwide movement to protect children from exploitation as cheap labor sources.

Consumers have tremendous power by refusing to purchase items that are produced as a result of the displacement of one group of workers and the exploitation of another group, such as children. The roots of social work are intimately connected to the consumer movement and are well reflected in the initiatives of persons such as Josephine Shaw Lowell and Florence Kelley, who organized the National Consumer's League.[32] A resurgence is needed in social workers' mobilization of consumers to boycott such goods, so that these interconnections in the well-being of workers, their children, families, and communities in the world family become clearer.

Without advocacy by social workers and others in deindustrializing and industrializing nations, the silence over the fallout from industrial practices may be misinterpreted as an absence of problematic conditions with which communities, developing welfare states, and work organizations must grapple. The radical restructuring of local economies that strikes at the very base of community life may thrust social workers in the United States into many of the same social development responsibilities as their counterparts in developing nations. U.S. social workers can help by disseminating more information on local economic development projects and initiatives, economic resources, and the requirements of knowledge and technical experience that may be applicable not just in distressed U.S. communities but in those in other nations.

Social workers in the United States must examine not just the human costs of unemployment and underemployment, but the costs of an insufficient balance between locally developed economic initiatives and resources devoted to building infrastructures for multilocal or multinational employers. Moreover, the cost of hosting a new business may far outweigh its profits, let alone the benefits it provides to the community. It can be shown, for example, that the billions of dollars that are spent by governments in cleaning up toxic waste are far greater than the actual multimillion-dollar profits acquired by polluting corporations.[33] Furthermore, the overpasses, bridges, and related infrastructures that are built to accommodate new businesses also have a steep price tag paid by taxpayers, as do the losses to the tax base from tax shelters, giveaways, and exemptions. Yet the funds that are available for the development of small businesses and the local economy and for welfare and unemployment insurance recipients to return to school or start their own business may be minimal at best. Likewise, a better balance needs to be struck between identifying declining mature industries that are at risk but that are salvageable through buyouts by workers and technical assistance and new industries whose relocation in the community may be more costly because of the need to develop the infrastructure and to provide tax giveaways. Such assessments may help counter the provision of services and loans to new outside developers and redirect these resources to indigenous populations, including some impoverished native American reservations, and other distressed groups of workers, and leaders who are promoting the revitalization of declining industries, towns, and communities.

Export of Practice and Knowledge

The infusion of new knowledge into the profession about employment, unemployment, and underemployment and the full employment and economic development initiatives that might combat them may help social workers reformulate their practice, missions, research focuses, and political agendas. This infusion is important not just for the sake of reclaiming some of the lingering economic agendas of the profession, but for reassessing whether social work practice and educational paradigms can be exported to other nations. Despite the diversity in roles and even practice paradigms in other countries, the application of U.S. practice and curricular materials in other parts of the world should be done with caution. Because much of our social work practice knowledge reflects adaptations to the political economy of our nation, its transfer to other political, economic, social, and cultural environments may be inappropriate, especially in the case of clinical practice models that focus on intervention with symptoms, rather than on the economic and employment precipitants of people's problems. Nevertheless, the international exchange of materials, innovations in practice, and research on the effects of economic conditions is essential for strengthening the debate about the role and practice mission of social workers in the restructured global economy.

Such debates are especially important for U.S. social workers, because some of the dynamics, conditions, causes, long-term consequences, and costs of joblessness may be understood best from the vantage points of practice in industrialized and developing nations. For example, even though the developing nations are increasingly exploited by U.S. corporations for their labor markets, expanded consumer markets, and sites for manufacturing and the extraction of resources, they are also repositories of knowledge about the dynamics of rapid economic decline and growth. What transpired during the Industrial Revolution in the United States and in European countries over several centuries is transforming developing nations in a matter of years. Thus, developing countries are succeeding the post-industrial countries as the new industrialized nations of the world. Four or five centuries of knowledge about industrialization should be critical to developing nations and especially their social welfare practitioners.[34]

International Network on Unemployment and Social Work

A constructive avenue of exchange for the social work community is the recently developed International Network on Unemployment and Social Work (INUSW). Coordinated by Hans Berglind of the School of Social Work, University of Stockholm, Sweden, this network fosters the global exchange of information on practice and research through a newsletter, international meetings, and scholarly publications. INUSW focuses on promoting unemployment as an issue for social work educators and practitioners. Hosting workshops in conjunction with the International Conference on Social Welfare, International Congress of Schools of Social Work, and the International Federation of Social Workers, INUSW addresses internationally relevant practice models and collaborative campaigns for economic and employment entitlements. Linking social workers in industrialized and developing nations, INUSW strengthens the sense of interconnectedness among social workers in dealing with the causes, consequences, and costs of economic and employment issues in various political economies around the world.[35]

As industrialized nations grapple with the problems of unemployment and stagnating economies, the similarities in the unraveling of what were once model welfare states committed to full employment provide an instructive basis for a campaign by social workers for international economic and human justice. International exchanges help to point out the commonalities in what might once have been seen as disparate or isolated experiences. For example, the collapse of the safety net in some countries owing, in part, to high unemployment may be paralleled by the unraveling of welfare state programs and entitlements in nations that have reneged on earlier commitments to full employment.[36] On the more positive side, countries that maintain a commitment to full employment through rigorous policy supports for the retention of jobs may do so despite the differences in their political economies.[37] Hence, cutbacks in entitlements in one country may be fought with data regarding the consequences of such cutbacks in another country. Clearly, the United States is a relevant laboratory for European nations whose welfare-state benefits are being cut back. In effect, the United States, through the findings of social workers and others, reflects a database on the predictable and rising casualties of such cutbacks in the midst of an unraveling economy.

Moreover, aberrant practices in one nation may give clues to the more subtle variations elsewhere. For example, the practices of expulsion and labor regulation in South Africa actually may be repeated in nations that seek ways to banish guest workers and their families when jobs are lost. Thus, as more workers become part of a world labor "surplus," welfare state programs—even in what had once been full-employment economies—may be challenged severely and begin to go down the path toward social Darwinism. This decline in programs may occur because there will be fewer pressures for the rehabilitative and mainstreaming functions of the welfare state when labor is displaced and discarded permanently. To counter such trends, tools are already in place to mobilize local social work efforts for global change. For example, the 1977 International Covenant on Economic, Social and Cultural Rights of the United Nations offers social workers the opportunity to press collectively for economic and human rights in their own nations.[38] To date, few nations have ratified this covenant; the United States has not been among the ratifiers.

Articles 1 through 8 of this covenant state that everyone has the right to freely chosen gainful work, fair wages, and equal remuneration for work of equal value; the right to a decent living; the right to safe and healthy working conditions; and the right to form trade unions and to strike. Its other articles include the rights to Social Security, social insurance, the equitable distribution of the world's food resources, and the promotion of highest attainable standards of physical and mental health. The covenant also requires the full development of the human personality and sense of dignity through education.[39] This covenant was to be ratified and adopted

by nations that would provide statements of the progress they had made
in achieving these goals. A recently appointed 18-member committee of the
United Nations has been convened to accelerate the review of the progress
reports submitted by countries that have ratified the covenant.[40]

The Challenge

Social workers stand between the political and economic institutions
that may harm or nurture and the people who may be deformed or aided. The well-being of the human community has never been so precarious
owing to the threat of nuclear obliteration and the unmitigated forces of
greed that are blunting the development of individuals and communities
while irreversibly pillaging the human and natural resources of the world.
The bond that unites the lone social worker, a small cadre of practitioners,
or entire work force of social workers in a nation to those in the world
is the promotion of human, community, and global well-being.[41]

Few would disagree with the goal of promoting well-being. Taking action to prevent harms or to stop laissez faire practices is the collective
heritage and mission of social work. After all, each time a social worker
intervenes to help a person, group, or community, the very ability to *act*
is a unique attribute of the profession. In fact, the profession's historic
claim to taking action when others remain immobilized or are constrained
by laws or ideologies that promote benign neglect, survival of the fittest,
or irresponsible abandonment of those in need gives the profession a legacy
of power. Because power implies, in part, the ability to act, the capacity
of the profession to germinate similar power in others is its collective
strength. As multiethnic groups, feminists, sexual minorities, the aged,
the young, and persons with disabilities develop the tools and strategies
of empowerment, the framework for a revitalized professional mission is
being built. When power is seen as infinite and as maximizing win–win
situations, old definitions of power can be replaced by new ones that em-
phasize that the more power one has and shares, the more power everyone
has. Many others have similar human service goals or values and seek
to "collectivize" their visions and standards for human well-being in communities around the world. Many organizations, from the United Nations to the National Conference of Catholic Bishops, have values that
echo those of social work, as well as consistent models for the kind of social
and economic plans that must be mounted around the world.

Like jobless or underemployed workers, social workers stand at a crossroads in setting their own occupational goals and in repudiating the

dichotomy between economic and social welfare concerns. For some, the capacity to reassess their talents, given an earlier heritage of taking action and empowering others, may mean that they will be more explicit about their many different practice roles. For others, the tasks of promoting economic well-being and employment through empowerment may seem to have little to do with the conditions and symptoms that flood those they serve. Whether the goal involves increasing the time one spends on ecomomic and employment rights and needs and occupational problem solving by 5 percent or 50 percent, there is little value on going it alone. To this end, practitioners, as well as the profession, constitute not just a problem-solving force—a catalyst that stimulates others to act—but a resource base for testing and promulgating effective ways of helping those who are disenfranchised by the labor market.

Social work was borne of the struggle to affirm alternative values and visions. Given social work's earnestness to establish itself as a profession, some of these values, visions, and actions have fluctuated. We social workers will reclaim and strengthen them not to own them alone, but to reenergize in others, through helping them take action, shared values and perhaps diverse and even disparate solutions for change.

Such an appeal may come at one of the worst times in history. Rising caseloads and budget cutbacks may make such capacity-building, empowering, and energizing activities seem unachievable. But just as we help others move in small steps into major life changes, so, too, must we gradually reframe our mission and reclaim our goal of achieving economic and employment rights for clients. Indeed, many social workers are underemployed because they are unable to address the economic and employment conditions that shape or cause the stresses of those they serve. Such underemployment constitutes immeasurable losses to society and limits our contributions to those we serve, as well as to the well-being of society.

The reframing of our practice agendas and job descriptions is merely the starting point for promoting changes in other groups and systems. In 1930, the American Association of Social Workers issued a statement that Fisher described as a distinct departure from previous practice.[42] The statement, known as the "Responsibility and Contribution of Social Workers in Unemployment Crises," claimed that "social work was under an obligation as never before 'to bear witness'."[43] Moreover, it emphasized that social work must admit that the problems of the Great Depression were too big for the profession to solve alone—that it was a national, not a social work, emergency. These words are instructive and prophetic for today. We must take our findings to the public, to the press, and to legislative bodies. We must acknowledge that the tools in our repertoires, programs, and service systems are insufficient to deal with the causes and the symptoms of the economic chaos about us and among those we serve. The tools that are available to us to document and educate the public and policymakers are far greater than those on which our forebears could rely. We have the data, advanced communications systems, and ethical mandates to bring forth the facts as we see them. To let our sense of futility, adherence to patchwork resources and strategies, or tireless dedication to serving yet one more person in need derail us from exposing the conditions among those we serve is to betray inadvertently a long and proud heritage. Ultimately, our goal is to make economic and employment rights not just a social work issue, but an issue of worldwide human rights, human development, and human survival.

Notes and References

1. B. Bluestone and B. Harrison, *The Deindustrialization of America* (New York: Basic Books, 1982).

2. R. Batra, *The Great Depression of 1990* (New York: Simon & Schuster, 1987).

3. *See* R. Rosecrance, *The Rise of the Trading State* (New York: Basic Books, 1986). I also wish to thank Stan Eccles for his suggestions regarding world federalism.

4. "Should We Protect Jobs—Or Redefine Work?" *New Options,* 21 (October 21, 1985), p. 1. This point has been made by D. Macarov in a presentation for Working Group 9 on the Unemployed: Policies and Services at the 13th Regional Symposium on Social Welfare, International Council on Social Welfare, Turku, Finland, June 1985.

5. D. Carter, "Employers Must Straighten Up as Worker Pool Shrinks," *Seattle Post Intelligencer,* July 20, 1987, pp. C1, C3, C8.

6. M. W. Sherraden, *School Dropouts in Perspective* (Washington, D.C.: Education Commission of the States, March 1985).

7. For example, Hitler's rise to power in Germany can be attributed, in part, to the terrorizing effects of the world depression of the 1930s, including inflation and unemployment. It is a reminder that people become vulnerable and violent when faced with hopelessness and a resourceless existence.

8. G. Merritt, *World Out of Work* (London: William Collins Sons & Co., 1982).

9. R. R. Reich, *The Next American Frontier* (New York: New York Times Book Co., 1983).

10. Ibid.

11. Bluestone and Harrison, *The Deindustrialization of America*.

12. Ibid.

13. Ibid.

14. These perspectives are critiqued in ibid.

15. *Hometowns Against Shutdowns* (New York: New York City Labor Institute, January 13, 1986).

16. Personal communication from Tom Croft, Seattle Worker Center, Seattle, Wash., 1987.

17. Center for Popular Economics, *Economic Report of the People* (Boston: South End Press, 1986).

18. H. M. Wachtel, *The Money Mandarins* (New York: Pantheon Books, 1986).

19. Rosecrance, *The Rise of the Trading State*.

20. F. Levy and R. C. Michel, *The Economic Future of the Baby Boom* (Washington, D.C.: The Urban Institute, 1985).

21. Batra, *The Great Depression of 1990*.

22. J. K. Galbraith, "The 1929 Parallel," *Atlantic Monthly,* 259 (January 1987), pp. 62–66. *See also* R. Heilbroner, "Hard Times," *New Yorker,* September 14, 1987, pp. 96–109.

23. Batra, *The Great Depression of 1990*.

24. J. A. Schumpter, *Capitalism, Socialism, and Democracy* (New York: Harper & Row, 1975); and K. Witcher, "World Bank Approves Loan to Nigeria to Aid Nation's Bid to Liberalize Trade," *Wall Street Journal,* Friday, October 17, 1986, p. 30.

25. B. Mohan, "Unraveling Comparative Social Welfare," in *Toward Comparative Social Welfare* (Cambridge, Mass.: Schenkman Publishing Co., 1985), pp. 1–11.

26. G. G. Schwartz and W. Neikirk, *The Work Revolution* (New York: Rawson Associates, 1983).

27. T. Kieselbach and P. G. Svensson, "Health Policy Development in Europe in Response to Economic Instability." To be published in a forthcoming issue of *Journal of Social Issues.*

28. B. Gross and K. Singh, "The New Right in the 1980's." Paper presented at the Conference on the Crisis in the United States and Its Impact on Latin America, sponsored by Centro de Información, Documentacion y Analysis Sobre el Movimiento Obrero Latino Americano, held in Mexico City, May 1985.

29. This idea is derived, in part, from a course taught by R. Barsh in the School of Business, University of Washington, Seattle, 1984–1985.

30. Presentation by T. Mazzocchio, at the conference "Toward Full, Fair, and Gratifying Employment for Quality Life and a Liveable Earth," held at the University of California, Santa Cruz, May 29–30, 1987.

31. M. H. Brenner, *Estimating the Effects of Economic Change on National Health and Wellbeing* (Washington, D.C.: Joint Economic Committee, U.S. Congress, 1984).

32. *See* C. A. Alexander, "History of Social Work and Social Welfare: Significant Dates," *Encyclopedia of Social Work* (18th ed.; Silver Spring, Md.: National Association of Social Workers, Inc., 1987), pp. 777–788.

33. Mazzocchio presentation at "Toward Full, Fair, and Gratifying Employment."

34. T. N. Whitehead, *Leadership in a Free Society* (Cambridge, Mass.: Harvard University Press, 1936).

35. *See* S. McKay, G. Maslany, and G. Riches, "Private Troubles, Public Issues, Global Concerns: Developing an International Perspective on Unemployment and Social Work." Unpublished paper, Lakehead University, Thunder Bay, Ontario, Canada. *See also* A. Pilcher, minutes from the INUSW workshop, "Social Work and the Unemployed," Tokyo, Japan, 1987; and K. Windschuttle, "INUSW at the Tokyo Welfare Conference," *INUSW Newsletter*, 5 (October 1986), pp. 1–6.

36. *See, for example*, D. Piel, "West Germany Cuts Back Social Benefits," *Journal of the Institute for Socioeconomic Studies*, 8 (Autumn 1983), pp. 1–14.

37. H. Berglind, "Unemployment and Marginality in the Labour Market: What are the Counter-Strategies?" Paper presented at International Council on Social Welfare Symposium, Rome, Italy, 1987. *See also* G. Therborn, *Why Some Peoples Are More Unemployed Than Others* (London: Verso, 1986).

38. *See Human Rights: A Compilation of International Instruments* (New York: United Nations, 1983).

39. Ibid.

40. "Rights and Humanity: A New International Humanitarian Initiative," *Rights and Humanity* (London), 1 (December 1986), pp. 4–8. *See also* "Establishing Expert Committees on Economic, Social, and Cultural Rights," *Rights and Humanity*, 1 (December 1986), pp. 21–22.

41. J. Fisher, *The Response of Social Work to the Depression* (Cambridge, Mass.: Schenkman Publishing Co., 1980).

42. Ibid.

43. Ibid, p. 34.